BITTERLY DIVIDED

BITTERLY DIVIDED

THE SOUTH'S INNER CIVIL WAR

David Williams

THE NEW PRESS

NEW YORK
LONDON

Requests for permission to reproduce selections from this book should be mailed to:
Permissions Department, The New Press, 38 Greene Street, New York, NY 10013.

Published in the United States by The New Press, New York, 2008
Distributed by W. W. Norton & Company, Inc., New York

LIBRARY OF CONGRESS CATALOGING-IN-PUBLICATION DATA

Williams, David, 1959–
    Bitterly divided : the South's inner Civil War / David Williams.
        p. cm.
    Includes bibliographical references and index.
    ISBN 978-1-59558-108-2 (hc.)
        1. Confederate States of America—Social conditions. 2. United States—History—
Civil War, 1861–1865—Social aspects. 3. Social conflict—Southern States—History—
19th century. 4. Social classes—Southern States—History—19th century. 5. Southern
States—Race relations—History—19th century. I. Title.

F214.W564 2008
973.7'13—dc22   2007045285

The New Press was established in 1990 as a not-for-profit alternative to the large, commercial
publishing houses currently dominating the book publishing industry. The New Press operates
in the public interest rather than for private gain, and is committed to publishing, in innovative
ways, works of educational, cultural, and community value that are often deemed
insufficiently profitable.

www.thenewpress.com

Composition by Westchester Book Composition
This book was set in Janson

Printed in the United States of America

2   4   6   8   10   9   7   5   3   1

For Teresa
Forever and Always

Contents

BITTERLY DIVIDED

Introduction

"It is a certain fact that the Southern people are fast becoming as bitterly divided against each other as the Southern and Northern people ever has been." At the height of the Civil War, while battles raged on distant fields, a Georgia man named Samuel Knight wrote these words to Governor Joseph E. Brown as he outlined the many ways in which southerners themselves were working against the Confederacy. He concluded his observations by insisting: "I have not written this letter to exaggerate these things. I only write such as I know to be true."[1]

Knight saw clearly what generations of historians have too often neglected—that during its brief existence, the Confederacy fought a two-front war. There was, of course, the war it waged with the North, the war so familiar to almost every schoolchild. But, though schoolchildren rarely hear of it, there was another war. Between 1861 and 1865, the South was torn apart by a violent inner civil war, a war no less significant to the Confederacy's fate than its more widely known struggle against the Yankees.

From its very beginnings, the Confederacy suffered from a rising tide of internal hostility. Ironically, it was a hostility brought on largely by those most responsible for the Confederacy's creation. Planters excused themselves from the draft in various ways, then grew far too much cotton and tobacco and not nearly enough food. Soldiers went hungry, as did their families back home. Women defied Confederate authorities by staging food riots from Richmond, Virginia, to Galveston, Texas. Desertion and draft evasion became commonplace. By 1864, the draft law was nearly impossible to enforce, and two-thirds of the Confederate army was absent with or without leave. Many deserters joined guerrilla bands—"tory" (anti-confederate) or "layout" (deserter and draft-resister) gangs, which controlled vast areas of the southern countryside.

Southern Indians too, from the seaboard states to Indian Territory (now Oklahoma), though allied by most of their tribal governments with the Confederacy, increasingly resisted Confederate authority. And southern blacks made the force of their opposition to the Confederacy felt. From the war's outset, in what W.E.B. Du Bois called a general strike against the Confederacy, blacks resisted by subtle and overt means, undermining the Confederate war effort at every opportunity.

The South's inner civil war had deep roots in the antebellum period. Many southern whites, like North Carolina's Hinton Rowan Helper, saw plain folk as impoverished by the slave system. Slaves, too, like Frederick Douglass, were becoming more difficult to control. Though Helper and Douglass were exceptional cases, both represented a rising tide of resentment and resistance. By 1860, slaveholders worried that although Abraham Lincoln was a direct threat only to slavery's expansion, his election to the presidency might give encouragement to southern dissenters and resisters, making control all the more difficult. One planter asked nervously, "If the poor whites realized that slavery kept them poor, would they not vote it down?" Some feared that there might soon be "an Abolition party in the South, of Southern men." Another frankly admitted, "I mistrust our own people more than I fear all of the efforts of the Abolitionists."[2] Such fears among slaveholders, though publicly unacknowledged, were a major driving force behind the secession movement.

But how could a slaveholders' republic be established in a society in which slaveholders were a minority? A third of the South's population was held in bondage and could hardly be relied upon to support a government built on slavery. Of the South's free population, three-fourths of whom owned no slaves, most made it clear in the winter 1860–61 elections for convention delegates that they opposed secession.[3] Nevertheless, state conventions across the South, all of them dominated by slaveholders, in the end ignored majority will and took their states out of the Union. One Texas politician conceded that ambitious colleagues had engineered secession without strong backing from "the mass of the people." A staunch South Carolina secessionist admitted the same: "But whoever waited for the common people when a great move was to be made—We must make the move and force them to follow."[4]

Still, there was some general enthusiasm for the war among common whites in the wake of Lincoln's call for volunteers to invade the South. Whatever their misgivings about secession, invasion was another matter. And, despite Lincoln's promise of noninterference with slavery, "fear of Negro equality," as historian Georgia Lee Tatum put it, "caused some of the more ignorant to rally to the support of the Confederacy."[5] But southern enlistments declined rapidly after First Manassas, or Bull Run, as Yankees called the battle. Men were reluctant to leave their families in the fall and winter of 1861–62, and many of those already in the army deserted to help theirs.

The Confederacy's response to its recruitment and desertion problems served only to weaken its support among plain folk. In April 1862, the Confederate Congress passed the first general conscription act in American history. But men of wealth could avoid the draft by hiring a substitute or paying an exemption fee. Congress also made slaveholders owning twenty or more slaves automatically exempt from the draft. This twenty-slave law was the most widely hated act ever imposed by the Confederacy, especially for poor soldiers already in the ranks. Said Private Sam Watkins of Tennessee, "It gave us the blues; we wanted twenty negroes. Negro property suddenly became very valuable, and there was raised the howl of 'rich man's war, poor man's fight.'" He continued, "From this time on till the end of the war, a soldier was simply a machine. We cursed the war . . . we cursed the Southern Confederacy."[6]

To make matters worse, planters devoted much of their land to cotton and tobacco, while soldiers and their families went hungry. During the course of the war, planters committed the manpower equivalent of the entire Confederate army to cotton and tobacco production. In the spring of 1862, a southwest Georgia man wrote to Governor Joe Brown about planters growing too much cotton, begging him to "stop those internal enemies of the country, for they will whip us sooner than all Lincolndom combined could do it."[7] Thousands of planters and merchants defied the Confederacy's cotton export policy and smuggled it out by the ton. Most states passed laws limiting slaveholders' production of nonfood items, but enforcement was lax and planters ignored the law. With prices on the rise, many cotton producers and dealers were getting richer than ever. Some openly bragged that the longer the war went on, the more money they made.

The inevitable result of cotton and tobacco overproduction was a severe food shortage that hit soldiers' families especially hard. With their husbands and fathers at the front and impressment officers taking what little food they had, it was difficult for soldiers' wives to provide for themselves and their children. Planters had promised to keep soldiers' families fed, but they never grew enough food to meet the need. Much of what food they did produce was sold to speculators, who hoarded it or priced it far beyond the reach of most plain folk.

Desperate to avoid starvation, thousands of women turned to individual and mass theft. As early as 1862, food riots began breaking out all over the South. Gangs of hungry women, many of them armed, ransacked stores, depots, and supply wagons, searching for anything edible. Major urban centers, like Richmond, Atlanta, Mobile, and Galveston, experienced the biggest riots. Even in smaller towns, like Georgia's Valdosta and Marietta and North Carolina's High Point and Salisbury, hungry women looted for food.

In an open letter to the *Savannah Morning News*, one enraged Georgian was sure where the blame lay: "The crime is with the planters . . . as a class, they have yielded their patriotism, if they ever had any, to covetousness . . . for the sake of money, they are pursuing a course to destroy or demoralize our army—to starve out the other class dependent on them for provisions." The letter spoke for a great many plain folk. It seemed increasingly obvious to them that they were fighting a rich man's war, which made the problem of desertion that much worse. One Confederate officer wrote home to his wife that "discontent is growing rapidley in the ranks and I fear that unless something is done . . . we will have no army. The laws that have been passed generally protect the rich, and the poor begin to say it is the rich man's war and the poor man's fight, and they will not stand it."[8]

Desertion became so serious by the summer of 1863 that Jefferson Davis begged absentees to return. If only they would, he insisted, the Confederacy could match Union armies man for man. But they did not return. A year later, Davis publicly admitted that two-thirds of

Confederate soldiers were absent, most of them without leave. Many of these men joined antiwar organizations that had been active in the South since the war's beginning. Others joined with draft dodgers and other anti-Confederates to form tory or layout gangs. They attacked government supply trains, burned bridges, raided local plantations, and harassed impressment agents and conscript officers. Tory gangs were most numerous in the southern hill country and pine barrens, where they all but eliminated Confederate control by 1864. The Red River Valley of Texas and Louisiana served as a haven for those resisting the Confederacy, as did the Okefenokee Swamp in south Georgia.

Among the most enthusiastic southern anti-Confederates were African Americans, especially those held in slavery. The Confederacy's vice president, Alexander H. Stephens, had said in March 1861 that slavery was the natural condition of blacks and the cornerstone on which the new government was founded. With Lincoln's Emancipation Proclamation came a promise of freedom that enslaved blacks eagerly embraced. In fact, they were taking freedom for themselves long before the Proclamation took effect in 1863. From the war's outset, they began to travel at will, gather freely, refuse instruction, and resist punishment. In so doing they undermined both slavery and the Confederate war effort.

Blacks often went so far as to strike out openly against slaveholders and local authorities, sometimes cooperating in the effort with whites. Deserters escaping the Confederate army could rely on slaves to give them food and shelter on the journey back home. Others joined tory gangs in their war against the Confederacy. Two slaves in Dale County, Alabama, helped John Ward, leader of a local deserter gang, kill their owner in his bed. In the spring of 1862, three white citizens of Calhoun County, Georgia, were arrested for supplying area slaves with firearms in preparation for a rebellion. Two years later, slaves in neighboring Brooks County conspired with a local white man, John Vickery, to take the county and hold it for the Union. Tens of thousands of blacks fled to federal lines and joined Union forces. Of about two hundred thousand blacks under federal arms, over three-fourths were native southerners. Together with roughly three hundred thousand southern whites who did the same, southerners who served in the Union military totaled nearly half a million, or about a quarter of all federal armed forces.[9]

Like southerners generally, southern Indians too were divided in their feelings toward the Confederacy. Most were residents of Indian Territory, where slavery was permitted, and were only a generation removed from their native lands in the Southeast. Many had family ties to southern whites. Still, there were those who insisted on honoring treaty agreements with the United States, hoping to garner favor from the Lincoln Administration. Others, like John Ross of the Cherokees, tried to steer a neutral course. But after federal troops pulled out of the region in 1861, most native leaders allied themselves with the Confederacy, hoping that if the South could secure its independence, perhaps they could as well. Still, violent divisions remained. Such divisions often had deep roots going back generations and reflected much the same question that had long divided the natives—would cooperation with or opposition to the whites bring a better result? And with which whites should alliances, if any, be made? Those divisions also reflected class divisions within the Territory nations, which broke down largely along mixed-blood/full-blood lines. Slaveholding was more common among the dominant and affluent mixed-bloods, who tended to side with the Confederacy. Most full-bloods, like Opothleyahola of the Creek Nation, continued to oppose a Confederate alliance. By the winter of 1861–62, a full-blown civil war was under way among the Indians, adding a further dimension to southern disunity.

The important story of dissent in the Civil War South, buried for so long under a mountain of military/political tracts and Lost Cause hyperbole, has in recent years become something of a cutting-edge topic among professional historians. Though traditional histories still tend to downplay the significance of internal southern conflict, that is becoming more difficult as new studies of southern dissent, mostly state and local examinations, have appeared. The recent film *Cold Mountain* has gone some way toward showing the public another side of the southern experience. But it remains overshadowed in the public mind by pictures like *Gone with the Wind*, *Gettysburg*, and *Gods and Generals*, all of which foster the popular myth of wartime southern unity.

The myth is bolstered by some of our most widely read schoolbooks. Far too many texts continue to teach that the North's greater population and industry explain Union victory. Yes, the North had more factories. But the South imported and produced arms enough to keep its troops supplied. Never was a Confederate army defeated in battle for lack of munitions.[10] What the Confederacy lacked was sufficient food, mainly because planters grew too much cotton and tobacco. And the Confederates lacked consistently willing men to carry arms. Certainly the North's population was greater. But Confederate armies were nearly always outnumbered mainly because so many southerners refused to serve—or served on the Union side. The Confederacy could nearly have met the Union man for man had it not been for problems of desertion and draft dodging, which were far greater for the Confederates than the Federals. Furthermore, if the nearly half-million southerners who served in the Union military had been with the Confederates, the opposing forces would have been almost evenly matched.

Why that reality so often goes unnoticed has much to do with regional vanity, North and South. It seems to gratify the pride of most southerners, at least white southerners, to think that the wartime South was united. It seems also to gratify the pride of many northerners to think their ancestors defeated a united South. Few northerners seem willing to consider that the Union may not have been preserved, that chattel slavery may not have ended when it did, without the service of nearly half a million southerners in Union blue, not to mention the internal resistance of many more.

Our skewed image of the Civil War South also stems in part from the ways in which we emphasize the era's military and political aspects. The great mass of literature dealing with the war years focuses largely on battles and leaders. Such studies are crucial, to be sure. But focusing so much of our collective attention on those aspects tends to foster the myth of sectional unity, minimizing dissent or ignoring it altogether. In so doing, we paint all southerners, all white southerners at least, with a broad brush of rebellion. This oversimplified and often not-so-subtle effort to, in a sense, generally demonize white southerners has led to the mistaken idea that the terms "Southern" and "Confederate" were interchangeable during the war. They are used as such in most texts to this day. That firmly embedded misconception leaves little room in the popular and, too often, professional imagination for the hundreds of thousands of southern whites who opposed secession and worked against the Confederacy.

Though Americans today often fail to acknowledge it, southern disunity was widely acknowledged during the Civil War. Near the war's midpoint, one Alabama planter frankly admitted that the myth of the "faithful slave" was long since exploded. Slaves wanted freedom and were determined to undermine the Confederacy wherever they could. So were many southern whites. In 1863, one Georgia newspaper editor wrote of the South's inner civil war: "We are fighting each other harder than we ever fought the enemy."[11] That inner civil war made it increasingly difficult, and ultimately impossible, for the Confederacy to survive.

1

"Nothing but Divisions Among Our People"

A few weeks after Abraham Lincoln's election, in the Confederacy's future capital city, Virginia Unionists organized a mass meeting of the "working men of Richmond" to oppose secession. At a second such meeting, they upheld the federal government's right to suppress secession by force if necessary. Anti-secession mechanics in Frederick County, Virginia, met to denounce the "folly and sinister selfishness of the demagogues of the South." Workers in Portsmouth were equally stirred: "We look upon any attempt to break up this Government or dissolve this Union as an attack upon the rights of the people of the whole country."[1]

From western Virginia came word of Union meetings in Harrison, Monongalia, Wood, Tyler, Marion, and Mason counties. Preston County residents drew up a resolution declaring that "any attempt upon the part of the state to secede will meet with the unqualified disapprobation of the people of this county." A resolution from Wheeling insisted that "it is the sacred duty of all men in public offices and all citizens in private life to support and defend the Constitution . . . the election of Abraham Lincoln . . . does not, in our judgment, justify secession, or a dissolution of our blessed and glorious Union."[2]

There were similar sentiments in the Deep South. In the heart of Georgia's cotton belt, a large crowd of local citizens gathered at Crawfordville to declare: "We do not consider the election of Lincoln and

Hamlin[3] as sufficient cause for Disunion or Secession." A mass meeting in Walker County expressed the same sentiment: "We are not of the opinion that the election of any man in accordance with the prescribed forms of the Constitution is sufficient cause to disrupt the ties which bind us to the Union." In Harris County, the newspaper editor stated firmly that "we are a Union loving people here, and will never forsake the old 'Star Spangled Banner.'" To stress the point, he printed the names of 175 local men, all pledged to "preserve the honor and rights of the South *in the Union*."[4]

At Lake Jackson Church near Tallahassee, Florida, there assembled a crowd of 400 "whose heart beat time to the music of the Union." A convention of laborers in Nashville, Tennessee, declared their "undying love for the Union" and called secessionist efforts "treason . . . by designing and mad politicians."[5] All across the South, thousands of worried southerners did their best to head off secession. While most had opposed Lincoln's candidacy, a similar majority saw no reason to destroy the country over his election. Three-fourths of southern whites held no slaves and tended to believe that, as one Georgia man wrote, "this fuss was all for the benefit of the wealthy."[6]

Still, slaveholders pressed their advantage in the face of popular opposition. Alfred P. Aldrich, a South Carolina legislator and staunch secessionist, acknowledged that most southerners opposed disunion. "But," he asked, "whoever waited for the common people when a great move was to be made—We must make the move and force them to follow."[7] Senator Robert Toombs of Georgia likewise expressed his determination to see the South out of the Union whether most southerners supported it or not. "Give me the sword!" he blustered. "But if you do not place it in my hands, before God *I will take it*!" When he learned of Toombs's threat, one Georgia newspaper editor wrote: "Let him take it, and, by way of doing his country a great service, let him run about six inches of it into his left breast."[8]

Secessionists employed more than words in pursuing disunion. One southerner recalled that secessionists "used the most shameless and unconcealed intimidation" to suppress their opponents. A secession meeting in Richmond turned violent when twenty or so "muscular young men" attacked several Unionists who tried to disrupt a secessionist speech by whistling "Yankee Doodle." That was hardly the worst of it. In Mississippi's Panola County, a group of vigilantes announced their intention to "take notice of, and punish all and every persons who may . . . prove themselves untrue to the South, or Southern Rights, in any way whatever." There was no mistaking their meaning. In Tallahatchie County, a secessionist gang of Mississippi "Minute Men" lynched seven local Unionists. In Florida, secessionists formed armed bands of "Regulators" who ambushed Union men by night.[9]

So the Civil War did not begin at Fort Sumter. It did not even begin as a war between North and South. It began, and continued throughout, as a war between southerners themselves.

Animosities that tore the South apart from within had been building for decades and had much to do with a widening gap between rich and poor. On the Civil War's eve, nearly half the South's personal income went to just over a thousand families. The region's poorest half held only 5 percent of its agricultural wealth. Land and slave ownership dominated the South's economy, but most white southerners held no slaves, and many owned no land. According to one antebellum resident, in southwest Georgia's Early County "there was a body of land east of Blakely . . . which made 216 square miles, and not one foot of it was owned by a poor man." John Welch, a poor farmer in western Tennessee, complained that the slaveholders of his district "owned nearly all the land and they wanted to keep it."[10]

Opportunities for upward mobility had not been so limited just a generation earlier. Land had been relatively cheap in the 1820s and 1830s after the Indians were forced into western exile. Wealthy men from crowded coastal regions bought much of the land, but small farmers too could get loans to buy land and slaves. Cotton prices were on the rise, and there was every reason to expect that loans could easily be repaid. Some yeoman farmers who were lucky enough to have good land and good weather became affluent slaveholders and even planters.[11]

But with a single act, Congress put an end to the hopes of millions. So did the resulting economic depression, known as the Panic of 1837. A year before, at the urging of Andrew Jackson—proclaimed friend of the common man—Congress had passed the Specie Circular Act, which made it difficult for small farmers to buy land. No longer would the government accept banknotes in payment for former Indian lands. Only gold or silver would do. Plain folk seldom had the required "hard money" on hand, nor did they have the collateral with which to borrow it. Successful loan applications fell dramatically, and small banks across the country began to fail. The depression that followed helped drive cotton prices down as well, and they continued falling into the 1840s. With their staple crop income cut nearly in half, debt-ridden farmers found it impossible to keep up loan payments. Their land and slaves were repossessed and sold at auction, usually to already well-established slaveholders. The sheriff in Henry County, Alabama, auctioned off so many small farms that enraged locals demanded his resignation.[12]

Some farmers were able to keep a few acres and eke out a living as lesser yeomen. But many lost everything and fell into tenancy and sharecropping. When the cotton market finally recovered, affluent slaveholders held nearly all the South's best land. Most other farmers found themselves trapped in a system of poverty from which few could ever escape. One contemporary described tenants in the South Carolina upcountry as "poor people who can neither buy [land] nor move away." Even for those who managed a move to cheaper western lands, disappointment most often awaited them. Historian Victoria Bynum recently noted that "most poor whites' geographic mobility grew out of class immobility rather than frontier opportunities. . . . Many moved time and again in search of elusive prosperity."[13]

"The slaveholders buy up all the fertile lands," recalled a disgruntled Mississippian who witnessed the process firsthand. "Hence the poor are crowded out, and if they remain in the vicinity of the place of their nativity, they must occupy the poor tracts whose sterility does not excite the cupidity of their rich neighbors." That gap between rich and poor continued to widen through the 1850s. Planters bought more and more land, forcing a rise in land prices and making it nearly impossible for smaller farmers to increase their holdings or for tenant farmers to buy any land at all. Wealth in terms of slaveholding was also becoming concentrated in fewer hands. During the last decade of the antebellum period, the proportion of slaveholders in the free population dropped by 20 percent. Economic circumstances beyond their control forced many yeomen into landless tenancy—so many that some commentators predicted the complete disappearance of small independent farmers. By 1860, at least 25 percent of southern farmers were tenants, and more were joining their landless ranks every day.[14]

"The Hell of Slavery"

At the bottom of the social scale, in a caste of their own separate and distinct from the white class structure, were free blacks and slaves. Numbering roughly four and a half million in 1860, they made up nearly a sixth of the nation's population and well over a third of that in the slave states. A total of about four million were held in slavery.

Despite the social chasm between them, living and working conditions for slaves were not altogether different from those of many southern whites. In describing a typical day's labor, one slave remembered getting up every morning before sunrise to work in the fields. After a short dinner break at noon, it was back to the fields until dark. And the women, she said, worked just like the men.[15] The same was true among white tenant farmers, sharecroppers, and lesser yeomen of both genders. Similarly, neither slaves nor poor whites had much hope of ever improving their condition. Poor whites may have been free in the strictest sense, but freedom meant little without opportunities for economic improvement. On the other hand, African Americans held by law as property bore physical and psychological burdens from which poor whites were mercifully free. Threats of violence and forced separation from loved ones were constantly present in the slave's life. Inevitably, to every extent possible, slaves pushed back against those threats.

Slaveholder claims to the contrary, the "wise master," in the words of historian Kenneth Stampp, "did not take seriously the belief that Negroes were natural-born slaves. He knew better. He knew that Negroes freshly imported from Africa had to be broken into bondage; that each succeeding generation had to be carefully trained. This was no easy task, for the bondsman rarely submitted willingly. Moreover, he rarely submitted completely. In most cases there was no end to the need for control—at least not until old age reduced the slave to a condition of helplessness." Control of elderly slaves was hardly a concern in any case. Less than four in a hundred ever lived to see age sixty.[16]

Slave resistance took many forms, the most celebrated of which was the Underground Railroad. Harriet Tubman, perhaps the most successful of the railroad's "conductors," led hundreds of slaves to freedom. Rewards offered for her capture totaled upwards of $40,000, but she was never caught. Neither was Arnold Gragston, an enslaved Kentuckian who ferried hundreds of fellow bondsmen and women across the Ohio River before making his own escape. Harry Smith helped escapees cross the river at Louisville but never escaped himself because he did not want to leave his family. Thanks to Tubman, Gragston, Smith, and so many others like them, well over one hundred thousand enslaved people had escaped by 1860.[17]

Though most blacks remained in bondage, they still resisted. Slaves organized work slowdowns. They feigned illness and ignorance. They sabotaged or destroyed equipment, or used the threat of such action as a bargaining tool for better treatment. If they failed to get it, suicide was not uncommon. Some slaves were treated so badly that death was a welcome relief. One Georgia slave took her own life by swallowing strychnine. In another case, two enslaved parents agreed to "send the souls of their children to Heaven rather than have them descend to the hell of slavery." After releasing their children's souls, they released their own. Another enslaved mother killed all thirteen of her children "rather than have them suffer slavery." Two boatloads of Africans newly arrived in Charleston committed mass suicide by starving themselves to death.[18]

Sometimes slaves killed their oppressors. Most famous for its violence was Nat Turner's 1831 Virginia rebellion in which well over fifty whites died. There were many others who fought back or conspired to do so. In 1800, over a thousand slaves marched on Richmond. The governor called out hundreds of armed militiamen to turn them back. When asked why he had rebelled, one slave calmly replied: "I have nothing more to offer than what General Washington would have had to offer, had he been taken by the British officers and put to trial by them. I have ventured my life in endeavoring to obtain the liberty of my countrymen, and am willing to sacrifice to their cause." There were similar efforts to gain liberty in Petersburg and Norfolk.[19]

In 1811, four hundred Louisiana slaves rose up for freedom. A year later, there was rebellion in New Orleans. In 1837, slaves near that city formed a rebel band and killed several whites before they were captured. Slaves fought back individually, too. In 1849, a slave in Chambers County, Alabama, shot his owner. In Macon County, a slave "violently attacked with a knife and cut to pieces" his overseer. A Florida slave killed his owner with an ax as the white man attempted to administer "punishment." When Edward Covey tried to bind and beat Frederick Douglass, he fought Covey off. From that day forward, Douglass later wrote, "I did not hesitate to let it be known of me, that the white man who expected to succeed in whipping, must also succeed in killing me." Covey never touched him again.[20]

Douglass was fortunate to escape slavery before resistance cost him his life. Most others were not so lucky. Slaves were defined as property by slave state courts and, in the Dred Scott case of 1857, by the United States Supreme Court. As personal property, slaves were subject to the absolute authority of slaveholders and to whatever controls they chose to employ. As one member of the Georgia Supreme Court insisted: "Subordination can only be maintained by the right to give moderate correction—a right similar to that which exists in the father over his children."[21]

There were, however, laws limiting abusiveness of parents over their children. Slaves enjoyed few such legal protections. And the definition of "moderate correction" was left entirely to the slaveholder. "Should death ensue by accident, while this slave is thus receiving moderate correction," recalled a British visitor, "the constitution of Georgia kindly denominates the offence justifiable homicide." The Reverend W.B. Allen, a former Alabama slave, personally knew those

On Christmas Eve, 1855, a slave patrol closed in on escaping fugitives from Loudon County, Virginia. The self-emancipated blacks brandished their weapons and held their ground. Ann Wood, the group's leader, dared her pursuers to fire. The patrollers backed off, and Ann led her friends on to Philadelphia. Rising resistence among slaves during the 1850s aroused worries about loss of control among slaveholders, which contributed to the move toward secession. Illustration from Still, *Underground Rail Road*.

in bondage who were beaten to death for nothing more than being off the plantation without written permission. Other offenses that might result in extreme punishment were lying, loitering, stealing, and "talking back to—'sassing'—a white person."[22]

Aside from the brutality they sanctioned, most state slave codes defined the limits of life for slaves far beyond their status as personal property. No slave could carry a gun, own property, travel without a written pass, testify against whites in a court of law, or learn to read or write. Slave gatherings, even for religious services, were forbidden without a white person present. Free blacks labored under similar legal restrictions. They had to have a white legal guardian and could not own property in their own names. In the words of historian James Oakes, "it was like turning the Bill of Rights upside down."[23]

"The Argument of the Cotton Gin"

By the mid-nineteenth century, the tools of slave control seemed to have firmly secured perhaps the world's most rigid system of racial caste. It had not always been so. Two centuries before, in the early decades of British North America, there had been no distinctions in law or custom between whites and blacks. In fact, the term "slave" was often used in reference to all those laboring as indentured servants. Like white servants, blacks typically gained freedom after serving a given number of years, usually seven. The servants themselves were, as historian Kenneth Stampp put it, "remarkably unconcerned about their visible physical differences." Black and white servants worked together, played together, lived together, and married each other. The harsher forms of racism that would become all too familiar to later generations of Americans were absent through most of the seventeenth century.[24]

That began to change as colonial elites, fearing rebellion from below, took steps to divide poor whites and blacks both socially and economically. The threat of rebellion was very real in a society where most people were servants, landless tenants, or small yeomen holding marginal lands that the gentry did not want. Few could vote or hold office. Those privileges were restricted by wealth throughout the colonies. As early as 1661, the Virginia assembly took a major step toward social division by defining blacks who had not already acquired freedom as "servants for life." It was not enough. In 1676, during Bacon's Rebellion, the under-classes of Virginia, black and white, united against their oppressors. They established fortifications all along the James River, marched against the colonial capital at Jamestown, and came close to seizing control of the colony before Crown forces put them down. Among the last to surrender was a band of eighty blacks and twenty whites.[25]

Bacon's Rebellion sent shock waves through the ranks of the ruling classes. Many feared that some future insurrection, perhaps larger and better organized, might succeed. What could be done to avert such a calamity? Their strategy became something akin to the military maxim "divide and conquer." In the words of historian Edmund Morgan: "For those with eyes to see, there was an obvious lesson in the rebellion. Resentment of an alien race might be more powerful than resentment of an upper class."[26] Encouraging a social distance between poor whites and blacks, assigning whites the superior position, might make the two groups less likely to unite.

In the late seventeenth and early eighteenth centuries, colonial legislatures throughout British North America passed a series of laws designed to do just that. They outlawed interracial marriage. They amended criminal codes to deal more harshly with blacks than whites. They defined black servants as slaves outright, the absolute property of slaveholders. They mandated limited lands for whites on completing their term of indenture and restricted the practice of most skilled trades to whites only. None of this was enough to qualify lower-class whites for voting or office holding. That would not come for another century or more. But it did instill in whites of all classes a sense that they were somehow "better" than those with even a drop of African blood—though many had a few such drops in their own bloodlines, whether they knew it or not.[27]

The strategy worked, and worked even better than elites had hoped. The new racism, they found, was a self-perpetuating thing passed on from generation to generation, keeping the poor divided and more easily controlled. Lower-class whites still resented their oppressors. There were any number of insurrections by poor whites in the eighteenth century—the Regulator Movement, Shays' Rebellion, and the Whiskey Rebellion among them. Slaves, too, occasionally rose in rebellion. But never again did poor whites unite with blacks against their common oppressor to the extent that they had in 1676 Virginia.

Ironically, the eighteenth century was also a time of changing attitudes toward slavery. The scientific revolution had shown that there were natural laws governing the physical universe. Some reasoned that perhaps there were also natural laws governing human interaction, that people even had natural rights. The most basic of these, as Thomas Jefferson wrote, would surely be "life, liberty, and the pursuit of happiness."[28] If so, was not slavery a violation of natural rights? The idea troubled many planters of Jefferson's generation, schooled as they were in Enlightenment philosophy. Most were not willing to give up slavery themselves, but they did see it as an unworthy institution. Some, like George Washington, freed their slaves in their wills. Even Virginia's arch-conservative John Randolph of Roanoke freed his slaves in his last will and testament.

Aside from the moral issues involved, most Americans of that era saw slavery as an economic dead end. The institution thrived only in the tobacco fields of the Chesapeake region and the rice country of coastal Carolina and Georgia. As the nation expanded, slavery would become proportionally less important to the nation's economy and would eventually die a natural death. But the development of an efficient cotton engine, or "gin," in the eighteenth century's last decade changed all that. The cotton gin became the vehicle by which slavery was carried across the Deep South. Not surprisingly, attitudes toward slavery changed with the institution's growing economic importance.

That change did not occur overnight. Antislavery sentiment in the South remained open and active through the early 1830s. As of 1827, 106 of the country's 130 abolitionist societies were in the South. To discourage the use of slave labor, some of those societies paid above-market prices for cotton produced without slave labor. North Carolina Quakers and Methodists repeatedly petitioned their state legislature for emancipation. In 1821, a leading Georgia newspaper insisted: "There is not a single editor in these States who dares advocate slavery as a principle." Far from advocating slavery, Alabama editor James G. Birney started an abolitionist newspaper. In 1827, the Alabama legislature passed a law prohibiting the importation of slaves from other states, and at every session throughout the decade, members proposed legislation favoring gradual emancipation. As late as 1831, a proposal to end slavery was introduced in the Virginia state assembly.[29]

But the early nineteenth century was also the era of Indian removal. In 1827, Georgia forced out its few remaining Creeks. Nine years later, Alabama did the same. The 1830s saw the Choctaws and Chickasaws driven out of Mississippi. And Georgia annexed Cherokee land following the 1829 discovery of gold there. In an effort that carried the hopes of all Indian nations with it, the Cherokees fought to keep their land through the court system. The United States Supreme Court finally responded in 1832 with its *Worcester v. Georgia* decision: by treaty obligation, by prior act of Congress, and by the Constitution itself, the Indians held legal title to their land. But President Andrew Jackson refused to enforce the ruling, and Congress declined to intervene. Georgia ignored the court order, and the Cherokees were driven westward on the Trail of Tears. A quarter of them died on that brutal forced march. In 1842, Florida's Seminoles became the last of the southern nations to be violently relocated to land that they were promised would be theirs for "as long as grass grows or water runs." At the time it was called Indian Territory. Today it is called Oklahoma.[30]

Indian removal completed the transition in slaveholder attitudes begun a generation earlier. Slaveholders no longer viewed slavery as a temporary necessity but held it to be a positive good, divinely ordained, for the slaveholder, the slave, the nation, and the world. Though religion, racism, pride, and fear were all used to bolster slavery at home and justify it abroad, the driving force behind planters' proslavery campaign was the same that caused their change of attitude in the first place—economic self-interest. Some planters, like Georgia's Benjamin Harvey Hill, were candid enough to admit it: "In our early history the Southern statesmen were antislavery in feeling. So were Washington, Jefferson, Madison, Randolph, and many of that day who never studied the argument of the cotton gin, nor heard the eloquent productions of the great Mississippi Valley. Now our people not only see the justice of slavery, but its providence too."[31] It was cotton, along with tobacco, rice, and sugar, all cultivated by slave labor, that gave planters their economic power. And it was this power that gave planters the political strength with which to control the South's lower classes and silence or exile slavery's opponents.

"The White Man Is Robbed by the Slave System"

Though most white males in the South could vote, and many did, there was not much for them to decide beyond the local level. Then as now, any successful bid for high political office depended as much on wealth as votes—and wealth went hand in hand with slavery. Both major parties, Whig and Democrat, centered more on personalities than issues, and both represented slaveholding interests. Fear of slave rebellion and abolitionism were always central campaign themes, with each candidate trying to "out-nigger" the other. But after the early 1830s, slavery's continued existence was rarely a topic of political debate in the South.[32]

The influence of planter wealth in politics was not lost on the plain folk. As one farmer noted, the planter "used money whenever he could. This fact usually elected him." A Tennessean noted that only slaveholders could afford "big barbecues during times of elections." In politics, said another, "it seemed that the slave holder had the fire-power." Another nonslaveholder observed that the wealthy bought "votes, with liquor and cigars." In Columbus, Georgia, a process of buying votes known as "penning" was so common that it came to be called "the peculiar institution of Muscogee County." On the day before an election, campaign workers would round up men off the streets, lodge them in local hotels, get them drunk, and then march them to the polls next morning. The party with the largest "pen" usually won the election.[33]

Obviously, these men felt that their right to vote meant little in the absence of real choices. Their interests would not be represented no matter who won. Donald Debats, in his study of the South's antebellum political culture, concluded that "far from encouraging citizen participation in the party system, the leaders of both parties discouraged grassroots politics. . . . Beyond the simple casting of a ballot, the role of the citizen in the party system was passive by design." Moreover, poorer men in some states were kept entirely out of the political process by long-established property qualifications, along with other restrictive devices, such as the poll tax.[34]

Slaveholder control of southern politics, at least at the state and congressional levels, was nearly absolute. One southerner complained that although a majority of qualified voters owned no slaves, "they have never yet had any part or lot in framing the laws under which they live. There is no legislation except for the benefit of slavery and slaveholders." The predominance of slaveholders in politics helped ensure that. During the 1850s, though the proportion of slaveholders in the South's general population was falling, their numbers in southern state legislatures were on the rise. In Mississippi, for example, the percentage of state lawmakers who owned slaves rose from 61 percent to more than 80 percent.[35]

It seemed that slaveholder dominance of the South was assured and that slavery as an institution was secure. But even as slaveholders consolidated their political control, cracks appeared at the base of the South's social pyramid. They had always been there, suppressed and controlled. As wealth became concentrated in fewer hands and opportunities for economic advancement were increasingly closed to yeomen and poor whites, those cracks began to grow.

"A renter had no chance to save anything," complained a western Tennessee tenant farmer. "Slaveholders were the only men that could save enough money to do anything." Another agreed, saying that slaveholders "kept the poor class of people down as much as possible." The social gap was just as obvious as the economic. A North Carolina tenant said slaveholders "felt biggety and above poor folk who did not have slaves." A Tennessee commoner noted that slaveholders "thought because they owned slaves they were better than any body." Another complained that even "slave holder children . . . made fun of the non-slave holders." J.C. Keysaer, a yeoman farmer in Tennessee, insisted that "slave holders always acted as if they were of a better class and there was always an unpleasant feeling between slave holders and those working themselves." William Johnson, also of Tennessee, put it more bluntly: "Those that didn't own slaves hated those that did."[36]

Despite the antebellum South's proslavery climate, there remained an undercurrent of antislavery sentiment that had never completely died away. Some nonslaveholders continued to view slavery as a moral evil. Others opposed it on economic grounds. Still others opposed slavery simply because they were too poor ever to own slaves themselves. Whatever the reasons, antislavery feeling was on the rise. In 1849, a Georgia carpenter openly declared his opposition to slavery. Competition with slave labor, he believed, kept his wages low. That same year, mechanics and workingmen in the slave state of Kentucky met at Lexington and drew up this statement: "Resolved, That the institution of slavery is prejudicial to every interest of the State . . . it degrades labor, enervates industry, interferes with the occupations of free laboring citizens, separates too widely the poor and the rich, shuts out the laboring classes from the blessings of education . . . and as slavery tends to the monopoly of as well as the degradation of labor, public and private right require its ultimate extinction."[37]

Experience suggested truth in that statement to southern laborers. Wage levels in the South were as much as 30 percent below those of the North. There was little southern workers could do about it, not when slave labor was so readily available. In 1830, out-of-work stone-cutters in Norfolk, Virginia, asked the Navy Department to stop using slaves in construction of a dry dock. The Navy refused. When the workers appealed to Congress, they were ignored. In 1847, when employees at Richmond's Tredegar Iron Works went on strike to protest the use of slave labor, some were hauled into court and prosecuted. So were New Orleans longshoremen when they walked out for higher wages. One observer wrote: "I have seen free white mechanics obliged to stand aside while their families were suffering for the necessaries of life, when slave mechanics, owned by rich and influential men, could get plenty of work; and I have heard these same white mechanics breathe the most bitter curses against the institution of slavery and the slave aristocracy." That aristocracy, wrote historian Roger Shugg, "was hardly of a mind to bargain with workers of one race when it owned so many of another."[38]

But there was danger in refusing to bargain, most of all to slavery's survival. If nonslaveholders felt thwarted by the institution of slavery, how long could it last? In 1850, an editorial in the New Orleans–based *De Bow's Review* pointed to the danger: "The great mass of our poor white population begin to understand that they have rights. . . . They are fast learning that there is an almost infinite world of industry opening before them, by which they can elevate themselves and their families from wretchedness and ignorance to competence and intelligence. *It is this great upbearing of our masses that we are to fear, so far as our institutions are concerned.*"[39] The most endangered institution to which the editor referred was slavery.

That danger seemed increasingly real to slaveholders, knowing as they did that there were southern whites who worked against slavery in any way they could, up to and including rebellion. Four white South Carolinians were thrown in jail for encouraging Denmark Vesey in his attempt to free the slaves around Charleston. In Mississippi, twenty-one "bleached and unbleached" men were hanged for plotting a slave revolt. A white Virginian was hanged near Lynchburg for trying to organize a slave uprising. So were several whites in Jefferson County, Georgia, for the same offense. And four "white abolition rascals" helped organize a slave insurrection at Iberville, Louisiana.[40]

Among the most outspoken southern opponents of slavery was Hinton Rowan Helper. Born the son of a yeoman farmer in North

Hinton Rowan Helper, born to a North Carolina farm family, wrote what has been called "the most important single book, in terms of its political impact, that has ever been published in the United States." In *The Impending Crisis of the South*, published in 1857, Helper argued vigorously that the "lords of the lash are not only absolute masters of the blacks . . . but they are also the oracles and arbiters of all non-slaveholding whites, whose freedom is merely nominal." Such attitudes pointed to cracks in the facade of white unity that caused deep concern among many slaveholders. Portrait from Helper, *Impending Crisis* (1860 enlarged edition).

Carolina, Helper wrote what one historian has called "the most important single book, in terms of its political impact, that has ever been published in the United States. Even more, perhaps, than *Uncle Tom's Cabin*, it fed the fires of sectional controversy leading up to the Civil War." In *The Impending Crisis of the South*, published in 1857, Helper argued vigorously that the "lords of the lash are not only absolute masters of the blacks . . . but they are also the oracles and arbiters of all non-slaveholding whites, whose freedom is merely nominal." Slavery, Helper pointed out, existed for the benefit of only a very few. Its existence kept most white southerners in ignorance and poverty. The region's economic development was so retarded that it was little more than a colony of the North, providing raw materials and buying back manufactured goods.[41]

Not only did slaveholders hinder economic growth and enslave both blacks and whites, but their concentration on cotton and tobacco production forced the South into a state of dependency. Imports of manufactured goods had always been high, but food imports were also on the rise. During the 1850s, Georgia's comptroller-general lamented that with regard to food, the South was "every day becoming more dependent upon those 'not of us.'" In Georgia alone, livestock production was declining, the corn crop was stagnant, and in just ten years, the oat crop had dropped by more than half. Helper calculated that the value of the North's food production outstripped that of the South by almost $45 million annually. In light of all this, he said, "the first and most sacred duty of every southerner who has the honor and the interest of his country at heart is to declare himself an unqualified and uncompromising abolitionist."[42]

For those who looked beyond the Old South's plantation facade, the system's disadvantages were obvious enough. Like other visitors of his time, Englishman James Stirling, who passed through the South in the 1850s, asked why the region lagged behind in "development and prosperity." He could find only one answer—slavery. "When Southern statesmen count up the gains of slavery," warned Stirling, "let them not forget also to count its cost. They may depend upon it, there is a heavy 'per contra' to the profits of niggerdom."[43]

In 1855, in what one biographer called "one of the most succinct and pungent analyses of the racist component of the capitalistic labor system in our literature," Frederick Douglass, himself a former slave, reached out to oppressed whites in *My Bondage and My Freedom*.

> The slaveholders, with a craftiness peculiar to themselves, by encouraging the enmity of the poor, laboring white man against the blacks, succeeds in making the said white man almost as much a slave as the black slave himself. The difference between the white slave, and the black slave, is this: the latter belongs to *one* slaveholder, and the former belongs to *all* the slaveholders, collectively. The white slave has taken from him, by indirection, what the black slave has taken from him directly, and without ceremony. Both are plundered, and by the same plunderers. The slave is robbed, by his master, of all his earnings, above what is required for his bare physical necessities; and the white man is robbed by the slave system, of the just results of his labor, because he is flung into open competition with a class of laborers who work without wages.[44]

"If Lincoln Is Elected"

Growing discontent within the Cotton Kingdom, of little concern to slaveholders only a decade earlier, was by the 1850s causing panic among many of them. As if to confirm Helper's and Douglass's arguments, one planter asked: "If the poor whites realized that slavery kept them poor, would they not vote it down?" Many were beginning to think they might. How could support for slavery be maintained among lower-class whites if they owned no slaves and had no prospects of ever owning any? Some defenders of slavery pushed for state laws mandating that each white family be given at least one slave. Others demanded a slave for every white person. Still others argued for reopening the slave trade from Africa to bring down the price of slaves. The African slave trade had been closed in 1808 with the backing of slaveholders who saw it as a opportunity to artificially inflate the price of their slaves.[45]

Slavery's supporters realized too that their difficulty stemmed not just from the expense of slaves but also the lack of land. There was only so much prime farmland to go around, and slaveholders already had most of it. The noted southern commentator J.D.B. De Bow wrote in 1853: "The non-slaveholders possess generally but very small means, and the land which they possess is almost universally poor and so sterile that a scanty subsistence is all that can be derived from its cultivation, and the more fertile soil being in the hands of the slaveholders." So long as the opportunity to acquire land was limited, support for slavery among poor whites would be uncertain. To slaveholders it was clear—slavery must expand or die.[46]

Most white northerners, upper class and lower, were just as determined to keep slavery confined to the South. Industrialists viewed the West as a region ripe for exploitation of natural resources. Working folk saw in the West a chance to escape their dismal urban lives. Neither group wanted to compete with slaveholders for western lands. Nor did they want to live among blacks, either in the West or the North. There were a quarter million blacks already in the North, and most whites wanted no more. If slavery could expand anywhere, they feared, it might expand northward too, bringing thousands of blacks with it.

Though northern whites opposed slavery's expansion, they also tended to support its continued existence in the South. Working-class whites feared job competition from migrating southern blacks should they ever be freed. Those fears were inflamed by northern industrialists, who encouraged whites to view blacks already in the North as the source of their economic woes. Industrialists themselves feared a sharp rise in the price of cotton should slavery ever end. Slavery kept blacks in the South and in the fields, just where most white northerners wanted them.[47]

The simmering pot of sectional tension began to boil over in 1854 when Congress organized the territory of Kansas under popular sovereignty, placing the issue of slavery in the hands of territorial voters. Northern Free Soilers rushed to get settlers into Kansas as quickly as possible. Southern proslavery men did the same. During legislative elections, thousands of "border ruffians" crossed over from Missouri to vote, giving the proslavery faction a victory. The territorial governor called the election a fraud but let the results stand anyway. The new proslavery legislature quickly expelled its few antislavery members and proposed a state constitution allowing slavery. Under the new government, to question the legality of slavery in Kansas was a felony. To aid or encourage an escaping slave was a capital offense. But antislavery men formed their own competing government and drew up a constitution excluding both slavery and free blacks from the territory. The controversy was by no means limited to political bickering. A proslavery raid on the town of Lawrence left one man dead. In retaliation, an antislavery band led by John Brown, later of Harpers Ferry fame, killed five proslavery men along Pottawatomie Creek. Violence spread quickly and by the end of 1856 over two hundred people were dead.[48]

Bloodshed in Kansas further polarized the politics of slavery's expansion. It drove a firm wedge between the Democratic Party's northern and southern wings. It destroyed the Whigs as a national force. And it gave rise to a political party that was doggedly determined to keep slavery confined to the South. This new Republican Party was composed mainly of former Free Soilers and northern Whigs, with some northern Democrats and those abolitionists who could swallow their principles and ally themselves with men who had no wish to see slavery ended, only limited. They ran their first presidential candidate, Georgia-born John C. Frémont, in 1856. Though they lost to Democrat James Buchanan, Republicans established a sectional hold by capturing most of the free states. Southern Democrats added fuel to the sectional fire by consistently painting opponents with the broad brush of abolitionism, calling all who dared challenge them Black Republicans.

Born in Savannah, Georgia, and raised in Charleston, South Carolina, John C. Frémont held strong antislavery convictions. After graduating from the College of Charleston, Frémont joined the army and made a name for himself exploring the West, gaining national acclaim as "The Pathfinder." In 1856, Frémont became the first presidential candidate of the newly formed Republican Party, dedicated to keeping slavery out of the western territories. During the Civil War, Frémont served as a general in the Union army and pushed hard from the start to make the war a crusade against slavery. Illustration from the Library of Congress.

The U.S. Supreme Court's attempt to settle the slavery question once and for all did little better. With its 1857 Dred Scott decision, the southern-dominated High Court cited the Fifth Amendment, which stated in part: "No person shall . . . be deprived of life, liberty, or property without due process of law." Slaves were not persons but property, claimed the justices, and could not be barred from the territories. By implication, neither could slaveholders be barred from taking their "property" anywhere the Constitution held force, free states included. With its ill-fated attempt to cool a heated atmosphere, the Court destroyed the very idea of free states and gave Republicans an issue on which they could build.

John Brown's raid did the same for southern Democrats. In October 1859, Brown led an attempt to seize the federal arsenal at Harpers Ferry, Virginia, and arm local slaves in rebellion. The effort failed, and a Virginia court sentenced Brown to hang for treason. Abolitionists now had a martyr, but the South's secessionist "fire-eaters" had something even more valuable to their cause. In the aftermath of Brown's raid, they easily played on southern white fears of northerners encouraging slave revolt. Fire-eaters pointed to Brown's black allies in the Harpers Ferry raid and described them as organized and led by "blatant freedom shriekers." Slavery's defenders warned their neighbors to be on guard. The whole South, they said, might be infested with "agents of the Black Republican Party."[49]

This volatile atmosphere of panic and paranoia formed the backdrop of the presidential campaign in 1860. Democrats met in Charleston, South Carolina, but could not agree on a policy regarding slavery in the territories. Southern delegates insisted on adhering to the Dred Scott decision, which opened the territories to slavery. Northerners held to popular sovereignty, arguing that territorial legislatures could still effectively bar slavery simply by refusing to enact slave codes protecting the institution. Unable to find common ground in Charleston, the party reconvened in Baltimore later that year. Again it reached an impasse, and most southerners walked out. The remaining delegates nominated Stephen A. Douglas of Illinois, who had championed popular sovereignty in the Senate for more than a decade. Southern Democrats held their own convention and nominated Vice President John C. Breckinridge of Kentucky for the presidency.

The Republicans met in Chicago and agreed on nearly everything but a candidate. Of the leading contenders, none had enough delegates to ensure nomination going into the convention. The party finally settled on a dark horse from Illinois who seemed to be everyone's second choice, Abraham Lincoln. As for slavery, their platform aimed to keep it confined to the South.

Some southerners, mainly Whigs concerned by the developing sectional nature of the campaign, formed the Constitutional Union Party. To represent their ticket, they nominated John Bell of Tennessee for president and Edward Everett of Massachusetts for vice president. The party's only platform was the "Constitution of the Country, the Union of the States, and the Enforcement of the Laws." Of the four candidates for president that year, none commanded a national following. Stephen Douglas was the only one who really tried.

Though often portrayed as such, the campaign was hardly a referendum on secession among southern whites. To the contrary, though Breckinridge was the most ardently "southern rights" candidate, he offered himself as the only man who could save the Union. Douglas

had no real chance to win, and neither did Bell. If the "Black Abolitionist" Lincoln came to office, argued Breckinridge and many of his
supporters, the pressures for secession would be overwhelming. A
breakup of the Union, insisted Breckinridge, was something he never
wanted to see. By playing both sides, he attracted votes from southern
secessionists and Unionists alike to carry eleven of the fifteen slave
states.[50]

Northern Democrats were as eager as their southern counterparts
to paint Republicans with the broad brush of abolitionism. Lincoln,
though he personally found slavery distasteful, repeatedly insisted that
he had no intention of ending slavery. Neither was he "in favor of
bringing about in any way the social and political equality of the white
and black races. . . . I as much as any other man am in favor of having
the superior position assigned to the white race." Still, Lincoln's opponents insisted that a Lincoln presidency would lead both to slavery's
end and black equality. "If Lincoln is elected," wrote the Democratic
New York Herald to the workers of that city, "you will have to compete
with the labor of four million emancipated negroes." Besides that,
"the normal state of the negro is barbarism," wrote the editor of the
Concord, New Hampshire, *Democratic Standard*. "Aided by the white
man, and only through the medium of slavery, he becomes partially
civilized and Christianized." Most northerners tended to agree. But
unlike the Democrats, Lincoln and the Republicans pledged uncompromising opposition to slavery's expansion and support for free
land in the West. That promise gained Lincoln 54 percent of the
free states' popular vote and enough electoral votes to make him
president-elect.[51]

"Strife Around Our Firesides"

With Lincoln poised to enter the White House, secessionists felt that
now was the time to push hard for disunion. Most slaveholders would
certainly support such a move. If nonslaveholders could be made to
see Lincoln as a John Brown writ large, they too might support leaving
the Union. Secessionist leaders had to act quickly before Lincoln took
office, or they might never have another chance.

"It is absolute submission to Black Republican Rule," insisted fire-
eating Alabama secessionist Hubert Dent, "or absolute resistance."

Henry Lewis Benning of Georgia warned that Lincoln and his "Black Republican Party" intended to end slavery and hang all who supported it. The only way to avoid the "horrors of abolition" was immediate secession. "Why hesitate?" he asked. "The question is between life and death."[52]

Southern plain folk tended to be less certain. Those who held a few slaves certainly saw Lincoln as a potential threat despite his insistence to the contrary. For lesser yeomen and poor whites, though they owned no slaves, they still had their racist pride. Would Lincoln really try to free the slaves and grant them equality, as secessionists claimed? Governor Joe Brown of Georgia, self-proclaimed friend of the common man, said it was true. He warned that poor whites would suffer more than planters if Lincoln ended slavery. Former slaves would, Brown insisted, "come into competition with [poor whites], associate with them and their children as equals—be allowed to testify in court against them—sit on juries with them, march to the ballot box by their sides, and participate in the choice of their rulers—claim social equality with them—and ask the hands of their children in marriage."[53]

Still, many commoners were leery of secessionist motives. From the Alabama hill country, James Bell wrote that he was "a heap freader [more afraid] of the disunions with their helish principals than I am of lincon." For years, men like Bell had been told to think of themselves as the planters' equal. In 1860, Alabama planter and future Confederate Senator William Lowndes Yancey called whites the "master race, and the white man is the equal of every other white man." Governor Joe Brown of Georgia insisted that plain folk belonged "to the only true aristocracy, the race of *white men*."[54] But most southerners hardly lived as the planters' equals. Nor did they have the economic opportunities that might make it possible for them to do so. Most blamed the planters themselves for that. It was just as clear to plain folk that planters did not view them as equals, no matter what they said in public.

Many planters had indeed come to view themselves as aristocrats and poor whites as little better than slaves. One planter, in a private letter to a friend, wrote of poor whites: "Not one in ten is . . . a whit superior to a negro." Most planters tried to keep such opinions concealed, lest their hypocrisy be exposed. Occasionally, though, suggestions of planter arrogance slipped into print. In his 1854 defense of slavery, *Sociology for the South; or The Failure of Free Society*, George

Fitzhugh not only insisted that slavery was "the best form of society yet devised for the masses" but also "that slavery, *black or white*, was right and necessary." Could white slavery result if the slave system continued to grow? Some were beginning to think it might.[55]

In 1859, one poor Hancock County, Georgia, laborer confided to an acquaintance that if it came to a war over slavery, he was going to fight against it. Without slavery, he felt that perhaps he could get better wages. That same year, a farmer in Georgia's Taliaferro County was convicted of hiding a runaway slave for three months. Yet another in Greene County was found making fake passes for slaves and "teaching them to write and cipher." In South Carolina's Spartanburg District, a poor white woman, Elizabeth Blackwell, was accused of helping runaway slaves. Poor whites living in and around the Great Dismal Swamp of Virginia and North Carolina commonly harbored black fugitives.[56]

Some were prepared to go much further. In 1860, a large group of Alabama planters gathered to discuss ways to keep "low down poor whites" from plotting to free the slaves and redistribute land, resources, and wealth. An Alabamian confirmed slaveholder fears by pointing out that "slaves are constantly associating with low white men who are not slave owners. Such people are dangerous to the community." In Tennessee, police arrested a white man named Williams along with thirty slaves for plotting rebellion. Three Louisiana whites were charged with the same offense. Two in Mississippi were implicated in a slave conspiracy. A white man named Edward Chandler of Brandon, Mississippi, just east of Jackson, hatched a plot to unite free blacks and slaves in an uprising. With various means and motives, white southerners increasingly worked to undermine the slave system.[57]

It seemed obvious to most slaveholders that growing numbers of people like these were potential recruits for the Republican Party. With Lincoln in the White House and discontent among nonslaveholding whites on the rise, a truly national Republican Party might become a reality. A writer in *De Bow's Review* reminded the periodical's generally well-to-do readers that many poor whites harbored "a feeling of deep-rooted jealousy and prejudice, of painful antagonism, if not hostility, to the institution of negro slavery, that threatens the most serious consequences, the moment Black-republicanism becomes triumphant in the Union." One secessionist warned that if the slaveholders did not take their states out of the Union, there would indeed soon be "an Abolition party in the South, of Southern men." Another frankly admitted, "I mistrust our own people more than I fear all of the efforts of the Abolitionists."[58]

And what of the slaves themselves? Though they argued otherwise, slaveholders knew very well that slavery did not come naturally to those of African descent. Slaves had to be controlled through fear and violence, though that control was never complete. In 1856, a posse of North Carolina slaveholders succeeded only in getting one of their number killed when they attacked a settlement of black escapees hiding in a swamp. The former slaves yelled at their attackers to "come on, they were ready for them again." That same year, Governor Henry Wise of Virginia sent state troops into Alexandria to quell a slave uprising. Along the Cumberland River in Tennessee, authorities arrested sixty-five slaves and executed nine for plotting rebellion. A Galveston newspaper wrote in 1856 that "never had so many insurrections, or attempts at insurrection, occurred as in the past six months."[59] There was much more to come.

In August 1858, over fifty slaves on a Mississippi plantation refused to take orders and refused to be whipped for it. It took seventy-five armed white men to restore the planters' authority. That year a Louisiana newspaper wrote that there were "more cases of insubordination among the negro population . . . than ever known before." A Mississippi paper noted that cases of slaves killing their owners were "alarmingly frequent."[60]

All across the South, rebellion was on the rise in the late 1850s. Slaves wanted freedom, and by 1860 they believed Lincoln was promising just that. How could they think otherwise, with secessionists ranting throughout the South that Lincoln's ultimate goal was to free the slaves? One freedman remembered that slaves "hoped and prayed he would be elected. They wanted to be free and have a chance." In the lead-up to the election that year, rebellions and rumors of rebellions were rife across the South.[61]

When Lincoln won the presidency, most slaves took it as a sign that their prayers had been answered. Some did more than pray. They took action, expecting Lincoln to back them up. One Mississippi slave roused his companions to rebellion with the promise that "Lincoln would set us free." In Virginia, Chesterfield County slaves planned an uprising, sure that Lincoln would come to their aid. Such plots were

James Madison Wells, a member of an old Louisiana family (his father attended the state constitutional convention in 1811), supported Stephen A. Douglas for president and led the fight against secession in upstate Louisiana. Though Wells was one of the wealthiest planters in Rapides Parish, he denounced the Confederacy's cause as a rich man's war and took up arms against it. From his Bear Wallow stronghold, Wells led a band of anti-Confederate guerrillas in attacks against Rebel supply lines. Portrait from the Old State Capitol Center for Political and Governmental History, Baton Rouge, Louisiana.

common in the weeks after Lincoln's election. Louisiana sugar planter Alexander Pugh wrote in his diary that "the negroes have got it into their heads they are going to be free [as] of the 4th of March [1861]," the day of Lincoln's inaugural. That thought made slaveholders' blood run cold.[62]

More than the abolitionists, more than Lincoln himself, slaveholders feared the South's slaves and nonslaveholding whites. Control of neither group had ever been easy. By the late 1850s, it was getting harder. A Lincoln presidency would make control even more difficult, even if Lincoln himself was no direct threat. If the slave states remained in the Union, most slaveholders feared that their "peculiar institution" might collapse as much from internal as external pressures. Outside the Union, controlling the lower classes might be easier and slavery might be safer. Other factors certainly helped fuel the crisis. Overestimation of abolitionist strength in the North, the issue of slavery's expansion, and personal political ambitions all played their part. But slaveholders' fear of their fellow southerners was a primary, though publicly unacknowledged, force driving secession.

Even so, slaveholders were not entirely united behind the movement. Secession found its most enthusiastic support among the more numerous "new money" planters and lesser slaveholders. Their

spokesmen tended to be young up-and-coming lawyer/politicians trying to carve out a niche for themselves at the expense of the old establishment. On the other side, wealthier and more conservative "old
money" planters tended to view secession as more risky than remaining in the Union. Some, like James Madison Wells of Louisiana, were
old-line Whigs who held a long-standing commitment to the Union.
Others viewed themselves simply as having a stake in preserving the
status quo. Still others felt that even if slavery within the Union was in
danger, they had enough capital and investments—much of it in the
North—to ride out slavery's demise. Whatever their situation, the
wealthier planters were generally more cautious than lesser slaveholders. Should withdrawal from the Union lead to civil war, business
dealings with the North would certainly be disrupted. Furthermore,
success for a southern confederacy would depend on widespread support from nonslaveholding whites. Some planters wondered how long
that support could last. Secession might actually hasten the end of
slavery rather than preserve the institution.[63]

That danger seemed clear enough to Texas Governor Sam Houston. "The first gun fired in the war," he warned, "will be the knell of
slavery." Thomas Peters of Lawrence County, Alabama, agreed. "As
the Negro is the sole cause of our present troubles," he wrote to his
friend, U.S. senator and Tennessee Unionist Andrew Johnson, "the
fury of the nonslaveholders will be turned upon him and his master."
Georgians Alexander Stephens and Benjamin Harvey Hill, future
Confederate vice president and Confederate senator respectively, expressed similar fears. Stephens stressed that as dependent as a southern government would be on plain folk, slaveholders could lose their
grip on the course of events. "The movement will before it ends I
fear be beyond the control of those who started it," Stephens said,
and southerners would "at no distant day commence cutting one another's throats." Hill was certain that a South divided by class could
not survive a civil war. The southern government would fall and slavery with it.[64]

Many of Hill's colleagues had similar fears. Shortly after Lincoln's
election, in what one contemporary called "a large meeting of the
Members of the General Assembly" at the Georgia capitol, legislators
called for thoughtful restraint. They appointed a committee of twenty-
two, including Hill, to draft a resolution urging Georgia voters not to
support secessionists in the upcoming election for convention delegates.

Immediate secession would, they insisted, lead to "nothing but divisions among our people, confusion among the slaveholding States, strife around our firesides, and ultimate defeat to every movement for the effective redress of our grievances."[65]

"They Did Not Stick to What They Said"

Such divisions set the stage for intense controversy at state secession conventions, at least in those states where secessionists had a strong voice. Though most slave states held elections for delegates to secession conventions, southern popular opinion ran so strongly against breaking up the Union that in the upper South and border states, comprising over half the slave states, an overwhelming majority of voters dismissed it out of hand. Only in the Deep South was secession an immediate threat. Even there, voters were deeply divided. So worried were secessionist leaders over the possibility of secession being voted down that they used intimidation and violence in their efforts to control the ballot box wherever they could. Samuel Beaty, a farmer in Mississippi's Tippah County who was physically threatened because of his Union sentiments, dared not go to the polls. "It would," he said, "have been too dangerous." Secessionists threatened to hang James Cloud, a crippled farmer in Jackson County, Alabama, after he spoke up for the Union.[66]

There were many who resisted such antidemocratic pressure despite the dangers. In some cases, there was a resistance of only one. In south Alabama, sixty-four-year-old Middleton Martin came "pretty near getting into two or three cutting scrapes" as he pleaded with his neighbors to support the Union. "I said to the men 'Don't for God's sake vote that secession ticket.'" When one local secessionist told Martin to shut up or be run out of town, the old man gave better than he got. "Do you see this knife?" Martin asked the man who had threatened him. "If you don't get away from here right away I'll cut your guts out!" Many Union men showed the same kind of grit on election day. At one Mississippi polling place, a lone Methodist preacher summoned up the courage to defy local secessionists.

Approaching the polls, I asked for a Union ticket, and was informed that none had been printed, and that it would be advisable to vote the

secession ticket. I thought otherwise, and going to a desk, wrote out
a Union ticket, and voted it amidst the frowns and suppressed mur-
murs of the judges and by-standers, and, as the result proved, I had the
honour of depositing the only vote in favour of the Union which was
polled in that precinct.

The preacher knew of many local men who opposed secession but
were so frightened by threats to their lives that they stayed away from
the polls.[67]

Due in large part to threat tactics, turnout in the popular vote for
state convention delegates across the Deep South dropped by more
than a third from the previous November's presidential election. In
Mississippi, the number of voters dropped by nearly half. Still, those
opposing immediate secession gave a strong showing. They ran almost
neck and neck with the secessionists in Alabama and Louisiana. Georgia's anti-secessionists polled a likely majority of over a thousand. In
Texas, two-thirds of voters opposed secession. Throughout the Deep
South, official returns gave secession's opponents about 40 percent of
the popular vote. However, fraud at the ballot box was so widespread
that the returns cannot be trusted as a gauge of popular opinion. Most
likely, anti-secession sentiment was considerably stronger than the
final vote would suggest.[68]

In any case, the balloting for state convention delegates makes clear
that the Deep South was badly divided. It also suggests that those divisions were largely class related. North Carolina's vote declining even
to hold a convention showed the state's electorate more clearly divided
along class lines than ever before. In Louisiana, nonslaveholding voters left little doubt that they saw the whole secession movement as an
effort simply to maintain "the peculiar rights of a privileged class." All
seventeen counties in northern Alabama, where relatively few voters
held slaves, sent delegates to the state convention with instructions
to oppose secession. In Lawrence County, voters elected anti-
secessionist delegates by a 90 percent margin. And in Texas, where 81
percent of slaveholders voted for secessionist delegates, only 32 percent of nonslaveholders did so. Slaveholders across the South, who
comprised barely a fourth of the electorate, consistently demonstrated
much greater support for secession than did their nonslaveholding
neighbors.[69]

A satirical, though not altogether inaccurate, view of how the South was voted out of the Union. During the winter of 1860–61, popular opinion in the slave states ran heavily against secession. Only in the Deep South was secession a serious threat. Even there, voters were deeply divided. Secessionists forced disunion on a reluctant South largely through subterfuge and intimidation. Samuel Beaty, a Mississippi farmer, was physically threatened because of his Union sentiments and dared not go to the polls. "It would," he said, "have been too dangerous." Illustration from *Harper's Weekly*.

Nevertheless, slaveholders commanded the dominant voice at all the cotton-state conventions. In Georgia, for example, while just over a third of qualified voters held slaves, 87 percent of the convention delegates were slaveholders. Similar statistics at all the conventions virtually guaranteed secession regardless of the popular will. Beginning with South Carolina in December 1860, secessionists took in order Mississippi, Florida, Alabama, Georgia, and Louisiana out of the Union. Texas finally went on February 1, 1861. Three days later, representatives from the seceded states met in Montgomery, Alabama, to form the Confederate States of America, with Jefferson Davis its appointed president.[70]

While many southerners welcomed the Confederacy's birth with enthusiasm, many others did not. In Honey Grove, Texas, Unionists burned a Confederate flag intended for the town square. Union men in Georgia's Pickens County kept the Stars and Stripes flying at the county courthouse for weeks after secession. The old flag continued to fly for a time in northern Alabama as well. Some in the Alabama hill country pushed for annexation by Tennessee, where secession had been voted down. Others thought the region should form its own state and ask for admission to the Union. James Bell of Winston County reasoned that north Alabama counties could certainly leave the state, "for they have the same Right as the state had to secede from the united states." After a Union rally in Huntsville, one worried secessionist wrote that the possibility of a new "state of Nickajack to be formed by the counties of North Alabama and possibly by adjacent counties of Georgia and eastern Tennessee, looms large."[71]

Many southerners continued to question the Confederacy's legitimacy and charged outright fraud. One furious Georgia voter accused Singleton Sisk, a Missionary Baptist preacher, of cheating Habersham County out of its anti-secession vote. In an open letter to the *Athens Southern Watchman*, he told how this "Janus-faced expounder of the Gospel" had declared himself a Union man to gain the nomination of Habersham's anti-secessionists. With their backing, he was elected to the state convention. "After the election, we find that he had privately promised the Secessionists that he would, in the Convention, support Secession." Sisk indeed betrayed his constituents and backed secession at the convention. Similar betrayals occurred among the representatives of at least twenty-eight other Georgia counties.[72]

So it was across the Deep South. John Powell, a Mississippi slaveholder, ran as the anti-secession candidate in Jones County. When the state convention met on January 9, Powell deserted his constituents and voted to make Mississippi the second state to leave the Union. Such fraud was common in Florida and Alabama, too. As one Florida resident complained: "The election machinery was all in the hands of the secessionists, who manipulated the election to suit their end." Jasper Harper, a disgusted voter from Marshall County, Alabama, complained bitterly: "I voted for those [delegates] who said the guns would have to be placed to their breast and the trigger pulled before they would vote for Alabama to go out of the Union, but they did not stick to what they said."[73]

Officials in Louisiana delayed releasing their questionable election returns for three months. So did Governor Joe Brown of Georgia, who did so only at the insistence of concerned voters. Even then he lied about the results. Brown falsely claimed that secessionist delegates had carried the state by over thirteen thousand votes. In fact, existing records from the time suggest that secession was probably defeated by just over a thousand votes.[74]

When Texas Governor Sam Houston, in accordance with his state's two-thirds vote against secession, refused to call a convention, an unofficial cabal of secessionists in Austin organized one for themselves. Houston was able to get the convention's secession ordinance submitted to the voters for ratification in what was a "free election" in name only. But in the other six seceding states, ratification was never placed in the hands of voters. One Louisiana delegate told his colleagues that in "refusing to submit its action to [the voters] for their sanction . . . this Convention violates the great fundamental principle of American government, that the will of the people is supreme." In March, the *New Orleans Picayune* stated plainly that secessionist leaders across the South were giving "new and startling evidence of their distrust of the people, and thus furnished strong testimony . . . that the South was divided, and that the movement in which we are now engaged has not the sanction of the great body of the people."[75]

In his seminal study of the secession crisis, David Potter looked at the popular vote for state secession conventions throughout the South and concluded:

> At no time during the winter of 1860–1861 was secession desired by a majority of the people of the slave states. . . . Furthermore, secession was not basically desired even by a majority in the lower South, and the secessionists succeeded less because of the intrinsic popularity of their program than because of the extreme skill with which they utilized an emergency psychology, the promptness with which they invoked unilateral action by individual states, and the firmness with which they refused to submit the question of secession to popular referenda.[76]

Throughout the secession crisis, southerners had worried about what the results of secession might be. Some feared that the federal government might try to hold the cotton states in the Union by force. The *Vicksburg Whig* warned its readers that not only was it "treason to secede" but also that such a move would bring "strife, discord, bloodshed, war, if not anarchy." It was a "blind and suicidal course." In an open letter, one southwest Georgia man was so sure civil war would come that he referred to secessionists as "the suicides." Others were just as certain that they were nothing of the sort. James Chestnut, a soon-to-be

senator from South Carolina, told enthusiastic crowds that he would
"drink all the blood spilled" resulting from secession. Georgia's *Albany
Patriot* assured its readers that the Yankees would never dare make war
on the South. "In all honesty we can say to our readers, be not afraid.
We will insure the life of every southern man from being killed in war
by the abolitionists for a postage stamp." The editor of Upson
County's *Pilot* was not sure what the outcome of secession might be,
but he was glad his county had voted against it. "If the demon of civil
war is to ravage our fields only to fertilize them with blood—we know
our Upson Delegates will be able, at the last dread account, to stand
up with clean hands and pure hearts and exclaim through no chatter-
ing teeth from coward consciences:—'*Thou canst not say we did it!*' "[77]

"Treasonable Sentiments Against the Southern Confederacy"

If most southerners opposed secession, most northerners opposed
civil war. "It cannot be denied," wrote the *New York Times* on March
21, 1861, "that there is a growing sentiment throughout the North in
favor of *letting the Gulf States go*." It was mainly business elites with
economic ties to the South, especially those with cotton interests, who
pressured Lincoln to hold the Union together by force if necessary.
But he could not do that without an army. What Lincoln needed was
an incident to fire northern nationalism and draw volunteers. Lincoln
got his incident on April 12 when, after he threatened to resupply
Union-held Fort Sumter in South Carolina's Charleston Harbor,
Confederate forces bombarded the federal garrison. The flag had now
been fired upon and Lincoln called forth 75,000 volunteers to defend
it. Four days after the Sumter incident, New York's *Buffalo Daily
Courier* wrote: "With the facts before us we cannot believe that Mr.
Lincoln intended that Sumter should be held. . . . War is inaugurated,
and the design of the administration is accomplished."[78]

Lincoln helped accomplish Jefferson Davis's design as well. The
certainty of invasion united white southerners behind the Confederacy as nothing else could. Within a few weeks, four more slave states—
Arkansas, Tennessee, North Carolina, and Virginia—left the Union.
So many men volunteered for service that the Confederacy was hard
pressed to arm them all. "The Union feeling *was strong* up to [Lin-
coln's] recent proclamation," wrote a North Carolina congressman on

April 26. "This War Manifest extinguishes it, and resistance is now on every mans lips and throbs in every bosom. . . . Union men are now such no longer."[79]

But that was not entirely the case. Despite the passionate post-Sumter excitement, there were large cracks in the facade of southern unity. Throughout the month of May, Unionists held anti-secession rallies all across Tennessee. At Strawberry Plains in eastern Tennessee, men at a Union rally exchanged gunfire with a passing train loaded with Confederate soldiers. In Knoxville, the Reverend William Brownlow, a newspaper editor and leading anti-secessionist, continued to fly the U.S. flag at his home. Early the next month, in an election hampered by fraud, manipulation, and intimidation on both sides, Tennessee voters ratified the legislature's secession ordinance by a two-to-one margin. But in the state's eastern third, the vote was more than two to one against.[80]

In North Carolina, there were reports that "Guilford, Randolph and adjoining counties are unshaken in their devotion to the Stars and Stripes." In Stanly County on May 13, the day of the vote for convention delegates, a yeoman farmer named Elijah Hudson was hauled before a secessionist vigilante committee for "using language against the interest of the South." There was intimidation in Henderson County as well, where known Union men were kept from the polls "with threats that all such would be hung or shot." When the sheriff of Madison County tried to shoot a Union man, he wounded the man's son instead. The enraged Unionist killed the sheriff, escaped that night to Kentucky, and joined the Union army.[81]

Despite intimidation, North Carolina Unionists managed to take about one-third of the delegate seats. At the convention, one Union delegate urged his colleagues to resist secessionist pressure: "Let South Carolina nullify, revolute, secess and be damned! North Carolina don't need to follow her lead!"[82] But by that time, Virginia had already left the Union too, and the convention voted to follow both states into the Confederacy.

In Virginia, there was no popular vote for convention delegates after the firing on Fort Sumter. That state simply used the convention elected in February to oppose secession—which on April 17 voted to support it. Though there was a popular ratification in late May, the balloting was rife with fraud and intimidation. In Floyd County, tenant farmer Charles Huff recalled "leading Rebels" warning residents "that those who refused to vote for secession would be hung." Threats to their lives, their families, and their property convinced many Unionists to vote the secession ticket. John Brunk did so "to protect himself and family from violence." So did David Rhodes for "fear of reprisal." Even so, there were those determined to have their say. Jacob Wenger was one of eleven known Unionists in his Rockingham County precinct who went to the polls in the face of lynching threats. Such courage seldom made much difference. At Mount Crawford, armed secessionist vigilantes forced those who had cast Union ballots back to the polls at gunpoint and made them change their votes.[83]

Such tactics had characterized Virginia's secession process from the outset. Within days of the firing on Fort Sumter and Lincoln's call for volunteers, former Virginia governor Henry Wise and his secessionist allies demanded that the sitting governor, John Letcher, take the federal arsenal at Harpers Ferry and the Gosport Navy Yard at Norfolk. Letcher refused and reminded his friends that Virginia's convention

In Floyd County, Virginia, tenant farmer Charles Huff recalled "leading Rebels" warning residents "that those who refused to vote for secession would be hung." Threats to their lives, their families, and their property convinced many Unionists to vote the secession ticket. John Brunk did so "to protect himself and family from violence." So did David Rhodes for "fear of reprisal." At Mount Crawford, Virginia, armed secessionist vigilantes forced those who had cast Union ballots back to the polls at gunpoint and made them change their votes. Illustration from Devens, *Pictorial Book of Anecdotes and Incidents.*

had not yet taken the state out of the Union. In what amounted to a coup d'état, secessionist leaders took control of volunteer troops and ordered assaults on the federal installations. Letcher reluctantly sanctioned the action a day later. When secessionists used mob tactics to intimidate the state convention, western Virginia took steps to split off and stay with the Union. In doing so, it joined the border slave states of Missouri, Kentucky, Maryland, and Delaware in rejecting secession.[84]

In eastern Tennessee, where only 30 percent of the fifty thousand votes cast favored ratifying the state's secession ordinance, there were also efforts to form a separate Union state. In Arkansas, the convention elected in February to oppose secession reconvened in May without popular sanction and voted enthusiastically to leave the Union. But that vote, as one analyst observed, "did not reflect a similar enthusiasm among the people." Anti-secession sentiment remained strong in the state.[85]

Even among Confederate volunteers, whose enthusiasm for the war was generally greatest, there were plenty of reluctant warriors. Family and community pressures pushed many hesitant men into the ranks. One group of well-to-do young women in Columbus, Georgia, advertised the formation of a Ladies' Home Guard for the "special protection of young men who have concluded to remain at home during the existence of the war." A southern belle in Selma, Alabama, put a halt to wedding plans when her fiancé refused to enlist. She sent him women's clothes along with a note reading, "Wear these or volunteer."[86]

Many of the unwilling still blamed slaveholders for instigating secession. One resident of Bedford County, Tennessee, who remembered the local gentry feeling "above those who did not own slaves," noted that class relations became increasingly strained as "the war clouds gathered." Those strains often showed up in the voting patterns for and against secession. In Tennessee's McNairy County, total property value of those who supported secession was twice that of those who opposed it. When war broke out, a Meigs County man confirmed that class interactions "became tense." But a Hickman County colonel argued that any concerns about the conflict's origins were now irrelevant. Such concerns among commoners were certainly dangerous to men of his class. "To arms!" he demanded in a circulating recruitment broadside. "Our Southern soil must be defended. We must not stop to ask who brought about the war, who is at fault, but let us go and do battle . . . and then settle the question who is to blame."[87]

Beyond the issue of blame, of more immediate concern to many poor southerners was secession's impact on their livelihoods. Economic disruptions that appeared on the heels of disunion threw thousands out of work and made taking a private's lowly pay of $11 a month the best option available to many poor laborers. When secession cut back the Mississippi's riverboat traffic, hundreds of Irish workers petitioned the British consulate in New Orleans for transport out of the South. Told that no funds were available, they had little alternative but to enlist. Many native southerners were in the same predicament. Paupers in the South's urban workhouses were released on the promise that they would volunteer. When the sheriff in Chatham County, North Carolina, arrested a poor transient for "refusing to do military duty and vagrancy," he was promised release if he would enlist.[88] That so many did on account of economic necessity foreshadowed the increasingly central role that class divisions would play in the wartime South.

Those divisions were made clear early, when commoners who went to the front lines quickly discovered that their personal sacrifice would be much greater than those few elites who joined them. Lacking weapons enough for all its volunteers, the Confederacy mandated that those who could not properly arm themselves enlist for three years or the war's duration. Those who could enlisted for one year only. That meant purchasing the expensive .577 caliber Enfield rifles, which few common soldiers could afford. Most volunteers were not informed until they reached the front lines that their squirrel rifles would not do for military service. Many poor soldiers found that their one-year enlistments had suddenly turned into three. As historian Paul Escott put it: "The price of being a patriot was higher for the common man than for the rich man, three times higher to be exact."[89]

"Many of us here is anxious to serve our country if needed," wrote one recruit to the War Department. But they were "mostly men of fameleys and cannot leave our families for so long a term as three years." Neither could a company of Georgia volunteers who felt that "twelve months will be best for us & our families." The Warrior Riflemen of Alabama's Walker and Winston Counties balked at the "three years or the war" rule but still offered their services for a year. The Mountain Rangers of Georgia's Meriwether County refused to enlist

at all when they got word of the three-year rule. They abruptly disbanded in June 1861 before being mustered into service.[90]

Second thoughts became increasingly common as enthusiasm gave
way to reality. Many of those early volunteers soon came to reconsider
their motives. Some acted on their doubts. In March 1861, four
months before the war's first major battle at Manassas (Bull Run), two
Georgia volunteers "took it into their heads to forego the honor and
glory of serving the Confederate States upon the tented field, and
without so much as saying to the officer in charge, 'By your leave,'
took the back track from Griffin to Atlanta." In May, three men of
Georgia's Second Infantry Regiment decided army life was not for
them and headed home. A month later in Virginia, two members of
the Macon Volunteers deserted to the Yankees. In June and July, five
men of Virginia's Floyd Guards deserted as well.[91]

What misgivings there were among the troops reflected even
greater doubts on the home front. Some continued to express those
doubts openly, despite the growing danger of speaking one's mind.
That danger was deadly real. At the height of post-Sumter excitement
in May, a man living just west of Auburn, Alabama, spoke out against
secession and was lynched for it. In southwest Georgia, George Martin was arrested on charges of "uttering treasonable sentiments against
the Southern Confederacy." Fearing for his life, Martin nearly killed
an army lieutenant while making his escape. Authorities offered a
$250 reward for Martin's capture—dead or alive.[92]

Secession also divided families all across the slave states. It pitted
fathers against sons, siblings against each other, and even wives against
husbands. A Union man in Kentucky was terribly embarrassed when
his wife "sang secessionism" to a group of their dinner guests. One
visitor called the man "henpecked" and referred to his wife as "unlady-
like." So fearful was a Confederate newspaper editor of similar embar-
rassment that he convinced his Unionist wife to live in England until
the war was over. A Confederate officer in Missouri had his wife committed to an insane asylum for her anti-secession views.[93]

Twenty-one-year-old Josie Underwood wrote that in her home-
town of Bowling Green, Kentucky, "all the men . . . of any position or
prominence whatever are Union men—and yet many of these men
have wild reckless unthinking inexperienced sons who make so much
noise about secession as to almost drown their fathers wiser council."
Josie could afford to be more open with her sentiments than her married

William G. Brownlow, a Tennessee preacher and newspaper editor, called the ordinances taking southern states out of the Union "covenants with death and agreements with hell! They are so many decrees to carry out the behests of *madmen* and *traitors*." He vowed to "fight Secession leaders until Hell freezes over, and then fight them on the ice." Confederates threw Brownlow in jail, then banished him to the North, where he toured speaking for southern Unionists. He also wrote a scathing indictment of his adversaries, *Sketches of the Rise, Progress and Decline of Secession*, known more popularly by the binder's short title, *Parson Brownlow's Book*. Illustration from the Tennessee State Library and Archives.

sister Juliet, who supported secession in the company of her Confederate husband but denounced it around her Union father. Women often took on the trying role of peacemaker within divided families. So difficult did it become for Sarah Glasgow of St. Louis, Missouri, that her sister encouraged her to be grateful for their father's death. Now Sarah would be free of the "serious disagreements" between her Confederate father and Union husband.[94]

For some, the bitterness born of seeing their country torn apart put any desire for reconciliation out of reach. Kentucky Unionist Maria Knott was mortified that her two brothers supported the Confederacy, writing "I want nothing to do with them." When Virginian George Thomas remained loyal to the Union, his two sisters turned his portrait to the wall and refused to correspond with him. From northern Alabama, Elissay Bell had written her brother Henry in Choctaw County, Mississippi, to "pick me out a Sooter" before she came for a visit. But she qualified her request when she learned that Henry was a secessionist. "If there is none but disunion men there for God Sake let them alone for I would distain to keep company with a disunionist."[95]

The Bell family's story was one of many that illustrates the sorrow and tragedy of families torn apart in a South at war with itself. In the spring of 1861, young Henry Bell wrote home to his Unionist family, calling them all tories for opposing the new Confederacy. As for their mostly Unionist neighbors, Henry denounced them as heathens. Henry's father John wrote back: "We ain't in a heathen land, or warent [weren't] until Alabama went out of the Union."

"I rather be called a Tory," John told his son, "than commit such treason against my country." He urged young Henry to recall a time when his ancestors marched over frozen ground with bleeding feet to establish the country and secure its liberties. "It is somthing strange to me that people can forget the grones and crys of our fourfathers So quick."[96]

Sadly, the family never had an opportunity to mend fences with Henry. In November 1861, he joined the Confederate army and left for the front. Four of Henry's brothers enlisted on the Union side. Three did not survive the war. One was killed in battle, another succumbed to "congestive fever," and a third died in prison at Andersonville. Henry himself died of disease in Chattanooga.[97]

"The Free State of Winston"

It was hard for many to forget their ties to the Union, especially those like John Bell, who carried long memories of family sacrifice. Alabama farmer Jacob Albright, whose father had fought in the Revolution, recalled after the war: "I told [the local pro-Confederate vigilance committee] that my father fought for the Union and I could not go against it . . . and that sooner than turn over [to the Confederacy] I would die right there." A fellow Alabamian, John Phillips, insisted that he "would never go back on 'Old Glory.' I had heard too much from my old grandparents about the sufferings and privation they had to endure during the Revolutionary War ever to engage against the 'Stars and Stripes.' "[98]

It was equally hard for large numbers of plain folk to forget that they had been cheated out of their vote. Had their voices been fairly represented at the state conventions, there would have been no secession and no war. One South Carolina aristocrat expressed deep concern on hearing poor farmers in his area saying "this is a rich man's war." They were saying the same all across the South. "What the hell's it all about anyway?" asked an angry speaker at the Texas state capitol.

"The nigger!" came a reply from the crowd. "I ain't got no nigger," yelled the speaker. "I ain't going to fight for somebody else's nigger." Such comments echoed what John Bell told his son Henry of the slaveholders: "All they want is to git you pupt up and go to fight for there infurnal negroes and after you do there fighting you may kiss there hine parts for o [all] they care."[99]

A month after the firing on Sumter, William Brooks, who presided at Alabama's secession convention, wrote a worried letter to Jefferson Davis. Brooks feared the sentiment among commoners that "nothing is now in peril in the prevailing war but the title of the master to his slaves." Already some had openly "declared that they will 'fight for no rich man's slaves.'" More and more, commoners were beginning to express their class resentment. If this trend continued, Brooks told the president, "I leave you to imagine the consequences."[100]

Those consequences were increasingly apparent. In June, a North Carolina man warned that Randolph County Unionists had as many men under arms as the secessionist home guard, and that anti-Confederates were "holding secret meetings in several places and have a roll or list of names of persons pledged to the support of the Union." On June 7 in Bradley County, Tennessee, word spread that Confederates were on their way to disarm local Union men. Though the rumor proved false, within twelve hours a thousand armed Unionists were assembled and ready to turn them back. Among the anti-Confederates of Walker County, Georgia, there was talk of forming a company "to defend the glorious Union." From neighboring Fannin County came word that "quite a number" were prepared to defend the old flag and help "whip Georgia and the South back into the Union."[101]

On July 16, 1861, an Alabama militia captain informed Governor Moore that "a very considerable number of the inhabitants of the Counties of Winston, Marion, Fayette, and some of Walker and Morgan, are . . . actually raising and equipping themselves to . . . sustain the old Government of the United States." In Blount County, there were large numbers prepared to resist Confederate authority by force. Already in Fayette County, Unionists were holding meetings to cheer for Lincoln and form armed companies "to protect themselves." Unionists in Limestone County established "an independent Union home guard" and held regular meetings to promote continued resistance.[102]

Charles Christopher (Chris) Sheats, was born in what is now Winston County, Alabama, in 1839. A teacher by profession, not a politician, his neighbors nevertheless elected him a Winston County delegate to Alabama's Secession Convention on the antisecession ticket. Sheats voted against the secession ordinance, refused to sign it after it passed, and took a leading role at the Looney's Tavern meeting where the "Free State of Winston" was born. Elected to the Alabama legislature in 1861, he was expelled for his Union sentiments and thrown in prison. When finally released, Sheats took refuge behind Union lines. Photo from Looney's Tavern Amphitheatre, Double Springs, Alabama.

There were perhaps no bolder Unionist leaders in northern Alabama than those of Winston County. There they organized a mass meeting at Looney's Tavern that was attended by up to three thousand people from all across the region. Charles Christopher Sheats was the main speaker. Sheats had been Winston's delegate to the state secession convention and was one of twenty-four delegates who refused to sign the secession ordinance. In a series of resolutions, Sheats and his colleagues at Looney's Tavern made clear that they would under no circumstances "shoot at the flag of our fathers, Old Glory," and further insisted that if a state could withdraw from the Union, then any county could legally break its political ties with the state. Dick Payne, one of the few Confederate sympathizers in the huge crowd, on hearing the resolutions read, sarcastically yelled out: "Ho! Ho! Winston secedes. The Free State of Winston! The Free State of Winston!" In fact, the county may as well have been called seceded from the state. A sizable majority of its people were Unionists, and they sent twice as many of their men to the Union as to the Confederate army. In any case, Payne's phrase stuck, and the county from that time on was popularly called the Free State of Winston.[103]

Eastern Tennessee may as well have been called seceded from the state, too. In the August 1861 balloting for the Confederacy's provisional congress, voters elected Unionist candidates T.A.R. Nelson and Horace Maynard by considerable majorities. Both Nelson and Maynard set out for Washington instead of Richmond, reasoning that since they had been elected by Unionists, they ought to sit in the United States Congress. Confederate authorities captured Nelson en route, but Maynard made the trip successfully and was granted his seat. Results of the balloting in Tennessee's second and third districts were so close that the Union candidates, Andrew Clements and George Bridges, claimed victory. Clements and Bridges followed Maynard to Washington, where they were both eventually granted seats in the U.S. Congress.[104]

In Mississippi too there were enclaves where Union sentiment remained strong. The summer of 1861 found a large band of Unionists in Greene County openly declaring that they would "fight for Lincoln." Local authorities suspected that the McLeod brothers, all nonslaveholding yeoman farmers, were leading the Unionists. When hauled in for questioning, Allen McLeod called Jefferson Davis "a murdering scamp & traitor." His brother Peter told the committee not only that there were plenty of men in Greene County ready to take up arms against the Confederacy but also that there were seven hundred to eight hundred men in nearby Choctaw County, Alabama, pledged to "fight against the South & slave owners." Perhaps most frightening to slave owners, the McLeods were also ready to arm and ally themselves with slaves.[105]

For generations, slaveholders had feared a union of slaves and nonslaveholders. That fear, in part, led many slaveholders to support secession, reasoning that they could control dissent more effectively in a regime dominated by slaveholding interests. But as early as spring and summer of 1861, secession was beginning to have the opposite effect. In Mississippi's Jefferson, Adams, and Franklin counties, slave conspiracies came to light, all of them involving whites. There was unrest in Georgia, too. In July, the *Columbus Sun* reported that a "vigilance committee" in southwest Georgia had uncovered plans for a slave uprising to be led by several local whites.[106]

Enslaved blacks hardly needed encouragement to reject the Confederacy. Comprising more than a third of the Confederacy's population, they could never be counted on to support a government whose "cornerstone" was, as Vice President Alexander Stephens put it in March 1861, "the great truth that the negro is not the equal of the white man." Stephens, like so many other whites, further insisted that slavery was the "natural and normal condition" of blacks. But he knew better. The fear that he and other slaveholders had of slave rebellion demonstrated their recognition that slavery did not come naturally to blacks.

Those fears were well founded. Though most slaves tended to adopt a wait-and-see approach in the war's early months, the mistaken notion that Lincoln intended to free them was enough to send many on the offensive. In April 1861, slaves rose up in Charleston, South Carolina. The next month, so did slaves in Kentucky's Owen and Gallatin counties. At the same time, in Georgia's Decatur County, Virginia's Charles City County, and Monroe, Arkansas, enslaved people developed plans for similar uprisings. Arkansas slaves laid plans to kill their owners and "march up the River to meet Mr. Linkum." In New Castle, Kentucky, a band of sixty slaves marched through the city's streets "singing political songs and shouting for Lincoln." No whites dared oppose them.[107]

Though blacks were ready to support Lincoln, he was not yet ready to support them. In his March 1861 inaugural address, Lincoln stated flatly that he had "no purpose, directly or indirectly, to interfere with slavery in the States where it exists." Congress agreed. In a nearly unanimous vote, it passed the Crittenden-Johnson resolution, assuring the nation that the war was being fought not to overthrow or interfere "with the rights or established institutions" of the slave states but only "to defend and maintain the supremacy of the Constitution and to preserve the Union." It hardly mattered what Lincoln or Congress wanted. What slaves wanted was freedom, and they were taking it. As early as spring 1861, self-emancipated former slaves were pouring into Union lines. Many offered their services as soldiers for Lincoln's army. Henry Jarvis volunteered at Fort Monroe, Virginia, but was told by General Benjamin Butler that "it wasn't a black man's war."

"I told him," Jarvis recalled, "it would be a black man's war before they got through." Escaping slaves would see to that.[108]

Stay-at-home slaves, too, were making it a black man's war. Arson was rampant in the early months of the war, and slaves were the primary suspects. May 1861 saw a dozen ships burned in New Orleans. There was little doubt that blacks were the culprits. That was the general feeling in Charleston as well when a massive fire destroyed six hundred buildings in the city. South Carolina authorities who became suspicious of the unusual frequency of black funerals followed one procession to a cemetery. There they found that the coffin was filled with weapons that were being transferred to a vault. Real funerals followed after nineteen of the conspirators were executed.[109]

At the height of the secession crisis, a newspaper editor in Augusta, Georgia, wrote an ominous warning to his fellow southerners: "The greatest danger to the new Confederacy arises not from without, not from the North, but from our own people." Virginia's *Richmond Examiner* agreed, admitting that the South was "more rife with treason to her own independence and honour than any community that ever engaged before in a struggle with an adversary."[110] It was clear even in its early days that the disunited Confederacy was in for a two-front war: one against the North, the other against its own people. If it could not win the war at home, it could hardly expect to win on the battlefield.

2

"Rich Man's War"

As the excitement of summer faded into fall, home-front opposition continued to undermine the Confederate war effort. Unionists in Walker County, Alabama, organized armed anti-Confederate companies and vowed to fight for Lincoln. Anti-Confederates were doing the same in Fayette, Randolph, Winston, and Limestone counties. One citizen in Georgia's Cass (later Bartow) County wrote directly to Lincoln, saying that he and other local Union men were "ready to sholder our guns" against secession. Joseph Cooper, a Tennessee farmer and Mexican War veteran, trained and drilled five hundred Union men in the Campbell County region. In Tennessee's Carter and Johnson counties, anti-Confederates killed two secessionists and ran others out of the area. Other Tennessee Unionists formed armed bands allied with the Federals and burned several bridges along an important rail line running through the state. When authorities jailed the Reverend William Brownlow of Knoxville in connection with the bridge burnings (although he had no direct part in the scheme), he was offered release if he would swear allegiance to the Confederacy. Said Brownlow: "I would lie here until I died with old age before I would take such an oath."[1]

Most southern whites were more acquiescent toward the Confederacy, but many continued to question service in the cause of what they saw as a "rich man's war." The price of that service was simply too high. Dependent as most women and children were on their menfolk, how would they get by without them? Who would work small farmers' land while husbands and sons were at the front? Planters had few worries there. Aside from the fact that few were enlisting, their plantations were worked by slaves. And taxes seemed to be going up on everything except slaves. As the fall 1861 elections approached, issues such as the war, enlistment, taxes, and even slavery were uppermost in the public mind. In September, Georgia voters who signed themselves "Many Anxious to Hear" addressed an open letter to their legislative candidates through state newspapers.

> Please give your views concerning our present condition—about the war, and the cause of the war . . . and our present condition of taxation for the support of the war. Is it right that the poor man should be taxed for the support of the war, when the war was brought about on the slave question, and the slave at home accumulating for the benefit of his master, and the poor man's farm left uncultivated, and a chance for his wife to be a widow, and his children orphans? Now, in justice, would it not be right to levy a direct tax on the species of property that brought about the war, to support it?

A week later, one editor apologized for printing the letter, saying that this kind of talk might cause class division.[2] In fact, the letter expressed an underlying class resentment that had long been there and was growing stronger by the day.

That those few planters who had joined the army as officers could resign at will added to class resentment. Just a week after the firing on Fort Sumter, one observer noticed that "there has been a withdrawing from the volunteer companies of men who have done their best to destroy this Union." An Arkansas man noted in his diary: "Most of those who were so willing to shed the last drop of blood in the contest for a separate Government are entirely unwilling to shed the first." In October 1861, one soldier wrote home from the Virginia front that "a great many of our commissioned officers are resigning and going home."[3]

For enlisted men, most of them nonslaveholders, resignation was forbidden. Such class distinctions were not lost on the men in the ranks, and the uneven treatment took its toll on morale. "The temper of the army is not good," wrote one Rebel soldier from Virginia during the winter of 1861–62. "The troops widely feel the unjust oppression and partial hand that is laid upon them, and in my opinion the spirit of the army is dying." Corporal James Atkins of the Twelfth Georgia Regiment, also stationed in Virginia, clearly reflected the army's declining morale. He wrote in December 1861 that "reflection has modified my expressed view of patriotism." Atkins had come to feel that it was "a strange virtue that clings to mere soil and in its defense will take the life of the dearest relatives; yet such is patriotism— *the love of dirt*." A few months after penning those lines, Atkins deserted.[4]

"Wholesale Conscription of the Poor"

Thousands of men like Atkins abandoned the army that fall and winter, but few were volunteering to take their places. In October came word from Greene County, Georgia, to the governor's office that "our people don't seem to be inclined to offer their services." That same month, an officer in Columbus reported that it was almost impossible to find volunteers. December found General Braxton Bragg writing to Richmond that he was having little success keeping the men he had, much less getting new volunteers. In February 1862, an Augusta recruiter wrote that he had been trying for two weeks to raise a company in what he called "this 'Yankee City,' but I regret to say every effort has failed." That failure could not be blamed on a lack of potential recruits. The *Augusta Chronicle and Sentinel* noted a week earlier that "one who walks Broad street and sees the number of young men, would come to the conclusion that no war . . . was now waging." From rural Brooks County in south Georgia, C.S. Gaulden reported that "several large families of young men in this county have not sent out soldiers." Another concerned southerner wondered, "How are the men to be got? . . . I have within a few days heard men say they would not go to the war; they had nothing to fight for and they would not go."[5]

Whether they had anything to fight for was beside the point as far as the government was concerned. Willing or not, the army had to have more men. In April 1862, the Confederate Congress passed its first Conscription Act, giving the president authority to force young men into the army. Under the terms of this act, commonly known as

John Joseph Kirkland, the author's great-great-grandfather, and his younger brother Jacob were among the many thousands of men who enlisted in early 1862 under threat of conscription. Those who volunteered received a $50 bonus and could serve with a unit of their choice. Those who awaited the conscript officer received neither privilege. A few weeks after they volunteered, Jacob died of disease in Virginia. John Joseph was nearly killed himself when he received a leg wound and underwent amputation just below the knee. One in four Civil War amputees died during or shortly after the operation. Kirkland was among the fortunate ones who survived. Photo courtesy of Martha Bush Kirkland.

the draft, white males between the ages of eighteen and thirty-five became subject to involuntary military service. As an inducement to enlist before the draft went into effect, the government offered a cash bonus to those who volunteered and allowed them to serve with units of their choice. Fearing they would be drafted in any case, thousands of reluctant men volunteered in March and early April. The Confederate War Department estimated that three-fourths of those who volunteered did so to avoid being drafted.[6]

One late-coming volunteer was John Joseph Kirkland, the author's great-great-grandfather. A slaveless yeoman farmer in Early County, Georgia, Kirkland had a wife and five children, with another on the way, when he enlisted as first corporal with the Early Volunteers in March 1862. He was thirty-three, only two years short of exemption. His younger brother Jacob joined the Early Volunteers too. A few weeks later, Jacob died in Virginia. John Joseph had the heartbreaking duty of escorting the body home to their mother. A year after that, having fought through the Peninsula Campaign, Second Manassas, Sharpsburg, and Fredericksburg, he was nearly killed himself when his right leg was shattered at the Battle of Chancellorsville. Kirkland's leg was amputated just below the knee.[7]

To common folk, the most offensive provisions of conscription were those allowing the wealthy to avoid service. Under the act, monied men could simply pay an expensive commutation fee to the government in lieu of service. Or they could hire a substitute, which was also very expensive. The going rate was $500 soon after the draft began. By late 1863, it ranged into the thousands—as high as $10,000 in some parts of the South. An advertisement for a substitute in one newspaper offered to pay "in cash, land, or negro property." Another offered a 230-acre farm. At least fifty thousand southern gentlemen politely sidestepped military service by hiring substitutes. So few men of means served that soldiers in Virginia sarcastically grumbled that it was easier for a camel to go through the eye of a needle than for a rich man to enter Camp Lee.[8]

Wealthy and well-connected men could avoid service in any number of other ways, legal or not. Some found bribing the local conscript officer to be cheaper than hiring a substitute. Colonel Carey Styles of southeastern Georgia sold exemptions for $1,000 to anyone who could afford to pay. Army surgeons got in on the action by selling medical exemptions. Other officers sold fraudulent substitute papers. The Bureau of Conscription's superintendent cited abundant evidence of actions "grossly criminal and mischievous, in the conduct of the officers of the army respecting substitutes."[9]

Elites could also use their influence with local judges like Richard Henry Clark of southwest Georgia, who granted exemptions to well-connected men on a regular basis. Such exemptions did not always come cheap. In Crawfordville, Georgia, several men paid one court official a $1,500 bribe in exchange for exemptions. Those with influence in government could also have themselves appointed to exempted positions. Sometimes it took more than influence. Appointments to such positions as postmaster, clerk, bailiff, or coroner could cost $500 or more. In North Carolina alone, Governor Zebulon Vance declared nearly fifteen thousand state employees, most with "above average connections," exempt from the draft. In Georgia, Governor Joe Brown did the same, extending protection to state militia officers as well. Those posts, noted one state paper, were "sought and obtained by young gentlemen." General Howell Cobb wrote to Brown complaining of able-bodied young men holding state militia commissions "to the exclusion of old men competent to fill the places. . . . This class I fear is large." An anonymous southerner wrote to the War Department, "It is a notorious fact, if a man has influential friends—or a little money to spare he will never be enrolled."[10]

Then there was the infamous twenty-slave law, which virtually excused planters outright from the draft. Though few in high office seemed to realize it at the time, this single law defined the entire nature of the war for southerners outside the planter class. "It gave us the blues," wrote Tennessee Private Sam Watkins. "We wanted twenty negroes. Negro property suddenly became very valuable, and there was raised the howl of 'rich man's war, poor man's fight.' " Watkins later recalled that "from this time on till the end of the war, a soldier was simply a machine. We cursed the war . . . we cursed the Southern Confederacy. All our pride and valor was gone." A soldier from North Carolina wrote to Governor Vance complaining of the law's "distinction between the rich man (who had something to fight for) and the poor man who fights for that he never will have. The exemption of the owners of 20 negroes & the allowing of substitutes clearly proves it."[11]

Reaction to the draft in general, and planter exemption in particular, was just as vicious on the home front. A Lafayette, Alabama, man warned his senator that the twenty-slave law was "considered class legislation & has given more dissatisfaction than any thing else Congress has done." A.W. Millican of Dirt Town, Georgia, wrote a biting letter to Joe Brown demanding that the governor firmly oppose "the centralized military despotism at Richmond." "Why didn't you hang the first minion of Richmond that called himself a Conscription officer for treason against the Government [of] Georgia?" Millican insisted that if Brown were not going to defend his people from Confederate tyranny, he should tell them how they might do it themselves. "You will very much oblige many men in Georgia if you will assist them in finding out whether they are *citizens* or *slaves*."[12]

To poor whites, eager to preserve their status as free men, conscription seemed to make them slaves of the Richmond government and those with power and influence who controlled it. As Frederick Douglass noted (see page 24), instead of being owned by a single rich man, poor whites were, in a way, owned by them all. "The common people is drove of[f] in the ware to fight for the big mans negro," complained one North Carolinian to the governor. Some were so incensed that they simply ignored the law. One newspaper reported that not a single man appeared at the April 1862 enrollment call in Savannah, Georgia. Nearly two hundred names of absentees were listed.

Around the same time, the entire Fourth Division of the South Carolina militia failed to report when called to service. Such displays of defiance could be dangerous. In the Alabama hill country, conscripts who declined to serve were tracked down with bloodhounds as if they were slaves. In Arkansas, General Joe Shelby sent his men after draft dodgers with orders to "use all force in your power, and when necessary shoot them down."[13] Slaves were hardly treated worse.

A North Carolina man wrote to his senator expressing hope that Congress would "never adjourn until you have ... placed our lives, our property and our liberties beyond the reach of Despots." If southerners gave up their freedoms, he felt, "then we shall be fit subjects for Slavery, and it matters not whether our Master be a Northern or a Southern tyrant." J.W. Reid of South Carolina felt the same way. In a letter to his wife, Reid called Jefferson Davis a dictator and could not decide whom he hated more—Davis or Lincoln.[14]

Many draft officials themselves were hardly enthusiastic about having to force men into service. Aside from finding the cruel nature of their work distasteful, some suspected that dragging unwilling men from their dependent families did the Confederate cause more harm than good. A North Carolina lieutenant assigned to enforce the draft wrote of the recruiting forays he made.

> While performing my duty as enrolling officer I witnessed scenes & compelled compliance with orders which God grant I may never do again. To ride up to a man's door, whose hospitable kindness makes you feel welcome & tell him, in the presence of his faithful & loving wife & sunny-faced children, that he must be ready in 10 minutes to go with you, and see the very looks of sadness and despair seize the wife & a cloud of apprehension cover the smiling faces of his children—their imploring looks and glances—the tears of sorrow—the Solemn silence—the affectionate clasping of hands—the fervent kisses—the sad & bitter Goodbye—the longing glance at the place most dear to him on earth, as he slowly moves out of sight—this is indeed a sad & unpleasant task. When we left doors on the road crowded with the faces of frightened & crying & helpless women ... made me ask often what have we gained by this trip?[15]

"They've got me in this war at last," complained a poor Georgia farmer to a neighbor after he was drafted. "I didn't want to have any

Shielded from the draft in various ways, most notoriously by the twenty-slave law, planters who wished to avoid military service had little trouble doing so. "Their negroes must make cotton," complained one Confederate soldier, and "the poor men must be taken from their families and put in the Army to protect their negroes. Was ever a greater wrong, or a more damning sin, perpetrated by men or devils?" Illustration from *Harper's Weekly*.

thing to do with it any how. *I* didn't vote for Secession—but them are the ones who have to go & fight now—and those who were so fast for war stay out." And so it was all across the South. "The brunt is thrown upon the working classes while the rich live at home in ease and pleasure," wrote one exasperated woman. That was evident on the draft rolls. Among conscripts in one regiment from eastern North Carolina, average personal property was under $100 and average real estate held was almost nothing.[16]

Pressured to rush men into service, draft officers took not only the poor but the sick, lame, and nearly blind as well. One distraught woman wrote that her conscripted husband could not see clearly enough to tell a black man from a white. Another man was hauled off despite a hacking cough and heart palpitations. One young conscript, described as "a helpless cripple . . . afflicted with epilepsy," was abandoned on the streets of Savannah after it became obvious to draft officers that he was incapable of military service. His father was fortunate enough to find the boy.[17]

Army nurse Kate Cumming wrote in her journal of two Alabama women wandering through the camps looking for their young sons, one of whom suffered with a facial cancer that had already eaten an eye out of its socket. "How can our people be guilty of such outrages?" Cumming wondered. "There is no punishment too severe for those thus guilty. But," she continued, "I have known conscript officers to take men from their homes whom the surgeons had discharged many times, and sent them to camp. We have had them die in our hospital before reaching the army."[18]

"It is strange to us," wrote the editor of southwest Georgia's *Early County News*, "that the Government allows its officers to conscript poor men who have the appearance of *dead men*, while they turn loose rich ones who are *young, hale and hearty*." That seemed strange to many others too. In a letter to the *Savannah Republican*, a resident of Valdosta, Georgia, wrote that "several healthy looking individuals have come home in Lowndes and Brooks counties, discharged as diseased" and that "most if not all of them *happened* to be men of means and influence, which looked strange." J.M. Radford of Virginia wrote to the War Department about the impact of such practices: "It is impossible to make *poor* people comprehend the policy of putting able-bodied, healthy, Mr. A. in such light service as collecting tithes and money *at home*, when the well known feeble & delicate Mr. B.—who is a poor man with a large family of children depending on him for bread—is sent to the front. . . . I beseech you to be warned of the coming storm—the people will not *always* submit to this *unequal, unjust* and partial distribution of favor and wholesale conscription of the *poor* while the able-bodied & healthy men of property are all occupying *soft places*."[19]

It hardly helped attitudes among common folk that wealthy men flaunted privileges in the faces of less fortunate neighbors. One young member of southwest Georgia's gentry ran an ad in a local newspaper reading "WIFE WANTED—by a young man of good habits, plenty of money, good looking and legally exempt from Confederate Service."[20]

"Endless Bales of Cotton"

Well-connected southerners held jealously to their exemption privileges. Planters in particular stressed their special role as food producers. The soldiers would need vast stores of food, and so would their families back home. With their prime lands and slave labor, who better to supply that food than the planters? Many agreed to "bonding" contracts that obligated them to contribute food or sell it below market rates to soldiers' families and the army. As soldiers left for the front, they were told to have no worries where food was concerned. They and their families would be well fed.[21]

But common folk quickly learned that planter patriotism was more apparent than real. Food production never came close to meeting demand because planters devoted far too much acreage to cotton and tobacco. In 1862, cotton production reached its second-highest level on record to that time, declining after that year due in large part to rising slave resistance. Even so, labor devoted to cotton in the growing alone, not to mention processing and transport, amounted to 2.3 million man-years between 1861 and 1864, more than went into defending the Confederacy.[22]

Confederate policy called for a voluntary embargo on cotton exports in an effort to force recognition from Britain and France, but Congress never enacted an outright ban. There were more than enough planters and planter influence in Congress to prevent that. It would likely have mattered little in any case. Even in the face of state restrictions, cotton growers and their agents easily ran cotton past the federal blockade fleet, sometimes with cooperation from federal officers. Over three-fourths of all ships attempting to run the blockade made it through. There was big money in cotton, as the planters well knew—much more than in food products. In April 1861, southern newspapers announced that raw cotton was going for "the enormous price of 12½ cents per pound. It has not been so high for years." Prices continued to rise as the war went on, reaching a dollar a pound by 1864. By war's end, it was nearly two dollars in some markets.[23]

"Plant corn! Plant corn!" demanded Georgia's *Macon Telegraph*. "We must have large supplies, or poverty and suffering will come upon us like a strong man armed." The *Richmond Examiner* agreed: "If all citizens were intelligent and patriotic, not another leaf of tobacco or pod of cotton would be seen in the fields of the South until peace is declared." The *True Democrat* in Little Rock, Arkansas, urged planters to put not a single cotton seed in the ground. Tallahassee's *Florida Sentinel* warned of famine in the land if planters continued their addiction to cotton. Open letters in southern newspapers repeatedly called on planters to plow up their cotton and replace it with corn. "Yes, plow it up," agreed one editor. "Look out for corn first, last and all the time." Another warned planters who continued to grow cotton and tobacco: "Look out, Gentlemen, the public eye is upon you, as will the public scorn unless you desist."[24]

Such warnings most often fell on deaf ears. During a land-buying trip to Alabama in February 1863, Mississippi planter James Alcorn wrote back home instructing his wife to "put in as much cotton as possible. You need not listen to what others say, plant corn to do you and the balance in cotton." Alcorn was sure that when the war was over, no matter which side won, cotton would be "worth a dollar a pound in good money." By "good money," Alcorn meant gold coins or Yankee greenbacks.[25]

Among the most reluctant to hold back on cotton production was General Robert Toombs of Georgia. Some reports from the summer of 1862 had Toombs planting close to nine hundred acres in cotton. Citizens' Committees of Public Safety near the Toombs plantation issued resolutions condemning Toombs and a half-dozen local planters for contributing to the South's food shortage. But condemnation could not compete with profits, and the resolutions had little impact. "My property," responded Toombs, "as long as I live, shall never be subject to the orders of those cowardly miscreants, the Committees of Public Safety. . . . You cannot intimidate me."

Ironically, just a year earlier, General Winfield Scott, a southerner who had remained loyal to the Union, wrote Toombs, asking him "to quit his rebel nonsense." Scott predicted that if the South continued on its imprudent course, it would eventually be starved to death. In reply, Toombs sent an ear of corn by express to his old friend. Said one southern editor, "We consider this one of Bob's best letters." But a year later, unable to shake his addiction to cotton, Toombs was among the thousands of planters helping Scott's prediction come true.[26]

By fall 1862, southern planters were growing so much cotton that the warehouses could not hold it all. In September, the firm of Dillard, Powell, and Company in Columbus, Georgia, ran this announcement in a local paper: "TO PLANTERS: Our Warehouse being full, Planters will please stop consignments of Cotton to our care until further notice." A worried Georgia citizen wrote to the governor begging him to force planters to grow more food, or "they will whip us sooner than all Lincolndom combined could do it." One disgusted editor wrote that if southerners refused to devote more land to food production, then they were "not only a blockaded but a block-headed people."[27]

Government response to cotton and tobacco overproduction was cursory and ineffective, often by design. After all, many legislators were themselves planters who were making huge profits from cotton and tobacco. Using the "state rights" dodge, Congress did no more than approve a nonbinding resolution asking planters to grow more food. For appearance's sake, some states did pass acts limiting production of nonfood items. Alabama placed a 10 percent tax on excess cotton. Arkansas limited growers to two acres in cotton for every slave owned or laborer employed. The limit per hand in Georgia was three acres. Other states made the limit four acres. Virginia set tobacco production at no more than 2,500 plants per hand. Such acts were barely enforced and almost completely ignored.[28]

A disgusted editor at the *Arkansas Gazette* complained that planters were "determined, notwithstanding the prohibition of the Legislature, to plant large crops of cotton." The same was true for tobacco. "Lynchburg has gone mad," wrote one exasperated Virginian, "stark mad . . . all tobacco—tobacco—from morning till night from night till morning." In the tobacco town of Danville, Virginia, businessmen cared more for the tobacco trade than the Confederacy. They balked at attempts by Confederate soldiers to tear up rail connections with Richmond to slow a Union advance. Most welcomed Union occupation, anticipating a more stable climate for business.[29]

Business was the priority for cotton dealers and growers as well. In Texas, one teamster recalled that throughout the war there was "a never ending stream of cotton pouring into Brownsville." In San Antonio, one witness saw "hundreds of huge Chihuahua wagons . . . waiting their turn to enter the grand plaza, deliver their packages of goods, and load with cotton" for the trip back to Mexico. At the border crossing of Eagle Pass, a customs inspector wrote that "there was scarcely a day that hundreds of bales were not unloaded . . . and crossed [over] . . . as fast as possible." On the coast, one seaman witnessed between 180 and 200 ships from various countries waiting their turn to be loaded with "endless bales of cotton."[30]

Along the Mississippi, cotton flowed as fast as the river could carry it and moved easily between Union and Confederate lines. "It seems incredible," wrote a Union colonel, "that in the midst of the most tragical scenes that war has ever created, the very arena of conflict should be the busy field of mercenary and lawless trade." Union officers themselves were often involved in the trade. After one federal official noticed some gunboats riding too low in the water, he found that they were all loaded with cotton.[31]

In the southeast, river systems like the Chattahoochee, Apalachicola, Tombigbee, Alabama, Altamaha, and Savannah all served as avenues of cotton smuggling. In March 1862, two men from Fort Gaines, Georgia, a port town on the Chattahoochee, told Governor Joe Brown that cotton smuggling was rife along the river. Steamboats typically made their way upriver, loading cotton as they went, with Columbus their supposed destination. But much of the cotton somehow found its way down to Apalachicola on the Gulf Coast, where it was transferred to

Despite the Confederacy's food shortage, and in violation of government policy, planters and merchants regularly produced and smuggled cotton out to an eager market. The *Shamrock*, built in Columbus, Georgia, during the war, hauled cotton downriver to the Gulf port of Apalachicola. There it was transferred to oceangoing vessels for transport to Europe and the North. With cotton prices at an all-time high, some planters bragged openly that the longer the war went on, the more money they made. Photo from the Florida State Archives.

vessels that took "pleasure excursions" out to see the Union blockading fleet. The vessels always returned with empty cargo holds. As late as March 1865, the steamboat *Comet* was caught on Georgia's Ocmulgee River with "a cargo of cotton designed for traffic with the enemy." General Howell Cobb, commanding reserve forces in Georgia, was implicated in the affair.[32]

Cotton moved along rail lines too, sometimes choking off transport of vital food supplies. In Albany, Georgia, there were a hundred thousand bushels of corn rotting in city warehouses while outbound trains loaded with cotton clogged the rails. "Is the Southwestern Railroad leaning to *favorites*, or speculating in the article themselves?" asked the *Albany Patriot*. Even wounded soldiers took a backseat to cotton. In November 1864, with Sherman's army bearing down, officers telegraphed Governor Brown from Macon about a state-owned train loaded with cotton: "We need the train to remove our sick from hospitals. I request your authority to use this train for the sick. . . . Please answer at once."[33]

Much of the Deep South's cotton traveled along rail lines into Tennessee and from there to points north. On March 12, 1862, a report was sent to Georgia's governor about two suspicious Tennessee men buying cotton in Macon. "It is believed they intend to let the Federals have it," read the communication. Two weeks later, an Atlanta newspaper published a letter warning that "uncompromising adherents to the Northern Government have been, for weeks, shipping cotton to East Tennessee. . . . Don't sell them your cotton. They are your enemies." It was not only Tennesseans who were engaged in the business. The paper's Chattanooga correspondent reported that "a few traitorous Georgians have a finger in the pie." Based on the amount of cotton exported during the war, the "traitors" numbered far more than a few.[34]

In direct violation of state law and Confederate policy, "planters insisted," as one historian put it, "on their right to grow unlimited amounts of cotton; to retain it for sale whenever they chose; and to sell it whenever, and to whomever, they chose." And it did not matter who the buyers were, even if they were Yankees. A neighbor wrote of one prominent South Carolina planter: "John De Saussure has sent a hundred bales to be sold. Says he knows they will slip into Old England or New England." The *Richmond Examiner* was furious at cotton planters "who were so early and furiously in the field for secession, who . . . are now raising cotton . . . and shipping it to the Yankees."[35]

Of the one and a half million bales that left the South during the war, two-thirds went to the North. Blockade runners carried much of it to Nassau in the Bahamas, where they sold it to buyers from New York and other northern import centers. But a good portion made its way north by more direct routes, with government officials on both sides, civil and military, accepting bribes along the way. Some producers reaped such profits from the cotton trade that they were not eager to see the conflict end. In a private letter, one planter wrote that he feared a "terrific fall" in cotton prices if the war ended. Others bragged openly that the longer the war went on, the more money they made.[36]

Trade between the lines enriched many planters and some merchants but did little to benefit the South generally, as the wealthy imported high-priced luxury items to maintain themselves in their accustomed lifestyle. A Mississippi congressman made that clear when he complained:

> The classes engaged in this nefarious traffic, to hide its enormity, would say that it was for the good of our people; that they were buying articles of necessity; that they were supplying the people with shoes, salt, etc. It was not so. If these men, who are trading with the enemy had been true to their specious professions every man and child in the

Confederacy would have a half-dozen pairs of shoes and the country would be knee-deep with salt. The evil has produced great disaffection among the people.[37]

Devoting so much land to cotton and tobacco produced hunger as well, which was a major source of disaffection. Concerned about the families of his men, Colonel J.L. Sheffield of the Forty-eighth Alabama regiment wrote to the governor:

I have, sir, made it my business to go through the country to ascertain the condition of families of *poor men* who are in the service. I find *hundreds* of them entirely destitute of everything upon which to live, not even *Bread*. Nor is it to be had in the Country. . . . Something should be done else they are bound to suffer. All they ask for is *Bread*.[38]

"The Money Thieves, Those Speculators"

Planters' reluctance to devote themselves to food production contributed not only to hunger but also to an inflationary spiral that began to spin out of control soon after the war started. During the war's first year, the South suffered a 300 percent inflation rate. It would only get worse as the war continued. Butter went from 12¢ a pound in 1861 to 75¢ two years later. By the end of the war, it was $5 or more. Bacon went from 12¢ to 50¢ a pound in the war's first year. Flour that sold for $9 a barrel before the war was going for $400 by war's end. Coffee went to $30 a pound shortly after the war began and from there to $60 and $70.[39]

Though the Union naval blockade contributed to rising prices, even more damaging to the economy was profiteering and speculation by planters and merchants. In his study of Columbus, Georgia, during the war, historian Diffee Standard concluded that the blockade was more an excuse than a reason for most price increases. So did Harriet Amos in her study of wartime Mobile, noting "the relative ease with which ships passed the Federal fleet." Wartime accounts support those conclusions. One southern editor boldly entitled his commentary "The Blockade No Excuse." For months he had heard merchants blaming the blockade for high prices. But he and many others observed that there were "dry goods alone within our southern limits sufficient to supply the wants of the people of the Confederate States for the next ten years to come. The blockade therefore is no excuse." In a private letter to a friend, one planter admitted as much. For years, southerners had been "abusing the Yankees for extortion and speculation, but [we are] quite as bad ourselves."[40]

The inflation that hit so many so hard sprang largely from inducements of the market. Merchants kept a tight grip on food and clothing resources, selling only to those who could pay top dollar, or holding out for even higher prices. Planters continued to focus far too much on increasingly profitable cotton and tobacco, leaving the South short of the food it needed. What edibles they did produce went not to support soldiers' families as promised, but to speculators who scoured the countryside buying up the scarce foodstuffs. Planters and merchants both took the same self-interested path that had served them so well before the war, following the dollar wherever it led. But in so doing, they left the interests of the soldiers, their families, and ultimately the Confederacy itself far behind.

As early as November 1861, one Georgian complained in a letter to Vice President Alexander Stephens that he and other "common farmers" were finding it difficult "to keep our heads above the flood of destruction" brought on by "the money thieves, those Speculators." Dependent as the Confederacy was on support from plain folk, if speculation forced them into ruin, the government would be ruined as well. That danger was clear to James Bethune of Columbus, Georgia. In a letter to the *Columbus Daily Sun*, Bethune warned that the avarice of southern elites was the Yankees' most powerful ally. He urged the well-off to contrast their own inconveniences with the hardships of poor soldiers and their families who were suffering and dying. "And now you complain of making sacrifices if you furnish bread for him at less than you might get for it from somebody else." E.H. Grouby, editor of Georgia's *Early County News*, saw the danger as well. He publicly denounced speculators as "home Yankees" who were "by far greater enemies to the South and do more to injure her cause than ten times their number of Yankees in the field."[41]

In a vein of religious bigotry and scapegoating, some editors openly associated speculation with southern Jews. Grouby's own *Early County News* carried on its masthead the legend DEATH ON SPECULATORS, JEWS, RASCALLY GOVERNMENT OFFICIALS. Other editors, though just as bigoted, were more broad with their criticism. The *Mobile News* observed that politicians, planters, and merchants generally had "out-Jewed Jews, out-traded the sharp Yankee trader, and descended from that exalted position known on earth—Southern gentlemen—to become nothing better than common hucksters." The *Richmond Examiner* agreed: "Southern merchants have outdone Yankees and Jews. . . . The whole South stinks with the lust of extortion."[42]

Nowhere was that more obvious than in Atlanta. As the Confederacy's rail hub, it became the South's commercial capital. Inevitably, it was soon swarming with a class of speculating industrialists and merchants whose "ruling passion," wrote one city editor, "is a lust for gain; their sordid souls care naught for the miseries of their fellow mortals, and [they] have no interest in the good of the country, if its ruin would advance their own personal aggrandizement." It seemed to this editor the height of hypocrisy for men who had, for the most part, supported secession to now benefit handsomely from the war they had brought on. And then to buy exemptions for themselves while preying on soldiers' families, keeping their wages low and cost of living high, was more than the editor could stomach. "Is it right that the war . . . with its carnage and woe, should work an absolute benefit to one class, while it ruins the rest? Shall those who are permitted to . . . be exempt from service on account of these employments out of which they are making such fortunes, amassing such wealth and splendor, in full view of want, poverty and destitution . . . not be required to contribute a portion of these gains for the benefit of the sufferers by the war?"[43]

In Tallahassee, the *Florida Sentinel* warned in November 1862 that "speculation and extortion are the great enemies of the Confederate cause. The rage to run up prices is going to ruin us if anything else does. It is impossible to overrate the degree of uncertainty, insecurity and alarm felt by the masses of the people from this cause alone." Of those masses, soldiers' families were perhaps the most enraged. Many blamed the wealthy and well connected for their men's absence and their own poverty. "My husband has been taken away," complained a North Carolina woman to Governor Vance, "by desyning men that wont go into the army themselves but prefer to stay at home & speculate by selling goods to the wives of soldiers at 500 per cent."[44]

A writer signing as "One of the People" in the *Lynchburg Virginian* demanded court-ordered price fixing to rein in speculators. He warned that if the courts did not take action, "the people would take the subject

As early as November 1861, one Georgian complained that common folk were finding it difficult "to keep our heads above the flood of destruction" brought on by "the money thieves, those Speculators." Soldiers' families were especially vulnerable. From Tallahassee, the *Florida Sentinel* warned that "speculation and extortion are the great enemies of the Confederate cause. The rage to run up prices is going to ruin us if anything else does." Virginia's *Richmond Examiner* agreed: "The whole South stinks with the lust of extortion." Illustration from *Frank Leslie's Illustrated Newspaper*.

of redress into their own hands." There were similar warnings in Burke County, North Carolina, where "capitalists" were "defrauding the helpless." One Texas man went a step further with a bold call: "Men of Austin, Arise!!!" He urged that they "mark forever with a brand of infamy" those extortioners "who no longer crawl like the slimy reptiles that they are, but boldly stalk through your streets, grinding at every step with their iron heels, deeper and deeper down, the poor man, the widow and the orphan." Some did take direct action. Nelson Tift, the founder of Albany, Georgia, was such a notorious speculator that a local court imposed pricing restrictions on him. Tift simply ignored the order. His neighbors sued him, then threatened him, and finally set fire to his Flint River bridge house.[45]

Speculation by southern planters and merchants marked the starting point of what became a vicious encircling trap for common people. Planters fed a lucrative cotton market, devoting not nearly enough acreage to food. Scarcity forced food prices up, and speculating merchants drove them even higher. Rampant inflation inevitably followed, making planters and merchants even less willing to exchange what food they had for the Confederacy's increasingly worthless currency. Lydia Brassfield of North Carolina's Orange County, a soldier's wife left with three children to care for, walked for five days in the winter of 1863 to buy corn, only to have merchants tell her that they would not sell for Confederate notes. In Georgia's Early County, a soldier's wife wrote to the local paper complaining of planters hoarding food and refusing to take paper currency. They would, however, take what little the poor had, if they had anything worth trading. "This is the only way many Soldiers' families in the county can get anything to eat," wrote this distraught woman. "Love nor Confederate money won't do it."[46]

Planters and merchants would also take gold or silver coin, which common folk rarely held. From Paulding County, Georgia, came a letter from J.B. Adair to the governor telling of local planters hoarding "considerable quantities" of corn. He singled out one for special censure: "Bennett Cooper of this County has about fifteen hundred bushels, more than sufficient to answer his purposes and refuses to sell a grain for anything except gold or silver." A Virginia soldier wrote that "hellish greed for gold" was throwing common folk into ruin.[47]

The editor of Georgia's *Athens Southern Watchman* felt the same way: "Some hard cases have come to our knowledge recently of men who were very active in bringing on the war, and who now vehemently urge its prosecution, and yet refuse to receive Confederate money in payment of notes given by poor men." An Alabama grand jury pointed out that "the man who refused to take this money is doing more damage to our cause, more injury to our soldiers and their families than if he were in the ranks of the enemy." And that was where some urged they be sent. One Georgia editor wrote that such men "should be drummed out of every respectable community, and sent heels over head to Yankeedoodledum, where they properly belong."[48]

If they would not take Confederate money, planters and speculators would take federal greenbacks, which smugglers who traded with the Yankees brought in across the lines. Such trade was so common in Vicksburg, Mississippi, that Confederate General Earl Van Dorn declared martial law and threatened those demanding Yankee money with fines and imprisonment. But such was the influence of Mississippi elites that they successfully pressured the Davis Administration to revoke Van Dorn's order. In so doing, Davis helped undermine his own currency. He also undermined troop morale. One disgusted Arkansas soldier wrote that "when it comes to that the citizens refuse to take their own currency I think it is time to quit." Davis was also undermining his ability to support the soldiers. If suppliers could not be forced to take Confederate currency from common folk, neither would they take it from the government.[49]

"Leeches and Sharks"

In 1863, the Confederacy determined that what it could not buy, it would take by force. That spring, Congress passed a series of taxes, the most far-reaching of which was a 10 percent levy on such agricultural products as livestock, wheat, corn, oats, hay, fodder, potatoes, peas, beans, and peanuts. Even this tax-in-kind did not provide enough food to meet the army's needs. So officers began to "impress" produce, and anything else they wanted, far beyond the 10 percent level. Though no member of any class held impressment in high regard, its weight fell heaviest on the plain folk. Only when poorer farms were stripped bare did impressment companies turn to the plantations. Even then, planters paid a proportionally lighter tax or used political connections to avoid impressment entirely. When Robert Toombs used his influence to dodge impressment, one newspaper editor lashed out: "We believe Toombs, because he is rich, does pretty much what he wants . . . if he were a poor man he would be hanged." The editor concluded that "a *poor* man in this world has no more showing than a blind dog in a meat house with a dozen starving Yankees after him."[50]

Some impressment agents could be ruthless. One seventy-year-old Georgia man who had sent five sons to Confederate service, two of them already dead, was threatened with a beating if he did not hand over his horse. Another was killed when he refused to give up his cattle. "Our own cavalry has been a great terror to our own people," wrote a man from northern Alabama to Governor Watts. "Stealing, robbing, and murdering is quite common." Some called impressment "pillaging." In January 1864, one Confederate official wrote a dire warning to Richmond after touring the countryside: "Great dissatisfaction prevailed in many sections, and generally among the masses. . . . In some localities all the cattle, hogs, and corn of farmers have been taken, and teams are not left to make a crop. Under this pressure the people have become, if not disloyal, at least indifferent . . . to the cause." When an impressment officer took two cows from a South Carolina farmer, the man thundered that "the sooner this damned Government fell to pieces the better it would be for us."[51]

Impressment was often accompanied by depredations of all sorts. A seventy-year-old man was threatened with a beating if he did not give up his horse. An impressment officer shot and killed a Georgia man who refused to hand over his cattle. When an impressment officer took two cows from a South Carolina farmer, the man thundered that "the sooner this damned Government fell to pieces the better it would be for us." Illustration from Ellis, *Thrilling Adventures*.

Governor John Milton of Florida wrote to the War Department complaining of impressment agents' "lawless and wicked conduct." So did Governor Joe Brown of Georgia, who warned that impressment's "baneful operations" were producing an "evil spirit, bordering already in many cases upon open disloyalty." And he was right. The *Atlanta Southern Confederacy* wrote of impressment officers: "We advise the people to resist them." So did the editor of Georgia's *Early County News*. Otherwise "our military officers will soon think they own the whole country." Judge James Bush, the author's great-great-great-grandfather, headed an assembly of Early County citizens who drafted a petition warning that impressment officers were so numerous and aggressive that they threatened to "alienate the affections of the people from the government." As the war went on, enforcing impressment

James Bush, the author's great-great-great-grandfather, headed a meeting of prominent citizens in Early County, Georgia, who drew up a petition warning that the government impressing supplies threatened to "alienate the affections of the people from the government." Among the county's wealthiest cotton planters, Bush and his fellow petitioners failed to acknowledge that it was in large part cotton overproduction that created food shortages, which led Congress to pass the impressment bill to begin with. Courtesy of the late Helen Kirkland Daniels. Photo in possession of author.

laws became more and more dangerous, with agents beaten up, shot at, and sometimes killed.[52]

What angered impressment's victims most, often to the point of violence, were the corrupt activities in which impressment agents frequently engaged. Mary Lane of Wilkes County, Georgia, complained that William Sneed, the local impressment agent, was feeding confiscated produce to his slaves. Other agents, civil and military, sold impressed produce on the open market and kept the money for themselves. Illicit trade in clothing occurred as well. Uniforms made by women in Augusta, Georgia, for donation to soldiers were "charged against the soldiers at full prices." An Augusta man wrote Governor Brown that army quartermaster officers in the city were "involved and complicated" with speculators. J.B. Jones, a clerk in the Confederacy's capital at Richmond, accused quartermaster officers there of the same. They were getting rich by passing army rations to speculators.[53]

As early as the fall of 1861, a Georgia farmer wrote to the *Athens Southern Watchman*: "I have never entertained the shadow of a doubt as to our success—our whipping out all the Yankees that can be produced—but God knows how we shall escape the *corruptions* of our own Government, and the *leeches and sharks* of our own people."[54]

Scandal rocked the War Department in 1862 when quartermaster officers were caught selling army rations to speculators. Congress responded by making it illegal for the public to buy military supplies from enlisted men but said nothing of officers. Small wonder that the act did little to stop corruption. It served only to emphasize the South's pervasive class divisions, and Georgia's *Early County News* denounced the legislation for its elitist overtones.

Why is it not also against the law to buy any of these articles from Quarter Masters, Commissaries, &c., when it is a well known fact that many of these swoll head gentry steal a great deal of this kind of Government property which they have in their possession, to be distributed among the needy Soldiers, sell them, and pocket the money? There is more rascality, according to the number, among officers than privates. Why are not officers bound up as tight as privates? There is altogether too much *favoritism* shown to little jackass officers by Congress.[55]

Corruption among quartermasters and commissary officers was even more obvious to soldiers in the field. An officer of the Fourth Alabama regiment wrote anonymously to one of his senators suggesting that "*every one of them* be beheaded at the expiration of their first 12 months in office. *Any man* who remains in either position longer will *steal*." Another exasperated southerner thought it would take more than that to stop the corruption. He added his voice to a swelling chorus when he urged his governor: "Do for God's sake put an end to this unrighteous war. We shall be eaten up by Confederate Office holders and Speculators."[56]

If common folk were being "eaten up" by officeholders, speculators, and other well-to-do southerners, the upper crust themselves ate well, despite food shortages. A Virginia belle recalled feeling "intensely patriotic and self-sacrificing" when she gave up ice cream and cake. She called it "putting our tables on a war footing." Many would not do even that. In Eufaula, Alabama, a guest of one upper-crust family described "a very nice table indeed, meats of various kinds, cakes, fruits, custards, floats and plenty of pure coffee." Coffee was one of the rarest commodities in the wartime South, but it was available to those with money. Blockade runners had long since reduced imports of basic necessities and even war matériel, preferring to smuggle in goods they knew would bring top dollar from rich southerners in gold, silver, or Yankee greenbacks. In the spring of 1863, Florida Governor John Milton made that point when he wrote to Jefferson Davis of the "villainous traffic" by smugglers and speculators who brought in rum and gin "but no arms or munitions of war." They were in it for the money, not the Confederacy.[57]

"Our Blood Rest upon the South"

While southern elites sacrificed ice cream and cake, Confederate soldiers were going hungry. According to one postwar report, the Confederacy "was barely able to scrape together, week by week, the stinted rations of bacon indispensable to keep life in the soldiers." Often it could not even do that. Cotton and tobacco overproduction, along with indifference among planters and their political allies, combined to keep Confederate soldiers in a state of near starvation.[58]

In September 1862, during the Army of Northern Virginia's campaign into Maryland, one observer felt that words were inadequate to express the soldiers' sad condition: "When I say that they were hungry, I convey no impression of the gaunt starvation that looked from their cavernous eyes." A Sharpsburg woman recalled that Lee's men "were half famished and they looked like tramps. They nearly worried us to death asking for something to eat." Most of the time, despite orders to the contrary, the soldiers did not ask. Living off the land, they gave in to the law of survival and took what they needed. It was the same wherever Confederate armies went. Confederate soldier John Hagan wrote in a letter to his wife: "I beleave our troops are doing as much harm in this country as the yankees . . . and in fact wheare this army goes the people is ruined." The situation only got worse as the war dragged on. By September 1864, one soldier wrote that the Army of Tennessee would "steal and plunder indiscriminately regardless of age or sex." Said another: "They talk about the ravages of the enemy in their marches through the country, but I do not think the Yankees are any worse than our own army."[59]

Starvation was also stalking soldiers' families back home, and letters from the men to their wives were filled with advice on how to get along until they returned home. In November 1863, William Asbell wrote to his wife Sarah: "I have received both of your letters and was glad to hear Through Them that you are all alive but sorry to know that the children are sick on your hands when I cannot be there to assist you with Them." William told Sarah to feed their hogs corn once a day and potatoes the rest of the time. "If the children are not able to dig the potatoes," he said, "fence of a portion of the patch for [the hogs]." As the weather grew colder and food ran low, William wrote his wife, "You had better try and sell one or other of the horses . . . as you are scarce of Provisions. You will have to do the best you can."[60]

Women were writing letters too. One South Carolina woman expressed general class resentment when she wrote to Jefferson Davis: "I wish you would have all the big leguslater men and big men about towns ordered in to confederate serviz. They [are] no serviz to us at home." Planters were a special target of the women's scorn. Many were obligated by law to assist needy soldiers' families when called upon to do so. But it was common for them to ignore the stipulations of their bonding contracts. Far from supporting soldiers' families, planters found it easy to run prices up for them. A disgusted Texas man recalled the promises planters had made to the soldiers and how often those promises were broken: "Most of them were induced to enlist, at the breaking out of the war, by promises made to them by planters, that if they would volunteer, their families should be supported. But, no sooner were the poor devils deluded from their homes . . . than the planters forgot their generous and patriotic promise, and, instead of assisting their families, extortioned on the soldiers' wives from one to three dollars a bushel for corn. Thus those cowardly vampires were fattening on the fat of the land, and enriching themselves on the misfortunes of their country and miseries of the poor."[61]

"It is folly for a poor mother to call on the rich people about here," wrote one hungry mother of three in an 1862 letter to Jefferson Davis. "[T]here hearts are of steel[.] [T]hey would sooner th[r]ow what they have to spare to their dogs than give it to a starving child." In Wilmington, North Carolina, a mother and her child were reduced to living in an outhouse, where they both starved to death. One group of Georgia women wrote to their governor that the planters "don't care what becomes of the poor class of people" as long as "they can save there niggroes."[62]

Thousands of letters from all across the South telling of starvation flooded into state and Confederate offices. Most were from soldiers' families asking for their discharge. A North Carolina soldier's wife wrote to Governor Zebulon Vance:

I set down to rite you a few lins and pray to god that you will oblige me I ame apore woman with a posel of little children and I wil hav to starv or go neked me and my little children if my husban is kep a way from home much longer . . . I beg you to let him come . . . if you cud hear the crys of my little children I think you wod fell for us I am pore in this world but I trust rich in heven I trust in god . . . and hope he will Cos you to have compashion on the pore.[63]

Ida Wilkom of New Iberia, Louisiana, wrote to Secretary of War Judah Benjamin, imploring him to let her husband come home. Her baby was dying, and her three other children were in dire need. She had done all she could to eke out a living, but death was now at the door. "I have tried every thing to submit to the will of God in tranquil resignation; but I find, a human being can suffer only according to his human strength."[64]

Almira Acors, a soldier's wife, bluntly wrote North Carolina's Governor Vance: "I do not see how God can give the South a victory when the cries of so many suffering mothers and little children are constantly ascending up to him." After asking for her husband to be sent home, another soldier's wife demanded of Vance: "I would like to know what he is fighting for." To her, the answer seemed clear: "I don't think that he is fighting for anything only for his family to starve." In northern Georgia, Marcella League and Ruth Nicholson, neither of whom could write, had a neighbor draw up a letter on their behalf to both the president and secretary of war, threatening to sue the Confederacy if their husbands were not immediately discharged. Both women signed the letter with an X.[65]

With hunger rampant and the elites refusing help, their families' survival was much more important to southern women than the Confederacy's fate. In September 1863 came a letter to Davis from soldiers' wives and widows in Miller County, Georgia.

Our crops is limited and so short . . . cannot reach the first day of march next. . . . But little [food] of any sort to Rescue us and our chil-

dren from a unanamus starveation. . . . We can seldom find [bacon] for
non has got But those that are exzempt from service . . . and they have
no humane feeling nor patraotic prinsables. . . . An allwise god [w]ho is
slow to anger and full of grace and murcy and without Respect of persons and full of love and charity that he will send down his fury and
judgement in a very grate manar [on] all those our leading men and
those that are in power ef thare is no more favors shone to those the
mothers and wives. . . . I tell you that with out som grate and speadly
alterating in the conduckting of afares in this our little nation god will
frown on it and that speadly.[66]

Another woman was just as direct in her letter to Davis: "If I and my
little children suffer [and] die while there Father is in service I invoke
God Almighty that our blood rest upon the South."[67]

Hunger was making outright Unionists of many southerners, especially those tormented by Confederate armies scouring the countryside for food. One old farmer near Vicksburg, Mississippi, told
Confederate troops plainly that "he would rather the hogs have his
vegetables than the soldiers." One soldier wrote to his wife, "We are
eating everything in our route, even milk cattle," as the army passed
through Arkansas. A Texas trooper wrote that "Arkansas is eat out, and
the citizens here are tired of us, and say that we are ruining their country and that if it wasn't for the Texas troops they would go back into
the Union." Some could not wait for the Confederates to leave, so
they fled to federal lines looking for food. One northerner described
civilians coming into Union camps in Arkansas as "poor, lean, hungry
looking creatures we could not help feeling sorry for. . . . We shall
have to open wide our store houses . . . to keep thousands of our
erring brethren from dying of actual starvation."[68]

As hunger grew worse, there were more and more calls in southern
newspapers for the rich to "Give to the Poor!" as many a headline
read. In February 1862, Georgia's *Milledgeville Confederate Union*
called on wealthy men of Baldwin County, "Come Up with Your
Money!" Soldiers' families were suffering, and the editor reminded
planters that they were obliged to help: "It is for you and your property that tens of thousands of poor men are now fighting. . . . What
are the rich men of Baldwin doing? Nothing. Wake up from your
slumber." A year later, the situation had not changed. As the *Union* editor wrote, "There are many men, in every county in the state, who

have fallen short of their duty. . . . When called on to make subscriptions to aid a poor disabled soldier, or help a soldier's suffering family, they have turned the back of their hands."[69]

Women could sometimes secure help for themselves and their children in exchange for sexual favors. In Columbus, Georgia, a disgusted citizen wrote to a city paper that women were frequently offered assistance only "at the sacrifice of their honor, and that by men who occupy high places in church and State." One southern editor expressed doubt that the southern gentry would ever change its self-serving ways: "To expect such miserable abortions of humanity, who have been living a lie for more than two years, to give in their property at anything like its value in Confederate money is to expect heat from ice or light from darkness."[70]

Officials at the state and local levels often tried to do what the wealthy would not, but relief efforts were frequently halfhearted and nearly always ineffective. All too often, funds slated for poor relief wound up in the pockets of corrupt officials. In Marion County, Alabama, the probate judge was found misappropriating money from a fund set aside for indigent families of soldiers. After a court in Augusta County, Virginia, appropriated funds to purchase twelve thousand bushels of salt, enough for twenty pounds per person, angry citizens demanded to know "why so many families have not been able to get a pound." George Cleveland of Miller County, Georgia, wrote to the governor accusing relief agents of "swindling." The state assembly had allocated $2.5 million in aid to soldiers' families, but none was getting through. In Valdosta, Thomas and Joshua Griffin, assigned to distribute government salt, sold it at more than twice what the state allowed and pocketed the difference.[71]

To keep their heads above the flood tide of corruption and speculation, many soldiers' families and other commoners were forced deep into debt, paying extortion prices for what little food was available. Most often the debt could not be repaid. Then, wrote a group of angry North Carolinians to their governor, creditors could "take there land & every thing they hav." A seventy-two-year-old widow with her only supporting son in the army wrote to Governor Vance for help when her small farm went on the auction block to cover a $50 debt. "It is with and aking hart and tremelous hand I seat my self this morning to inform you of my condition. . . . [T]he Specerlators will prove too hard for us . . . those that can assist the nedy will not do so . . . pleas

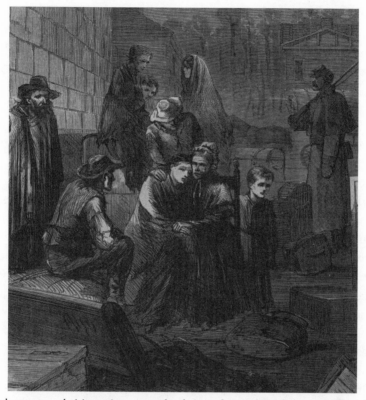

Food shortages and rising prices meant hard times for working folk, especially soldiers' families. Urban tenants, forced to choose between food and rent, were frequently thrown into the streets. In the North Carolina town of Wilmington, a mother and her child were reduced to living in an outhouse. There they both starved to death. One Columbus, Georgia, resident lamented that poor women were frequently offered help "at the sacrifice of their honor, and that by men who occupy high places in church and state." Illustration from *Harper's Weekly*.

excuse bad speling and writing and help me if you pleas." She was hardly alone. Thousands of such letters poured into government offices during the war.[72]

Reacting to the outcry, some states passed "stay laws" to prevent confiscation of soldiers' property in their absence or postpone it until after the war. But creditors would have none of it. Alabama planter John Horry Dent called indebted farm families "worthless and unprincipled" and called stay laws unconstitutional. Jonathan Worth—a North Carolina slaveholder, cotton planter, mill owner, and speculator—complained that the stay law "disorganized Civilized society." A fellow member of the North Carolina elite, B.F. Moore, called it "radical, unwise, demoralizing, disgraceful." Many such men simply used their influence with local magistrates to ignore the stay law and continue taking land. In North Carolina, they succeeded in having the stay law repealed after only four months. The result was that tens of thousands of Confederate soldiers returned home to find their families destitute and their land gone.[73]

"A Criminal Sort of Economy"

Some states also tried to relieve suffering by contracting with employers who promised to provide jobs for the poor at prescribed wages. But it was all too easy for government contractors to skim wages. In November 1862, a Georgia woman wrote that the wives of government contractors were bragging that they would be millionaires if the war went on much longer. Some employers paid their workers barely half the contracted wages, keeping the rest for themselves.[74] The practice was so common that citizens lashed out in editorials such as this one, from an April 1863 issue of Georgia's *Columbus Sun*, telling how local seamstresses were cheated.

> Only think of it. A sleek speculator growing rich by the labor of the poor half-famished needle woman, who gave up her husband as a sacrifice on the altar of our country! A man who forcibly wrests from the hands of starving children that which is to make him rich! A man who will deliberately rob the widow and orphan of their daily bread, that he may add to his opulence. A man who professes not only to be a patriot, but also a Christian, who would deliberately drive the poor sewing woman to choose between a life of shame or an ignominious death by starvation! How dare such a monster look his fellow man in the face without cowering in very shame? The milder forms of villainy, such as treachery and counterfeiting, sinks into insignificance when compared with such enormities.[75]

But the Confederacy refused to interfere with industrial operations on workers' behalf. Within a year of the war's outbreak, southern manufacturers were cranking out arms and supporting material at an astonishing rate. The Ordnance Bureau under Josiah Gorgas was especially efficient in producing and funneling military accoutrements to the field. So much was manufactured and transported that no Confederate army ever lost a major battle for lack of munitions. The Confederate government was prepared to pay well for their delivery, and it was not particular about where the money went.[76]

That lack of concern weighed heavily on working-class folk, especially soldiers' families. Late in 1863, "A Needy Soldier's Wife" of Montgomery, Alabama, wrote in a letter to the city press that she and her children simply could not survive on the small salary she got as a government seamstress. The cost of beef and other basic commodities was much too high. With winter coming on, she wondered how Montgomery's well-to-do could "enjoy their warm houses and comfortable beds" when so many poor women and children were in such dire straits. In a petition to President Davis, Montgomery women wrote that they were willing to "work to support ourselves and little ones" but they had to get more for their labors or perish.[77]

Despite enormous profits flowing into the pockets of southern industrialists, wages were generally low from the war's outset. In October 1861, a "poor mechanic" in Georgia wrote the *Athens Southern Watchman* complaining that he could not find work that paid nearly what he got before the war. With prices on the rise, he wondered how he was going to support his family. He was not alone. The paper's editor knew that many local workers faced similar hardships. The only thing he could add to the man's "words of truth and soberness" was "God help the poor day-laborers."[78]

Working conditions were just as appalling as wages. In some cases, they were deadly. Few industrialists saw much point in spending money on worker safety. The result was that throughout the war, the South's urban newspapers were filled with reports of fatal industrial accidents. One of the worst occurred at Augusta's Confederate States Laboratory, where gunpowder was made. In August 1864, eighteen thousand pounds of powder exploded at the granulating mill, killing nine employees. The concussion stripped leaves from neighborhood trees and broke windowpanes in all the surrounding buildings. According to one report, the victims were "blown to atoms. Hardly a vestige of them remaining. Portions of the bodies were found hanging on the trees—a most shocking spectacle."[79]

Many victims of industrial accidents were women. Fifteen female employees died in a Jackson, Mississippi, factory explosion. A cartridge manufacturing facility in Virginia blew up, "scattering workers like confetti." The mishap killed thirty-two women and injured thirty others. In Richmond, nearly fifty women died when an ordnance factory exploded.[80]

Children in the labor force were even more imperiled. Because they were usually unskilled and economically less valuable, they often performed the most hazardous jobs. One factory in Augusta, Georgia, had a special storeroom filled with caskets for its workers, most of them small. Young Martin Reilly, who worked at a Savannah foundry to support his widowed mother, was blinded in one eye when molten lead splattered his face. A falling timber killed John Henry, a boy of fifteen, at a mill near Augusta. His father had died earlier working at the same mill. Jack McElrath and John Madden, aged twelve and fifteen respectively, were horribly mangled when an artillery shell they were working on exploded at the Naval Iron Works in Columbus, Georgia. Both suffered through more than an hour of agony before they mercifully died.[81]

Facing dangerous conditions and low wages from the war's early days, workers often went on strike. In the fall of 1861, employees at Richmond's Tredegar Iron Works struck for more equitable pay, setting off a series of industrial strikes across the South. Influential manufacturers pressed the government for help. Such pressure, along with a lack of volunteers for the army, contributed to passage of the Conscription Act in early 1862. Under the legislation, certain categories of workers were declared exempt from the draft as long as they were employed. If they went on strike and lost their jobs, they could be hauled off to combat. Factory owners found the act an effective tool to keep workers in line and wages low. In one of the measure's first tests, Lynchburg machinists went on strike for a living wage. They were fired, then drafted. Telegraph operators in Augusta struck as well, with the same result.

Still, consumer prices outstripped wages so far and fast that workers frequently had to take action. In 1863, postal clerks in Richmond struck for a wage increase. The next year, gravediggers at the city's Shockoe Cemetery did the same. With the draft act in force, they risked more than just a loss of their jobs. When lithographers in Richmond went on strike, they were locked up in a military prison and threatened with conscription unless they returned to work. Managers at the Virginia and Tennessee Railroad used the same tactic when their workers went on strike. They contacted the local enrolling officer and had the strikers sent to the guardhouse. There was little legal recourse for the detainees.

With the writ of habeas corpus suspended, government officials could imprison almost anyone without warrant, charge, or trial.[82]

Such obvious extortion of labor, coercing men to live poor or risk death in battle, infuriated working folk. As some had feared even before the war, enslavement of whites had arrived and was backed by the Confederate government. Still, workers continued to resist. In early 1864, angry workers at the Mississippi Manufacturing Company in Bankston struck for better treatment, but Confederate cavalry arrived to disperse them. Reacting to similar heavy-handed actions, one enraged citizen wrote to a Georgia newspaper: "When this war broke out our people thought they had something to fight for, but now they have nothing, but to keep the Yankees checked, so that our own Government may oppress them more." The paper's editor was in full agreement. "Our freedom is now gone!" he declared. "May the devil get the whole of the old Congress!" One commoner spoke for many when he wrote that "freemen . . . are to day slaves—nay, worse than slaves." And in a way they were. Since a free man represented no investment, to the elites nothing was lost by his death either in the factory or on the battlefield. One disgusted southerner called the whole system of labor extortion "a criminal sort of economy."[83]

Common folk reserved their most intense scorn for those who brought on the war yet refused to serve in it or grow enough food to support it. "The crime is with the planters," wrote an angry Georgian to the *Savannah Morning News*. "As a class, they have yielded their patriotism, if they ever had any, to covetousness . . . for the sake of money, they are pursuing a course to destroy or demoralize our army—to starve out the other class dependent on them for provisions." Another asked: "What class has most interest in the war and has made the most money by it, *and sacrificed the least to maintain it?* . . . It is the class known as the planters."[84] One soldier called the planters

the most contemptible of all our public enemies. . . . These fellows talk loudly about *their* constitutional rights—that no body has a right to say how much cotton they shall plant and intend to put at defiance the law and the authorities. But listen again and you will hear them loud for the enforcement of the Conscript Law. Oh, yes! Their negroes must make cotton and whilst doing it the poor men must be taken from their families and put in the Army to protect their negroes. Was ever a greater wrong, or a more damning sin, perpetrated by men or devils?[85]

"Many Voters Who Are Not Planters"

Such attitudes produced a class-based political consciousness among commoners that made itself felt in the fall 1863 elections. Not all those who threatened to vote against incumbents were anti-Confederate, nor did they do so for entirely class-related reasons. That most of Tennessee and Arkansas, and much of Mississippi and Louisiana, were already in Union hands—together with the losses at Gettysburg and Vicksburg that summer—also eroded support for the Confederacy. Yet amid the discouragement over Confederate military failures, there were also clear signs of class resentment. In September 1863, just before fall elections, this broadside circulated in Texas:

Common Sense

It is high time for the people of Texas to determine whether they will invite the fate of Louisiana and Mississippi, and allow a few men more distinguished for shallow brains and loud talk, than other capacity, and who have little stomach for the suffering they prepare for others, to drag them down to inevitable ruin.

The author signed himself "One who was at Vicksburg."[86]

Some plain folk were even more direct with their expressions of class antagonism. In an open letter to the *Savannah Morning News*, southeast Georgia commoners called on two of their state assemblymen to make public their positions on a recent state tax hike: "There was a tax act passed at the last session for the support of indigent widows and orphans of deceased soldiers, *from which the planters were specially exempted.* Did you, or either of you, vote *for that exemption*, or oppose it? And how did you manifest your opposition to that gross and palpable injustice?" They signed themselves "Many Voters Who are not Planters."[87]

Planters and their allies increasingly became worried that their political control might be slipping away. "The poor hate the rich," wrote South Carolina planter James Henry Hammond, "& make war on them everywhere & here especially with universal suffrage." So great were elitist fears of rising voter disaffection that some called for class-based restrictions on voting rights. Some demanded an increase in the poll tax to discourage poorer citizens from casting ballots. Others suggested banning them from politics entirely with property qualifications for voting and officeholding. As early as November 1861, a committee assigned to consider revising Virginia's state constitution called for more restricted suffrage and fewer popularly elected offices. In May 1863, the Reverend H.W. Hilliard, a former member of Congress from Georgia, spoke out publicly for a more restricted suffrage. When word of Hilliard's remarks reached Athens, a local paper wrote that "the most unfeeling, unjust and cruel wrong we have ever witnessed, is this effort of designing politicians and juggling priests who are lying about home doing nothing, and worse than nothing, to disfranchise the brave and noble poor men who are fighting the battles of the country."[88]

Such efforts on the part of elites served only to inflame common folk and further undermine Confederate support. By 1863, many were openly demanding peace. In North Carolina, there were peace rallies throughout the mountain regions. In Georgia, the editor of Griffin's *Southern Union* called for an end to the war, and reunification with the North. Several candidates for Georgia's General Assembly from Gilmer and surrounding counties ran on the Union ticket. So did candidates in northern Alabama. In parts of Mississippi, so numerous were Union men that cavalry units were posted to keep them away from the polls. Still, armed bands of deserters showed up at Mississippi polling places defying arrest and demanding their right to vote. In Floyd County, Virginia, Confederates guarded every precinct to prevent deserters from voting. Nevertheless, so many local deserters' relatives went to the polls that they elected a pro-Union sheriff, Ferdinand Winston, and several other Unionist county officials. In Mississippi's Tishomingo County, Confederate officials were so worried about a Union victory at the polls that they suspended elections entirely.[89]

Fear, intimidation, and despondency kept many alienated voters away from the polls. And because the Confederate Constitution gave the president a six-year term, Jefferson Davis was in no danger of losing his office. Even so, the election returns brought discouraging news for the Davis Administration. In North Carolina, candidates for the Conservative Party, composed mainly of longtime secession opponents, won nine of ten congressional seats—and eight of them were "reported to be in favor of peace." George Logan of the Tenth District was nominated at a peace rally. Both of the state's gubernatorial candidates were Conservative Party men.

In Texas, half the incumbent congressmen lost their seats. Of Georgia's ten congressional representatives, only one was reelected. The state's 90 percent freshman rate was the highest in the Confederacy. Eight of Georgia's new representatives ran on an anti-Davis platform. Alabama voted out its staunchly pro-Davis governor. Four of the state's new congressmen were suspected of being outright Unionists. The new legislature was made up mostly of men inclined to sue for peace. One Alabamian wrote that the election results showed a "decided wish amongst the people for peace." In all, nearly half the old Congress was turned out. Two-thirds of the newly elected members had long opposed secession. The congressional freshman rate would likely have been much greater had it not been for the large bloc of returning members representing districts under federal occupation who were "elected" by refugees, by soldiers, or by general ticket in a given state's districts still held by the Confederacy.[90]

Plain folk had an impact on local elections as well, especially in urban areas, where turnout tended to be higher. Some commoners even formed their own political alliances. In Columbus, Georgia, they organized and offered a slate of candidates for city office on the Mechanics' and Working Men's Ticket. According to the *Enquirer*, the new party "prevailed by a very large majority." Its success sent shock waves through the ranks of the city's political establishment. The *Enquirer*'s editor voiced upper-class fears just two days after the vote when he chastised plain folk for their "antagonistic" attitude and condemned the "causeless divisions of our citizens into classes." The *Enquirer* conceded that because of their numbers the city's commoners could control any election in which they were united. But he insisted that this fact alone was among the strongest reasons why they should not unite. "Nothing can be more mischievous in any society," he warned, "than antagonistic organizations of its classes. Such divisions are more bitter in their alienations than any other political parties, and are far more apt to produce hurtful collisions."[91]

Reaction to the *Enquirer*'s criticism was swift and direct. On October 13, a competing city paper, the *Daily Sun*, ran a letter it received from a local man signing himself "Mechanic." He argued that mischief had already been done by the well-to-do. Common folk were trying only to protect themselves from further harm.

Voting by Classes

Editor Daily Sun:—I notice in the Enquirer, of Friday evining, an article complaining bitterly of the people voting by classes, in which both classes are accused of clannishness, but the burden of his complaint seems to rest on mechanics and working men. He says, "there is certainly no ground for any antagonism in the city." In this the Enquirer is mistaken; for any man, woman or child can see that the people are dividing into two classes, just as fast as the pressure of the times can force them on. As for example: class No. 1, in their thirst for gain, in their worship of Mammon, and in their mighty efforts to appropriate every dollar on earth to their own account, have lost sight of every principle of humanity, patriotism, and virtue itself, and seem to have forgotten that the very treasures they are now heaping up are the price of blood, and unless this mania ceases, will be the price of liberty itself; for we know something of the feeling which now exists in the army, as well as in our work-shops at home. The men know well enough that their helpless families are not cared for, as they were promised at the beginning of the war. . . . They know, too, that every day they remain from home, reduces them more and more in circumstances, and that by the close of the war a large majority of the soldiery will be unable to live; in fact, many of them are ruined now, as many of their homes and other effects are passing into the hands of speculators and extortioners, for subsistence to their families. Thus you see, that all the capital, both in money and property, in the South, is passing into the hands of class No. 1, while class No. 2 are traveling down, soon to take their station among the descendants of Ham. You can easily see who are class No. 2. The soldiery, the mechanics, and the workingmen, not only of Columbus, but of all the Confederate States. In view of these things, is it not time that our class should awake to a sense of their danger, and in the mildest possible manner begin the work of self-defense, and endeavor to escape a bondage more servile than that imposed by the aristocracy of England on their poor peasantry? Then we claim the right, as the first alternative, to try and avert the great calamity, by electing such men to the councils of the nation as we think will best represent our interests. If this should fail, we must then try more potent remedies.[92]

"Amazonian Warriors"

Destitute and desperate, many thousands of southerners had been resorting to "more potent remedies" for some time. As early as July 1861, a crowd of New Orleans soldiers' families numbering ten thousand gathered outside the mayor's office insisting on aid for food and rent. Some were taking more direct action. In June 1862, a group of soldiers' wives in Bartow County, Georgia, descended on Cass Depot and demanded cotton to make clothes for their families at home and their husbands in the field. They intended to pay, but the agent refused to deal with them. That would not be the end of it. Returning later that day, the women "called for the Agent as a witness of their doings, and cut the rope from one bale, took a supply of cotton, and marched very quietly home with it." In November, a "party of Ladies . . . driven by necessity" raided a store in nearby Cartersville. The next month, twenty women shouting "Salt or blood!" marched on the depot in Greenville, Alabama, and took what they needed. With desperate times calling for desperate measures, others across the South soon followed their example.[93]

In February 1863, as the war's second winter was depleting private food stocks, a band of "regulators" in North Carolina's Bladen County sent their governor an ominous warning.

> The time has come that we the common people has to hav bread or blood & we are bound booth men & women to hav it or die in the attempt. . . . the common people is drove of in the ware to fight for the big mans negro & he at home making nearly all the corn that is made, & then becaus he has the play in his own fingers he puts the price on his courn so as to take all the Solders wages for a fiew bushels & then . . . [extend credit] until the debt will about take there land & every thing they hav & then they will stop all & if not they will hav to Rent there lands of there lords Sir we hoos sons brothers & husbands is now fighting for the big man's negros are determined to hav bread out of there barns & that at a price that we can pay or we will slaughter as we go.[94]

It was no idle threat. Shortly after the letter was sent, hungry women attacked a government depot in Bladenboro, taking six sacks of corn and one sack of rice.[95]

Women's riots were breaking out all over the Confederacy during the spring of 1863. In late March, a crowd of at least fifty ax-wielding North Carolina women appeared at the government supply depot in Salisbury demanding food. When an agent tried to send them away, they stormed the building and stole ten barrels of flour. A few weeks later in Guilford County, as Nancy Mangum reported, "a crowd of we Poor wemen went to Greensborough yesterday for something to eat as we had not a mouthful [of] meet nor bread in my house[.] what did they do but put us in gail. . . . they threatened to shoot us and drawed their pistols over us." Such threats did nothing to address the problem of hunger. Nor did they deter North Carolina women. A short time later, women were again rioting in nearby High Point.[96]

The largest of the women's riots took place in the Confederacy's capital city of Richmond, Virginia. Like so many of the South's urban areas, the city was thronged with soldiers' wives and widows left on their own and barely surviving. With planters growing too much tobacco and cotton, there was never enough food on the shelves. The resulting high prices were driven even higher by speculation. And the paltry wages paid to those women fortunate enough to find work were falling further behind rising prices. After two years of wartime suffering and little or no help from elites in the public or private sector, poor women were at the breaking point. When Richmond's city council refused even a slight increase in funding for poor relief that spring, it was the last straw. On April 1, several hundred women gathered at Oregon Hill Baptist Church to discuss how they were going to feed themselves and their children. One fiery speaker named Mary Jackson said out loud what they were all thinking. They needed food, and they needed it now. If merchants would not sell at prices the women could afford, they would have to take what they needed.

The next morning, hundreds of women assembled at Capitol Square and headed for the business district. Hundreds more joined their ranks as they went. Soon the surging crowd of women, and some men, numbered over a thousand. They hit the clustered shops like a human hurricane, smashing down doors, looting stock, and sending terrified merchants running for their lives. Governor John Letcher called out the City Battalion and threatened to shoot the rioters if they refused to turn back. They ignored him and continued their rampage. City officials turned fire hoses on the looters. Still they pushed ahead. Finally, Jefferson Davis himself appeared on the scene. Mounting a drayman's cart, he threw what money he had to the crowd but also threatened to order them shot if they did not disperse. Many of the rioters, with all they could carry, were beginning to scatter in any case. The police hurried after them, arresting a few who later received jail time ranging from weeks to months. Among them was Mary Duke, a poor soldier's wife who was sentenced to six months in prison. Her young son Andrew begged for his mother's release in this undated letter addressed to Governor Letcher.

> I am a poor boy, the oldest of four children & I am only 15 years old. My father is in Genl Lee's army & my mother is in prison—and we are left to ourselves, dependent on my labor to support us. When my mother was first put in prison, a lady came to stay with us but she says that she cannot stay no longer—and these little children will be left alone.
>
> Our poor Mother did very wrong, but she has suffered greatly—all the rioters that have been tried have been discharged from the prison but her—she is in a decline and suffers in mind & body.
>
> Four little children appeal to you for clemency and ask you for their sake & for their father's sake who is fighting for the country, to pardon our sick mother and let her come back to our humble home. My little sisters are 10, 7 and 2 years old.
>
> I sell news papers to feed us & try to save a little to help pay her fine which by the help of friends I can do if you will show us mercy.
>
> Do good Governor, and four little hearts will rise up and call you "blessed." I served 10 mos [months] under the good Jackson in Co. C, Irish batt. [battery]—as drummer.
>
> Don't be angry that a poor boy troubles you to read this. He asks most respectfully mercy for his mother, Mary Duke who was imprisoned 12 May last.

Letcher quietly pardoned Mary Duke on July 1, 1863.[97]

The day after the riot, soldiers patrolled Richmond's business district and artillery guarded its streets. Hoping to keep news of the riot suppressed, government officials ordered telegraph operators and newspaper editors not to mention it in their communications. Obligingly, the *Richmond Dispatch* entitled the next day's lead editorial "Sufferings in the North." But word of rioting in the capital quickly leaked out and filtered through southern newspapers over the next few weeks.

It would have made little difference even if the news could have been contained. Widespread as hunger was that spring, the Richmond riot was but one of many that broke out almost simultaneously across the South.[98]

In April, when speculators drove up the price of bacon in Mobile, Alabama, dozens of women marched through the city with banners reading BREAD OR BLOOD and BREAD AND PEACE. One witness reported that this "army of women" carried "axes, hatchets, hammers and brooms." And they were prepared to use them. As they reached each grocery store, if the doors were not already open they tore them down and helped themselves to ham, flour, and any other supplies. Army officers sent in Confederate troops, but the soldiers refused to level their

Women in Miller County, Georgia, wrote to Jefferson Davis warning that God would "send down his fury and judgement in a very grate manar [on] all those our leading men and those that are in power ef thare is no more favors shone to those the mothers and wives." But they were not waiting for God or Davis. With a fury of their own, southern women from Virginia to Texas—including those in Miller County—looted stores, depots, and warehouses for food. Illustration from *Frank Leslie's Illustrated Newspaper*.

rifles at the women. According to one merchant who witnessed the scene: "The military was withdrawn from the field as soon as possible—for there were unmistakable signs of fraternizing with the mob." By the time Mobile's mayor arrived to appeal for calm, women with armloads of food were making their way home.

Elsewhere in Alabama, women were banding together both to take what they needed and to send a strong message. Barefoot women in Talladega stormed a local store and ransacked its supply of shoes. In Lafayette, fourteen women armed with "guns, pistols, knives and tongues" marched on a grist mill and took what flour they wanted. Knowing that cotton overproduction was a major cause of food shortage and high prices, a band of about forty enraged women in Calhoun County attacked local plantations and destroyed the cotton fields.[99]

Georgia was a hotbed of women's riots that spring. On March 16, about a dozen women raided a store on White Hall Street in Atlanta. Their leader, "a tall lady on whose countenance rested care and determination," asked about the price of bacon. When she heard it was a dollar a pound, she said that the women in her group were wives and daughters of soldiers and could not afford to pay such prices. To demonstrate her seriousness, "this tall lady proceeded to draw from her bosom a long navy repeater, and at the same time ordered the others in the crowd to help themselves to what they liked." They cleared the room and made off with nearly $200 worth of bacon. A few weeks later in Cobb County, just north of Atlanta, a black man driving a wagonload of goods to Marietta was robbed of several bales of yarn by a "gang of women."

On April 10, women entered a store near Augusta's Upper Market and asked about prices for shoes and calico. The proprietor sensed mischief afoot, so he closed his store due to "pressing business" elsewhere. The women moved to another store but took nothing and dispersed after authorities came on the scene. They arrested one man for "telling the women they did perfectly right." One Augusta newspaper labeled the women "Amazonian warriors." A few days later, Columbus newspapers gave accounts of that city's "seizing party." On April 11, a group of women numbering about sixty-five rallied at the intersection of Broad Street and Franklin (now Fourteenth Street) and marched down Broad Street "to raid the stores of speculators." Armed with knives and pistols, the rioters shouted curses as they went. They first struck George A. Norris's dry goods store and "commenced helping themselves to whatever they wanted." Police arrived in time to disperse the mob before it could reach other stores. A man named Shanghai Brooks, described by the press as a vagabond, was arrested for encouraging the women. Seven months later, Columbus women warned the governor by letter that they would again organize a mob and take provisions if they received no relief. Brown forwarded the letter to Muscogee County's inferior court justices, "requesting them to take such action in the premises as the court might think proper."

Women in Georgia's state capital of Milledgeville seized items from a dry goods store on the morning of April 14, 1863. They dispersed only when a city magistrate promised immediate relief. The women agreed and were issued funds directly from the city treasury. Macon saw its women rioting that same month as well. In what one editor called "The Women Rising," a crowd armed with pistols and knives attacked the Rosenwald & Bro. store on Second Street to seize calico and other supplies. The proprietor grabbed one of his assailants, wrestled a Bowie knife from her, and retrieved two bolts of calico. The other women escaped with their loot.

Later in April, a band of twenty-eight women, most of them armed with pistols and knives, robbed a freight wagon headed from a factory in Butts County to the rail depot at Forsyth. The editor of the *Macon Telegraph* called on officials "to nip this dangerous business in the bud." Sensing class animosities reflected in the riots, the editor emphasized that protection of private property for both elites and commoners was at stake. "The rich can better afford to be robbed than the poor, and when that game is set afoot the poor will be the greatest sufferers." But from a commoner's perspective, the rich had robbed them through speculation and impressment. They saw themselves as taking back only what was, in a general sense, theirs by right.[100]

At the height of the spring riots, Congress passed a joint resolution urging that planters, "instead of planting cotton and tobacco, shall direct their agricultural labor mainly to the production of such crops as will insure a sufficiency of food for all classes, and for every emergency, thereby with true patriotism subordinating the hope of gain to the certain good of the country." The resolution was merely a suggestion. It carried no force in law. Nor did efforts on the part of cities like Richmond to set up "free markets" for the destitute. Such markets did ward off further riots in some urban areas, but they were usually underfunded and often relied more on private charity than public finance. Predictably, most wealthy folk ignored government pleas and continued, as one Georgia editor wrote, to "carry their patriotism in the *pocket-book*."[101]

Later that year, eleven women in Georgia's Pickens County stormed the tanyard at Talking Rock. According to one report, they "helped themselves to as much leather as they could well carry off." They boasted of having protection from menfolk home as paroled prisoners of war, and threatened to raid other businesses. One local merchant wrote to Governor Brown begging him to stop the riots and to protect the community from those "who have not our cause at heart."[102]

In the late fall of 1863, starving women rampaged through Thomasville, Georgia, for the "purpose of supplying themselves with goods." Threats of further violence caused such fear among city officials that they called for help from as far away as Valdosta, fifty miles to the east. Thannie Wisenbaker, a Valdosta resident, later remembered when the town's home guard

> was ordered to Thomasville where some great excitement was reported. My! Such preparation in getting ready for the trip! Everything that they imagined they might need was gotten ready. Old muskets, used in the war with the Indians, shot-guns and such old pistols that they had on hand, were readied. . . . The men rushed hurriedly from place to place, pressing into use every horse and mule available, until at last they rode off to Thomasville. But alas! For their hopes and dreams of meeting and subduing the enemy. When they arrived in Thomasville, they learned, to their utter chagrin, that some soldiers' wives had threatened to break into the government commissary to obtain food for their hungry children.[103]

It was the only time Valdosta's home guard was ever called to service.

At its December session, the Thomas County Superior Court called the riot a "disgraceful act," and warned that "all such misguided females" should refrain from "unlawful demonstrations in the future." Driven by continuing hunger, women did not always heed such warnings. Some months later, six Thomas County women armed with rifles stopped a wagon and stole its cargo of corn.

"Women Outrages"

Another wave of rioting struck Georgia in the spring of 1864, this time focused on the state's southern half. In April, newspapers reported a "daring robbery" in Savannah. A number of women entered the stores of A.F. Mira on Whitaker Street, John Gilliland on Congress Street, W. and R. McIntire on Saint Julian Street, and a Mr. Stroup on Bryan Street, helping themselves to bacon and other items. Mira was preparing to sell the women bacon but was forced into a corner while they helped themselves. One of the McIntires offered the women rice and sugar free of charge, hoping to avoid a general ransacking; his gesture appeased them. They moved on to Gilliland's store, where they stole all his bacon. Gilliland tried forcibly to retrieve some of his pork, but most of the women escaped with their plunder. Sheriff Cole of Chatham County arrested three women and placed them in jail. Mary Welsh, charged with taking bacon from Gilliland's store, was turned over to the magistrate for prosecution. Anne McGlin and Julia McLane were charged with disorderly conduct. In the end, none of the women were prosecuted. There was too much popular sympathy for them, especially since they were soldiers' wives.

On April 19, E. Yulee of Stockton, Georgia, wrote Governor Brown that "thirteen women made their appearance here armed with pistols and knives and demanded admittance to the depot containing the provisions collected as tax in kind." Three guards at the depot tried without success to "pacify" the women. They shoved the guards aside, broke open the door, and took over one hundred pounds of bacon. Yulee believed that these women would steal more supplies now that they knew they could "seize them with impunity." He suggested that the civil courts might offer a remedy, but "unfortunately these are now silent in the middle of our troubles." Most of the governor's incoming correspondence was read by clerks who wrote a short description on the outside of envelopes or letters for faster processing. Yulee's letter was marked, "women outrages."

Just to the west of Stockton, Lowndes County saw more female lawlessness that month. A group of Valdosta women marched on a local store and tried to buy cotton yarn, but the proprietor refused to take Confederate money. He would, however, trade for bacon. Having no bacon to exchange, the women "forcibly took all the yarns in the store." In the same neighborhood, a dozen or more women, at least one armed with a pistol, broke into a government warehouse and stole a wagonload of bacon. At about the same time, the small Lowndes County settlement of Naylor had troubles of its own. A mob went on a rampage "for the purpos of taking of spun yarn cloth and bacon." Among the participants were three members of Union Primitive Baptist Church. Hetta Peters, Rachel Chitty, and W.S. Peters came under the "displeasure" of the congregation for their role in the riot. According to church minutes, "W.S. Peters cleared himself; Hetta Peters confessed and was forgiven with joy." Chitty, apparently unrepentant, refused to answer the church summons and was turned out of the congregation.

In May 1864, Campbell County Justice of the Peace B.D. Smith found himself in an uncomfortable situation over women taking impressment into their own hands. In a letter to Governor Brown, Smith outlined the circumstances that led two men to accuse him of "up holding the women presying provisions." The men in question were trying to avoid conscription by having Smith call bailiff elections and running for the positions themselves. Once elected, they would not have to report for duty. To force the issue, they had tried to frighten a sixty-one-year-old bailiff into quitting his post. But neither Smith nor the bailiff would be intimidated. In retaliation, the two men accused Smith of supporting women who forcibly took what they needed. He denied the accusation but wrote, "I did not blame the women." Smith told of a gentleman who was "staying at home" only to profit from a war in which he refused to fight. Though the man was well aware of how badly soldiers' wives needed provisions and had "a right smart to spair, he would not let them have it neither for money nor work but was speculating on it." Careful not to alarm the governor, Smith noted that the women's actions were peaceful. He refused to call the impressment a raid, insisting that no such incident, with all its violent connotations, had ever taken place in Campbell County.

Destruction of property was usually not a part of women's plans for justice. But there was at least one raid that resulted in severe property damage. In June 1864, a number of armed women in Pierce County, Georgia, broke into a storehouse, "carried off several wagon-loads of bacon, and burned some houses." These women boasted that they had plenty of men, including deserters hiding in the Okefenokee Swamp, who would back them up should they meet resistance. According to one source, "the people of property were much alarmed"—so much so that one "prominent citizen" took the train from Blackshear to Savannah and personally reported the attack to authorities.[104]

It was the same all over the South. A letter to Florida's Governor Milton reported that starving soldiers' families in Hernando County "are becoming clamorous for meat, and are killing people's cows where ever they can get hold of them." About a dozen women in Floyd County, Virginia, ransacked a Confederate supply depot and stole a large supply of bacon. Fifty miles to the west, a dozen mountain women brandishing pistols and knives descended on Abingdon and looted the town. The raid's success inspired a second band of women, who shortly afterward swept through Abingdon taking what was left. In Raleigh, North Carolina, about twenty soldiers' wives fell on a government depot and took all the flour and grain they could carry. In Yancey County, 50 women did the same. In the state's port city of Wilmington, women were involved in an attack on a blockade runner in which most of the cargo was stolen. When authorities ordered members of the home guard to fire into the crowd, they refused. There were other riots in Barnwell, South Carolina; Archer, Florida; and Waco, Texas. On the Texas coast, Galveston citizens assembled at the local Confederate commander's home, demanding access to commissary provisions. And in the north Texas town of Sherman, 125 armed women ransacked town stores for what provisions they needed.[105]

As the war entered its final months, the plight of the southern women grew even more desperate, and they continued their robberies and raids. During the winter of 1864–65, soldiers' wives and children were regularly seen stealing livestock in southwest Georgia's Early and Miller counties. One man, who signed himself "A Stock Raiser," placed a notice in Blakely's *Early County News* demanding that the thievery stop. He insisted that he had already given generously to local relief efforts and was sorely disappointed in the women. He threatened to publish their names in a later issue of the *Early County News* if they did not stop their criminal ways. "What would your husbands and fathers think if they should see your names in a public print as *stock stealers?*"

John Davis of Miller County, a well-to-do slaveholder and stock raiser, complained about women stealing his sheep's wool. The sheep were being caught, sheared, then released back into the woods. He, too, warned that unless the women stopped their "nefarious business," he would have their names published in the local paper. Besides, Davis insisted, these apparently desperate women were not needy at all. It was simply, he said, their nature to steal. "They are now acting as they always would have done, had they the same opportunity."[106]

Such attitudes were common among the upper classes. Godfrey Barnsley, a wealthy Georgia planter, complained that "the character of the population here . . . is growing worse." "Thieving," he said, "in no small way" was among their character flaws. J.A. Turner, who published Georgia's *Turnwold Countryman* on his Putnam County plantation, held females who resorted to theft in particularly low regard. "Women do not transgress the bounds of decorum so often as men, but, when they do, they go [to] greater lengths." The editor continued: "For with reason somewhat weaker, they have to contend with passions somewhat stronger. Besides, a female by *one* transgression forfeits her place in society forever." According to Turner, a woman's modesty was her greatest asset. If she engaged in stealing and rioting, she forfeited her heavenly "ornament" forever. Turner ended his condemnation of such women by saying that "if an angel falls, the transition must be to a demon."[107]

Newspapers all over the South were quick to describe destitute women in such unflattering ways, some denying they were destitute at all. Wrote an Alabama editor: "The class composing the mobs are of the lowest—prostitutes, plug uglies . . . and those who have always been a nuisance to the community, and who are not in a perishing, or even suffering condition, for want of food." A Georgia editor insisted that the rioters were little more than loafers, vagrants, and loose women who used the pretense of necessity to justify their theft. Virginia's *Richmond Examiner* suggested that many were not even southerners, calling them "prostitutes, professional thieves, Irish and Yankee hags, gallows-birds from all lands but our own." Few were bold enough to acknowledge the obvious link between desperate circumstances and desperate acts.[108]

One brave soul who did was the editor of Georgia's *Athens Southern Watchman*. In a lengthy and painstaking editorial, he looked for the root cause of the riots and concluded that ultimate blame lay not with the women but with self-interested moneymen, especially planters and speculators, who cared more for profit than patriotism. He begged the wealthy to change their ways while there was still time: "In the name of our beloved country—in the name of outraged humanity—in the name of that religion they profess to reverence—in the name of the God they pretend to fear—we call upon these men to change their policy before it shall be too late!" But his plea fell mostly on deaf ears, relief never came, and rioting went on.[109]

In February 1865, fifty women raided the government depot in Colquitt, Georgia, the seat of Miller County. Armed with axes, they broke open the doors and took close to fifty sacks of government corn, or about one hundred bushels. It was reported that the women were soldiers' wives and that the judges of Miller County's inferior court, responsible as they were for poor relief, bore most of the blame. In an open letter, one local resident accused the judges of being more focused on their own concerns than the well-being of the destitute women and children. The accusations of callousness did not stop with local officials; state officials, including Governor Brown, were also at fault. Singling out the governor, the writer had always thought of Brown as a "complete demagogue" and an "out and out humbug."

The *Augusta Chronicle and Sentinel* shared the writer's sentiments, especially about the lack of proper administration of poor relief. Commenting on the Colquitt raid, the editor wrote: "The Government has lost the corn. Would it not have been much better to have given it freely to the sufferers? We think so." Those who were the women's staunchest supporters—their husbands and sons—very much agreed. Shortly after the Colquitt raid, Georgia soldiers from Hart County arrived home and were appalled at the destitution they found among their families. Realizing that no help was coming from the county's inferior court justices, these men raided a gristmill and distributed sacks of flour to local women.[110]

"Every Soldier on Each Side Ought to Run Away and Go Home"

In the spring of 1863, Daniel Snell of Harris County, Georgia, wrote home to his wife Sarah: "You spoke of a riot in Columbus . . . it is no more than I expected. I understand there was also one in Augusta. . . . What will become of the women and children with the food situation?"[111] More and more soldiers were wondering how their families would get along in their absence. Others knew all too well. Said one man serving in the Army of Tennessee:

I have been in all the battles of the West, and wounded more than once, and my family, driven from their home, and stript of everything, are struggling in Georgia to get a shelter and something to eat . . . Little sympathy is shown my suffering wife and children—they are charged three prices for what scanty accommodation they get, and often are nigh starvation. We might as well be under Lincoln's despotism as to endure such treatment.[112]

Rural women might have been able to get along well enough had it not been for government impressment agents taking much of what they had. Urban women might have fended for themselves if not for rampant hoarding and speculation. Perhaps neither impressment nor speculation would have been so widespread and devastating had the planters grown more food and less tobacco and cotton. But impressment, speculation, and cash-crop overproduction were facts of the wartime southern economy, much to the despair of common folk. To them it was clear that the war was little more than a profit-making enterprise for speculators in money crops and other commodities. One southern woman wrote to her soldier husband: "I do believe every soldier on each side ought to run away and go home and let them that wants it carried on for the purpose of speculation carry it on themselves. I hear some saying they would not have it stopped for know price. I do think hanging would be too good for such men."[113]

Tens of thousands of women wrote such letters, begging their men to come home. One such desperate letter read: "Last night I was aroused by little Eddie's crying. I called and said, 'What is the matter, Eddie?' and he said, 'O, mama, I am so hungry!' And Lucy, Edward, your darling Lucy, is growing thinner every day. . . . I would not have you do anything wrong for the world, but before God, Edward, unless you come home, we must die." To women with families nearing starvation, it could not be wrong for a man to look to his family's survival. A mother encouraged her soldier son to "think the time past has sufficed for *public* service, & that your own family require yr protection & help—as others are deciding."[114]

In Lee's Army of Northern Virginia, a group of angry North Carolina soldiers wrote to their governor insisting that he make good on his promise that their families would be cared for: "Very many of our wives were dependent on our labor for support before the war when articles of food and clothing could be obtained easier than now. At this

Letters from home telling of family hardships, and the government's failure to respond, led many a soldier to question the cause. A young Georgia volunteer wrote to a friend: "I don't want mother to suffer for anything as long as I live. I am willing for her to work and I know she will do it; but when I hear she is in want of provisions and cant get them, I am going home. . . . The last two letters I received from her don't suit me." Soldiers were acting on such resentment. By September 1864, two-thirds of Confederate soldiers were absent with or without leave. Illustration from *Harper's Weekly*.

time they are alone, without a protector, and cannot by hard and honest labor, obtain enough money to purchase the necessaries of life." The letter contained a veiled and portentous threat: "We cannot hear the cries of our little ones, and stand." A young soldier from Columbus, Georgia, was more blunt in a letter to a friend: "I don't want mother to suffer for anything as long as I live. I am willing for her to work and I know she will do it; but when I hear she is in want of provisions and cant get them, I am going home. . . . The last two letters I received from her don't suit me."[115]

Tens of thousands of soldiers were acting on their resentment. "My men are deserting fast," wrote a Rebel captain to his wife in January

1864. "The laws that have been passed generally protect the rich, and the poor begin to say it is the rich mans war and the poor mans fight, and they will not stand it." Private James Zimmerman of North Carolina wrote home in October 1863: "If you will show me a man that is trying to compel soldiers to stay in the army he is a speculator or a slave holder, or has an interest in slaves." A group of men signing themselves "Many Soldiers" wrote to Jefferson Davis asking "what are we fighting for?" They were "tired of fighting for this negro aristockracy," tired of fighting "for them that wont fight for themselves." "This war," they insisted, with all its "hardships and dangers must fall on all classes alike or we are determined it shall cease as far as we are concerned." To Jasper Collins of Mississippi, the twenty-slave law exposed the Confederacy's struggle as a "rich man's war and poor man's fight." Soon after its enactment, he deserted.[116]

Angry as they were that the financially well-off could avoid service, most galling to soldiers was what the rich were doing to their families back home. A Virginia soldier wrote home in 1862: "I begin to hear a good deal of murmuring & complaint among the soldiers & reproaches thrown at 'the rich' who have no mercy in grinding every cent out of the poor." With prices high and wages low, it seemed to the soldiers that they were fighting mainly to protect the ability of the rich to grow richer at their expense.[117] The rich did not see it that way. To them, their wealth bestowed the liberty to do as they pleased. Those with little or no wealth had liberty to do only what pleased the rich.

Soldiers with suffering families were anything but pleased with such an arrangement. That was especially true among Confederate soldiers for whom slave property had for decades been an obvious mark of class distinction. In February 1863, Private O. Goddin of the Fifty-first North Carolina wrote to Governor Vance:

> Now Govr. do tell me how we poor soldiers who are fighting for the "rich mans negro" can support our families at $11 per month? How can the poor live? I dread to see summer as I am fearful there will be much suffering and probably many deaths from starvation. They are suffering now. . . .
>
> I am fearful we will have a revolution unless something is done as the majority of our soldiers are poor men with families who say they are tired of the rich mans war & poor mans fight, they wish to get to their families & fully believe some settlement could be made were it

not that our authorities have made up their minds to prosecute the war regardless of all suffering. . . . A man's first duty is to provide for his own household the soldiers wont be imposed upon much longer.[118]

To men in the ranks with destitute families, their higher duty was clear. Their loved ones came first. "My family are nearer and dearer to me than any Confederacy could be," wrote Private Edwin Hedge Fay. "My first allegiance is to my family." Asked another Confederate soldier, "If I lose all that life holds dear to me, what is my country or any country to me?"[119]

To Lieutenant A.H. Burch of Alabama, such attitudes were hardly surprising. Late in the war, in a letter to Governor Thomas Watts, he stressed the obvious connection between suffering among soldiers' families, the class-based root of that suffering, and desertion.

Is it any wonder that our armies are decimated by desertion and dissatisfaction prevails throughout the poor classes when such nefarious practices (i.e. buying up corn in middle Alabama and selling it at eight dollars a bushel) are allowed to be carried on at home by wealthy men and officers . . . how many families who have not means to purchase . . . and are suffering while Messrs. ———— and ———— wealthy citizens and one of them a Government official of conscript age, hiding in a bomb-proof behind a miserable little tax collector's office, are speculating upon the bread that ought to go into the mouths of poor women and children, many of whom have husbands and sons now for four years defending the lives, liberty and property of these miserable, avaricious and cold blooded speculators.[120]

With most of the war's home-front burden borne on the shoulders of wives and mothers, it was their letters that directly or indirectly brought their men home. So clear was the connection between bad news from home and men leaving the army that many, especially among the upper crust, ignored the roots of family destitution and placed blame for desertion squarely on women. In February 1864, a North Carolina government official wrote: "Desertion takes place because desertion is encouraged. . . . And though the ladies may not be willing to concede the fact, they are nevertheless responsible."[121]

Many women were not at all reluctant to concede that they encouraged desertion. Like thousands of others, one woman told her husband in no uncertain terms to come home. The children were barefoot and cold, and there was almost nothing in the house to eat. "My dear, if you put off a-coming, 'twont be any use to come, for we'll all hands of us be out there in the garden in the old grave yard with your ma and mine." Another woman not only conceded her encouragement of desertion, she made it publicly clear. At the rail depot in Charlotte, North Carolina, she called to her deserter husband, who was being dragged back to the army: "Take it easy, Jake—you desert agin, quick as you kin—come back to your wife and children." As the distance between them grew, she yelled even louder. "Desert, Jake! Desert agin, Jake!"[122]

In April 1863, a brigade commander in the Army of Northern Virginia told General Lee that his regiments were being reduced by desertion far more quickly than they had ever been by combat. A Virginia colonel tried to stop desertion in his regiment by posting guards around the men. When that failed, he went "into a perfect rage." He cancelled furloughs, got drunk, and yelled at his troops that they could "go to hell for all he cared." By late 1863, close to half the Confederate army had deserted and, according to one soldier, half those desertions were caused by depressing letters from home. Less than a year later, President Jefferson Davis publicly admitted that "two-thirds of our men are absent . . . most of them without leave."[123]

Deserters usually slipped away individually or in small groups. Desertion gradually wore away Company E of the Twenty-first Virginia Cavalry. By spring 1864, it simply ceased to exist. Sometimes whole units deserted en masse, as when a regiment of Arkansas Confederates went over to the Federals. So did the Third Alabama. In May 1863, when ordered to Vicksburg, so many men from the Sixteenth, Seventeenth, and Twenty-fourth South Carolina regiments deserted that the units were of little use for battle. A year later, as Yankee forces advanced on Atlanta, Company D of the Fifty-fourth Virginia broke ranks and headed back home. As for the Fifty-eighth North Carolina, almost the entire regiment disappeared when it was stationed near Jacksboro, Tennessee, just 150 miles from the men's Ashe County homes.[124]

As early as 1862, so common was desertion in the Army of Northern Virginia that Robert E. Lee began ritual executions soon after he took command that summer. It was hardly welcome news for the soldiers. Just before the Battle of Second Manassas in August, three members of the Tenth Virginia and one from the Fifteenth Virginia became, as Private John Casler recalled, "the first that had been sentenced to be shot for desertion in our division." One made his escape during the night. The other three were shot to death the next day. When all three officers who had sat on their court-martial were killed or mortally wounded in battle a few days later, "most of the soldiers," wrote Casler, "looked upon it as a judgment."[125]

In the Army of Tennessee, Braxton Bragg was notorious for executing his men. He ordered five Alabama men shot for an unauthorized absence of only three days. One soldier in Bragg's army wrote that "almost every day we would hear a discharge of musketry, and knew that some poor trembling wretch had bid farewell to mortal things here below." Sergeant William Andrews of Lee's Army of Northern Virginia wrote that it was "an everyday occurrence for men to get letters from home stating that their families are on the point of starvation. Many a poor soldier has deserted and gone home in answer to that appeal, to be brought back and shot for desertion." He wrote, "Thank God I have no wife and children to suffer on account of an ungrateful government."[126]

Despite the dangers, soldiers continued to desert by the tens of thousands. And the more men deserted, the easier desertion became. When Lee detailed a fifty-man detachment of the Twenty-fifth North Carolina to return home and track down deserters, every man in the detachment deserted as well. Members of the Sixty-second and Sixty-fourth North Carolina regiments did the same. North Carolina was the destination for its deserting native sons, but it was also a waypoint for deserters from the Army of Northern Virginia traveling south and those from the Army of Tennessee going north. One state resident observed that "a good many deserters are passing the various roads daily." If challenged, "they just pat their guns and defiantly say, 'This is my furlough.'"[127]

"Fighting Each Other Harder Than We Ever Fought the Enemy"

Deserters who made it home found plenty of neighbors willing to help them avoid further entanglements with the Confederacy. That was obvious even from distant Richmond. A disgusted head of the Bureau of Conscription complained that desertion had "in popular estimation, lost the stigma that justly pertains to it, and therefore the criminals are everywhere shielded by their families and by the sympathies of many communities." A resident of Bibb County, Georgia, wrote that the area around Macon was "full of deserters and almost every man in the community will feed them and keep them from being arrested." In Marshall County, Mississippi, a witness noted that "many deserters have been for months in this place without molestation. . . . Conscripts and deserters are daily seen on the streets of the town." When deserters were arrested in Alabama's Randolph County, an armed mob stormed the jail and set them free.[1]

In Georgia, Augusta's *Chronicle and Sentinel* warned in June 1863 that the South contained "a large number of persons who not only sympathize with the Federals, but who are doing all in their power to injure us in every possible manner." Samuel Knight of southwest Georgia wrote to Governor Brown with a similar warning. After three months of "mingling freely with the common people," Knight reported that "among that class generally there is a strong union feeling."[2]

From Russell County, Virginia, came word in March 1862 that there were "plenty of Union men here." There were plenty in Arkansas, too. A former Confederate general declared in an 1863 address: "The loyalty to Jeff. Davis in Arkansas does not extend practically beyond the shadow of his army, while the hatred of him is as widespread as it is intense. The Union sentiment is manifesting itself on all sides and by every indication—in Union meetings—in desertions from the Confederate army—in taking the oath of allegiance [to the United States] unsolicited—in organizing for home defense, and enlisting in the federal army."[3]

When the Confederacy's "Ole Stonewall" succumbed to complications from wounds received at Chancellorsville in May 1863, a young North Carolina woman wrote that "some of the people about here actually rejoiced at the death of Genl Jackson!" That same year, an exile from Mississippi told a northern audience: "The question has been asked, is there any Union sentiment in the South? I reply that there is strong Union sentiment, even in Mississippi. . . . I make this statement without fear of successful contradiction, that the majority of the white inhabitants of the South are Union-loving men." Though most southern whites were hardly outright Unionists, it was "a certain fact," as Samuel Knight wrote in his letter to Governor Brown, "that the Southern people are fast becoming as bitterly divided against each other as the Southern and Northern people ever has been."[4]

Knight hardly needed to exaggerate in making his point. Brown could find abundant evidence of dissent simply by reading the newspapers in his own state capital of Milledgeville. Letters to the editor were filled with nearly constant criticism of Brown, Davis, the war, and the Confederacy. Some wrapped their dissent in humorous parody. In the summer of 1864, with verse patterned after Shakespeare, one farmer voiced his feelings on the war—and those of many rural men—in a Milledgeville paper.

To Go or Not to Go
To go or not to go, that is the question:
Whether it pays best to suffer pestering
By idle girls and garrulous old women,
Or to take up arms against a host of Yankees,
And by opposing get killed—To die, to sleep,
(Git eout) and in this sleep to say we "sink

To rest by all our Country's wishes blest"
And live forever—(that's a consummation
Just what I'm after). To march, to fight—
To fight! perchance to die, aye there's the rub!
For while I'm sleep, who'll take care Mary
and the babes—when Billy's in the low ground,
Who'll feed 'em, hey! There's the respect
I have for *them* that makes life sweet;
For who would bear the bag to mill,
Plough Dobbin,[5] cut the wheat, dig taters,
Kill hogs, and do all sorts of drudgery
If I am fool enough to get a Yankee
Bullet on my brain! Who'll cry for me!
Would patriotism pay my debts, when dead?
But oh! The dread of something after death—
That undiscovered fellow who'll court Mary,
And do my huggin—that's agony,
And makes me want to stay home,
Specially as I aint mad with nobody.
Shells and bullets make cowards of us all,
And blam'd my skin if snortin steeds,
And pomp and circumstance of War
Are to be compared with feather beds,
And Mary by my side.[6]

"Murdering Union Men"

Most southerners were hardly eager to fight. Had they been so, no draft would have been needed to force them. A majority had opposed secession to begin with. Even those who lent support to the cause of southern independence early on found plenty of reasons to disown the Confederacy as the war continued. That seemed obvious to John Wood of Mississippi, who wrote that "the power which wealth always gives has been brought to bear most heavily upon the poorer classes, producing a degree of suffering almost incredible in a country professing to be free." It was producing disaffection as well. South Carolina's commandant of conscripts reported that the state's hill folk were "little identified with our struggle."[7]

Sam Scott found the same to be true in southwestern Arkansas, attributing antiwar sentiment in part to the twenty-slave law. He reported that "the old cry of poor men being obliged to fight for the rich may be heard on all sides." Mississippian James Phelan warned Jefferson Davis that "never did a law meet with more universal odium" than the Conscription Act and its exemption of planters from the draft. "Its influence upon the poor is most calamitous, and has awakened a spirit and elicited a discussion of which we may safely predict the most unfortunate results."[8]

Privileges for planters made disaffection among plain folk predictable enough. Just as predictable were the results of speculative profiteering. Cotton and tobacco overproduction, along with speculation on what foodstuffs there were, led commoners to conclude that the Confederacy held little but misery for them. An army officer in South Carolina wrote to his superiors after a failed attempt to talk a group of deserters back into service that they were outraged over "speculations and extortions so rampant throughout the land. . . . They swear by all they hold sacred that they will die at home before they will ever be dragged forth again to do battle for such a cause." With prices high and food scarce across the South, small wonder that one North Carolinian wrote to his brother in the army telling him not only to desert but desert to the Yankees: "I would advise you to . . . go to the other side whear you can get plenty and not stay in this one horse barefooted naked and famine striken Southern Confederacy."[9]

Planters had promised to provide food for soldiers and their families but instead usually sold it to speculators, giving plain folk little reason to view the conflict as anything but a rich man's war. Georgia's *Early County News*, after reflecting on planter indifference to starving soldiers' families, asked, "Ain't it a pity but what the Yankees would take every thing such men have, and leave them without a single mouthful of anything? We hope to live to see the day." When told that a Union fleet was on its way down the Mississippi, a nonslaveholder from Jefferson County said publicly that he "wished the Gun Boats would shell every God Damn plantation on the River."[10]

Such language could be dangerous. One resident wrote to her mother that there were many Unionists in Randolph County, North Carolina, "some of which have had to leave for their large talking in favor of Lincoln. Others keep quiet and are let alone." But silence was not always a sure safeguard. F.A.P. Barnard, chancellor of the University of Mississippi, revealed his support of the Union only in private correspondence, but local secessionists got wind of his sentiments. They made life in Oxford so unpleasant for Barnard that he resigned and fled the state, finally settling in Virginia.[11]

Robert Guttery of Walker County, Alabama, recalled after the war that it was no uncommon thing "for union men to be arrested, put in the county jail, others sent to military prisons, some hung and others shot." It was a fair summation of what Union families suffered during the war. Simply declining to volunteer was often enough to have a man arrested for treason. In March 1862, a month before the draft law took effect, Levi Naron was thrown in a Corinth, Mississippi, jail because he would not enlist. There he "found some two hundred citizens, and learned that most of them were there on the same pretext as my own case, that of not belonging to any regiment . . . and were, in consequence, suspected of being Union men."[12]

The draft law became one more excuse to go after suspected Unionists. Some units harassed civilians whether suspected of Unionism or not. Eight members of the Fifty-fourth Alabama from Barbour County wrote to Governor Shorter (also from Barbour County) infuriated that cavalrymen were "prowling through our county on pretense of getting deserters" but were in fact "mistreating our aged fathers, mothers," and other locals. "Soldiers' families are insulted, there stock killed and there houses plundered." Some deserter hunters killed more than stock. One Tennessee man complained that when a conscript company showed up in Carter County it "appeared to have no desire whatever to engage in any other business but that of murdering Union men, and plundering their houses and robbing their families of what little provision they might have to keep them from starving."[13]

In Mississippi, a Presbyterian minister lamented that "the rebels punished with death any who declared himself in favor of the Union. In my presence at Tupelo, they were taken out daily and shot for expression of sentiments adverse to the rebellion." Floyd County, Virginia, Unionist Hyram Dulany casually remarked that he was "glad to hear of the death of Henry Lane in the Battle of Cedar Run [and] that he hoped he was in Hell where all secessionists ought to be." Local secessionists heard of the comment and shot him for it.[14]

Mississippi secessionists raided the home of a suspected Union man and decided to execute him on the spot when he refused to recite a Confederate loyalty oath. According to one account of the murder,

> He had a large family of small children, who, together with his wife, begged that his life might be spared. He himself had no favours to ask of the secessionists. Among his foes, the only point of dispute was, as to the mode of his death. Some favoured shooting, some hanging; but the prevailing majority were in favour of scalding him to death. And there, in the presence of his weeping and helpless family, these fiends in human form *deliberately heated water, with which they scalded to death their chained and defenceless victim.* Thus perished a patriot of whom the State was not worthy. The corpse was then suspended from a tree, with a label on the breast, stating that whoever cut him down and buried him, should suffer the same fate.

Defying the threat, some of his neighbors took the body down that night and secretly buried it deep in the woods to prevent further desecration.[15]

Even ministers of the gospel were afforded little protection if they expressed, or were suspected of harboring, Union sentiments. In southeast Alabama's Dale County, rumor had it that the Reverend Bill Sketoe was somehow involved with a gang of Unionist raiders. For Captain Joseph Breare of the local home guard, that was all the evidence needed to convict Sketoe. Breare's men dragged Sketoe from his home in Newton and hauled him just north of town near the Choctawhatchee River bridge. There they prepared to hang him.

Just as the rope was being tied off, Captain Wesley Dowling, a Confederate soldier at home recuperating from a wound, came riding across the bridge and tried to stop the lynching. Breare warned Dowling off, saying that if he did not move on he would "get the same medicine." Breare then turned to Sketoe and asked if he had any last words. The preacher began to pray aloud, not for himself but for his murderers. "Forgive them, Lord, Forgive them." Sketoe's pious pleading so enraged the guardsmen that they threw the noose around his neck before he had finished his prayer. They shoved Sketoe onto a buggy, pulled the rope tight over a tree limb, and slapped the horse, jerking the buggy from under him. But in their haste to lynch Sketoe, the guardsmen had tied the rope over a weak branch. When it caught Sketoe's full weight, it bent down just low enough for the preacher's toes to touch the ground. One of Breare's men rushed over and dug a hole under his feet. Now swinging freely, Sketoe strangled to death within a few minutes. His body was cut down next morning, and he was laid to rest at Mt. Carmel Church cemetery on the outskirts of Newton.[16]

The Reverend James Pelan, pastor of the Presbyterian Church in Macon, Mississippi, was hardly outspoken about his Union sentiments. Nevertheless, his refusal to preach secession brought close scrutiny and eventually attempts on his life. One night while he was on his way home, bushwhackers shot and nearly killed him. As he was recovering, three men showed up at his door and asked if he and his wife could spare some food for supper. As was the custom, the Pelans invited them to sit at their table. When Pelan's wife left the room to see to preparations for the meal, the three men stood up and yelled at Pelan, "All the supper we want is to kill you, you infernal Unionist and abolitionist." A blast of gunfire brought Pelan's wife rushing back to the dining room. As she cradled her dying husband in her arms, Pelan managed to whisper, "Father, forgive them, they know not what they do."[17]

A fellow Mississippi Presbyterian, the Reverend John Aughey, nearly suffered the same fate for his own Unionism. A gang of armed secessionists attacked the Aughey home one night, but were foiled when several of them fell into an unfinished well. On a later evening, an assassin named Smith approached, the Aughey home, caught sight of a minister, and drew his pistol. He fired a single shot and killed the man—the wrong man. Lying dead on the ground was a local preacher whom Smith had mistaken for Aughey.

Where assassins had failed, Confederate authorities nearly succeeded. They arrested Aughey, imprisoned him at Tupelo, and were about to execute him for treason when, with the help of sympathetic friends, he escaped and made his way to federal lines. From there he traveled north and in 1863 published a book recounting his experiences entitled *The Iron Furnace: or, Slavery and Secession*. In its preface, Aughey wrote with sympathy of the "many loyal men in the southern States, who to avoid martyrdom, conceal their opinions . . . they now 'bide their time,' in prayerful trust that God will, in his own good time, subvert rebellion, and overthrow anarchy, by a restoration of the supremacy of constitutional law. By these, and their name is legion, my book will be warmly approved."[18]

John Aughey was a Mississippi minister and staunch anti-secessionist. In 1862, Confederate officials arrested Aughey and imprisoned him at Tupelo. They were on the verge of executing him for treason when, with the help of local Unionists, he escaped and made his way to federal lines. From there he traveled north and in 1863 published a book recounting his experiences, entitled *The Iron Furnace: or, Slavery and Secession*. In its preface, Aughey wrote of the "many loyal men in the southern States, who to avoid martyrdom, conceal their opinions. . . . they now 'bide their time,' in prayerful trust that God will, in his own good time, subvert rebellion. . . . By these, and their name is legion, my book will be warmly approved." Illustration from Aughey, *Iron Furnace*.

Among those who did *not* approve was Jefferson Davis. Still, he knew Aughey was right about one thing at least—that by the hundreds of thousands, southerners worked against the Confederate cause. Davis's reaction to dissent was much the same as Lincoln's. Though both professed to be fighting for liberty, both took steps to undermine personal liberties guaranteed by their respective constitutions. In January 1862, Congress authorized Davis to declare martial law and suspend the writ of habeas corpus. Civilians could now be arrested and held without charge. Even if they were charged, they could be tried by military courts in areas where martial law had been declared.

Davis wasted no time in identifying hotbeds of dissent, beginning with Richmond itself. The Confederate capital was so rife with anti-Confederates that it was one of the first cities to have martial law imposed upon it. Its military governor, General John H. Winder, was soon rounding up civilians he considered dangerous. Among them was the Reverend Alden Bosserman, who had publicly prayed for Confederate defeat. Winder also went after John Minor Botts, a former U.S. congressman from Virginia, when word got out that Botts was working on a manuscript exposing the secession movement as a conspiracy of southern Democrats. Winder arrested so many Richmond civilians that they took up the entire second floor of Castle Thunder military prison.[19]

It was the same across much of the South. One witness recalled that among the inmates of a Columbus, Mississippi, prison were "a number of political prisoners. . . . about one hundred and fifty Mississippi citizens, such as were suspected of Union sentiments." The prisoners included "three clergymen—one a Presbyterian, one a 'United Brother,' and the other a Methodist." Without the ear of some sympathetic judge, such men were beyond the reach of any legal remedy. Even to seek legal redress could be dangerous. William Hyman, a young defense attorney in Alexandria, Louisiana, was arrested in January 1864. Though there was no evidence of his being a Unionist, he had tried to secure the release of several "illegally conscribed persons" by applying for writs of habeas corpus. In doing so, he had made himself "obnoxious to the authorities," and soon found himself lodged in jail with his clients.[20]

"Trying to Keep Out of the Army"

It was hardly unusual for questions to be raised about the legality under which "conscribed persons" were drafted. According to one account, conscript officers went "sweeping through the country with little deference either to the law or the regulations designed to temper its unavoidable rigor." A man in Troup County, Georgia, wrote to General Howell Cobb, commander of the Confederate military district that included Georgia, complaining that "the poppinjays employed as enrolling officers . . . delight in harassing and putting to expense everybody." A resident of Georgia's Clay County wrote that conscript officers were everywhere, "watching for some poor devil who is trying to keep out of the army." He told of conscript companies running men down with hounds and dragging them off to the army in chains. One draft dodger was caught in Albany, Georgia, disguised as a woman. The man was chained and delivered to his company wearing the dress in which he was captured.

Not all men of military age were necessarily subject to the draft. Beyond those who held twenty slaves or who could afford to buy their way out, the Confederacy, unlike the Union, exempted any number of occupational positions. Government employees and officeholders, men engaged in river, rail, or marine transportation, workers in certain military support industries, mail carriers, telegraph operators, hospital staff, druggists, ministers, college professors, and teachers with at least twenty pupils were all legally excused from the draft. Still, in their zeal to reach enrollment quotas, draft officials frequently rounded up such men and herded them off to conscript camps. In August 1863, sixty people from the small community of Attapulgus in Decatur County, Georgia, signed a petition urging Governor Brown to have their postmaster discharged from the army. "If our Post office is permitted to go down for the want of a P.M.," they insisted, "our nearest office will be Bainbridge distant—12½ miles."[21]

Though they were not always a guaranteed draft dodge, exempted positions became the most sought after, and among the most corrupt, in the Confederacy. Schools were suddenly opened all over the South by men with little if any formal education. Their founders were often willing to teach for free if only they could get twenty students to enroll. Drugstores sprang up too, run by druggists who, according to one southern editor, "could not analyze the simplest compound or put the plainest prescription in a satisfactory manner if his life depended upon it." In Early County, Georgia, thirty-seven candidates vied for five seats on the Inferior Court. "But there was no politics in the race," said one county resident. "The candidate just wanted the office to keep him out of the war." So did candidates in Randolph County, Alabama, where officeholding was "more sought after than Heaven." In Florida's fall 1863 elections, most of those winning county offices were Confederate soldiers, some of them already deserters, looking for a legal way to stay home.[22]

One of the most common ways of dodging the draft was to join a home guard or militia company. Nearly every town and county had such units, which were supposed to be manned primarily by old men, young boys, and the physically disabled. There were a few home guard companies, like the Nancy Harts of LaGrange, Georgia, made up entirely of women. Invariably, there were also many healthy men of draft age in home guards claiming exemption from conscription on that basis. In January 1864, four young men from Columbus, Georgia, who had just reached draft age organized a home guard company of younger boys for the alleged purpose of "guarding bridges" and performing other light duty. According to one local citizen, their action was prompted only by fear of being sent to the front lines. John Smith of Cherokee County, Alabama, said derisively of the local home guard, "Their business was to gather up conscripts and deserters from the Confederate army, but their main business was to keep from going to the front themselves and to do as little as possible and stay about home."[23]

Those who objected to the war on grounds of conscience refused to do military service of any kind. Among the most confirmed objectors were members of pacifist sects such as the Dunkers, Nazarenes, Mennonites, and Quakers, most of whom were also forbidden by their faith to hold slaves. In Virginia's Floyd County, one unsympathetic man wrote that local Dunkers refused to "bear arms in the defense of their country's rights . . . alleging that it is not right to fight." Pacifists paid a high price to secure the rights of conscience. According to county resident Willis Reed, who had friends among the Dunkers, local Confederates saw no difference between pacifists and Unionists: "All that class of people were persecuted and abused." Several groups of Dunkers and Mennonites were thrown in prison after being caught fleeing to Union lines. Others were murdered. The persecution became so intense in some areas that congregations suspended their worship services or held them clandestinely.[24]

Confederate policy at first refused exemptions for religious objectors. But, like anyone, they could buy their way out of the draft if they could afford to do so.[25] Even those who could often refused on religious grounds. They would not support the war directly or indirectly, even when forced to serve. Christian Good, a Mennonite ordered into the 146th Virginia Militia, made it clear that though he was placed on the firing line, he would not kill his fellow men. As a friend of Good's related the story,

> Over and over he was forced into battle but he would not shoot anybody. At the first battle the captain came up and asked him if he shot. He said, "No, I did not shoot." Sometime afterward he got into another battle. After it was over the captain came to him and asked him whether he shot. He said, "No, I didn't see anything to shoot at." The captain asked, "Why, didn't you see all those Yankees over there?" "No, they're people; we don't shoot people."[26]

General Thomas J. "Stonewall" Jackson observed that Dunkers and Mennonites, even when they fired their weapons, refused "to take correct aim." He suggested that they be sent back home so "that they may produce supplies."[27]

Resistance among members of pacifist sects was so persistent and troublesome that in June 1864 the Confederacy finally exempted them from the draft. However, the act applied only to men who had been members as of October 11, 1862, when the Second Conscription Act took effect. Viewing their religion as a sanctuary for anyone who wished to join, Quakers petitioned Congress to exempt all their adherents, regardless of when they joined. Their request was ignored, but they and other pacifists continued to resist the draft as best they could.[28]

But how to resist the conscript law? That was the question dissenters faced throughout the war. Many of those who could do so simply left the Confederacy. Most headed north, but escaping dissenters in the western Confederacy often went south. A thriving anti-Confederate community of exiled Texans, Hispanic and Anglo alike, sprang up just across the Rio Grande from Brownsville in Matamoros, Mexico. Immigrant Germans too were among the exiles. They had come to the United States escaping Europe's turbulent revolutions of 1848, and wanted nothing to do with rebellion. When Confederate officials tried to conscript them, hundreds struck out for Mexico. In August 1862, one group of families totaling sixty-one individuals assembled

When Confederate officials tried to conscript antiwar men in Texas, hundreds struck out for Mexico. In August 1862, one group of families assembled west of Kerrville and headed for the border. Most never made it. On August 10, just a day's ride from Mexico, they were ambushed near the Nueces River by pursuing Rebel cavalry. About half were killed on the spot, some after they had been wounded and taken prisoner. Of those who escaped the Nueces Massacre, several were later shot trying to cross the Rio Grande. Illustration from *Harper's New Monthly Magazine.*

west of Kerrville and headed for the border. On August 10, just a day's ride from Mexico, they were ambushed in Kinney County near the Nueces River by pursuing Rebel cavalrymen. About half were killed on the spot, some after they had been wounded and taken prisoner. Of those who escaped the Nueces Massacre, six were later shot trying to cross the Rio Grande.[29]

Those dissenters for whom exile was not an option were no less determined to escape conscription. In January 1863, at a conscript camp in Magnolia, Arkansas, about fifty draftees lined up on the parade ground, announced their refusal to be inducted, then marched out of camp. One observer reported that the conscript law was "making Union people fast" in Arkansas. Hardly pacifists, such men were prepared to defend their right of dissent by force if necessary. In Clay County, Georgia, a conscript officer was nearly killed when he tried to enforce the draft. Threats to his life became so serious that he fled the state. The Dial brothers of North Carolina wrote to Captain Quill Hunter, telling him that "if yo Ever hut for us a gin I will put lead in yo god dam your hell fired Sole. . . . If this don't give yo warning enough the next warning we will give yo with powder and lead take the hint."[30]

The wise draft officer did not take such threats lightly. Putting the word of resisters to the test could be plenty dangerous. In the Nolichucky Valley of North Carolina, when conscript officials went after a professed Unionist and draft dodger, the man and his three daughters stood them down. "Old Yank," as he was later known, told a visitor: "I just reached 'round the door and pulled out my Henry rifle, an' my gals understood it an' got their double-barreled shotgouns, an' I just told them boys I had lived too long in the mountains to be scared that way, an' if they . . . laid hand on an ole man like me they'd never do it agin, fur my gals had the bead on 'em." They left Old Yank alone. In Rapides Parish, Louisiana, two draft officers were fired on, and one was badly wounded. Draft resisters in Jones County, Alabama, killed a local enrolling officer. In Virginia, officer John Payton went after draft dodgers on Bent Mountain and was shot dead from his horse.[31]

Stories of such violent draft resistance survive in southern family traditions to this day. Descendants of Newton Knight, a Confederate deserter from Jones County, Mississippi, still tell of how he killed Major Amos McLemore for hunting conscripts. As Ethel Knight tells the story, McLemore was a "hot-headed young fellow" who was "warned that he was treading on dangerous ground but he refused to heed the warning." A similar tale has been passed down in the author's own family. His great-great-grandfather Frank Williams was born to a nonslaveholding farm family in Dooly County, Georgia. Frank reached draft age in 1862 but never served in the Confederate army. After Frank's father, Asa, stabbed a man, perhaps a draft officer trying to conscript Frank, the family left Dooly County and settled in Miller County a hundred miles to the southwest.[32]

Large areas of the Confederacy became so dangerous for some conscript companies that no one could be found to fill their ranks. Even where such companies could be formed, the troops often displayed more sympathy for their neighbors than for the Confederacy. That was the case in Austin County, Texas, where authorities could not trust the local militia to enforce conscription. In southeast Georgia, when Colonel Duncan Clinch sent the Fourth Georgia Cavalry to round up deserters and draft evaders, some of his men deserted and joined the resistance. So did members of the Sixteenth South Carolina Infantry in Greenville, Pickens, and Spartanburg counties. One dis-

Stories of draft resistance survive in southern family traditions to this day. One such tale has been passed down in the author's own family. His great-great-grandfather Frank Williams, shown here in a postwar photo with his wife Nancy Newberry, was born to a nonslaveholding farm family in Dooly County, Georgia. Frank reached draft age in 1862 but never served in the Confederate army. After Frank's father, Asa, stabbed a man, perhaps a draft officer trying to conscript Frank, the family left Dooly County and settled in Miller County a hundred miles to the southwest. Photo from the author's collection.

gusted officer wrote in 1863 that in those and surrounding counties, it was "no longer a reproach to be known as a deserter."[33]

For deserters and draft dodgers who were captured, punishment was not guaranteed. When a conscript company in Franklin County, Georgia, rounded up several deserters, the local jailer refused to lodge them. In White County, a band of forty men broke into the Cleveland jail and released a draft dodger. In Alabama's Randolph County, armed men forced a jailer to surrender his keys and released the deserters he was holding. When five Winston County anti-Confederates were arrested and told to "join the colors or be shot," a detachment of local men serving with the Union army in Decatur made an all-night ride back home, freed the men, burned down the jail, and killed the jailer.[34]

So strong was antiwar feeling in some parts of the South that judges could not hold court on dissenters without a military escort. Even when trials were held, convictions were rare. Juries consistently refused to return guilty verdicts against those who opposed the war. Georgia's General Howell Cobb conceded in August of 1863 that to drag antiwar men into court was "simply to provide for a farcical trial." Later that year two Lumpkin County men, John Woody and John A. Wimpy, were tried on charges of treason. In the face of strong evidence against them, and after Woody confessed his opposition to the war, local juries acquitted both men. Soon after, Woody left for Tennessee and joined the Union army.[35]

From north Georgia's Fannin County, deserter John Hopper wrote in September 1863 assuring his brother, who was still in the army, that "there is no dificulty now in staying at home [and] no opposition from the citizens. I can tell you if you can only get here with out being took up it is all right—for in the place of opposition you will have protection." Augusta County, Virginia, was another place where deserters could find protection. Confederate authorities advertised the names of 181 area deserters in a local paper, offering $30 reward each to anyone turning them in. After five months, hardly any names had been stricken from the list. One disgusted officer reported from Louisiana that the draft law was "a dead letter" within a fifty-mile radius of Lafayette, such was the "universal hostility of the people."[36]

In Madison County, North Carolina, when enrollment companies came around, draft dodgers took to the hills while friends and family kept them informed of their pursuers' movements. In South Carolina's Greenville and Pickens counties, draft resisters found protection in numbers by moving from farm to farm in a group, working each other's land as they went. Farmers like Willis Bone of Irwin County, Georgia, and David Weddle of Floyd County, Virginia, offered havens on their property for deserters and draft dodgers who worked the land in exchange for lodging. The resister community on Weddle's lands numbered as many as 150 men. Other Floyd County Unionists, like Tilman Overstreet and Eli Epperly, offered help to deserters because doing so would also help "brake up the war."[37]

"Hanging Is Getting to Be as Common as Hunting"

Offering help to layouts could be a dangerous undertaking. By law, anyone who fed, harbored, or aided the escape of a deserter could be fined $1,000 or imprisoned for up to two years. In practice, penalties could be much worse since those charged with enforcing the law often paid little attention to it. In the hill country around Fredericksburg, Texas, Confederate patrols took whole families into custody and confiscated their farms. "It was a pitiable sight," wrote a sympathetic Rebel soldier, "to see all these poor folks stripped of their property, such as it was, earned by hard toil and exposure to a dangerous frontier." For the deserters themselves, treatment was far worse. When one happened to fall into the hands of local home guards, recalled one witness, "he is dealt pretty roughly with and generally makes his last speech with a rope around his neck. Hanging is getting to be as common as hunting."[38]

In April 1863, Isaac Miller, a War of 1812 veteran, gave the following testimony after the home guard in Randolph County, North Carolina, murdered his son, a draft resister: "Then they come and taken me and put me in Jale and kep me thare twenty four days and then turned me out and made me pay for my Board and I am a man About Eighty Eight years old and I was A soldier in the jackson wars." Another North Carolina man told of "one old helpless bed-ridden mother, with 3 sons in the army (C.S.A.) and 3 in the bushes" who had been "dispoiled of her property" by Confederate soldiers, part of a force sent from the Army of Northern Virginia to hunt for deserters. "Many deserters families have been deprived of all means of subsistence & left to starve this winter," complained the writer. "Is this not making war on women & children?"[39]

Sympathetic southerners often tried to help needy families of men resisting the Confederacy, even at the risk of their own lives. Thomas Sawyer of Blount County, Alabama, a farmer and miller exempted from the Confederate draft on account of being "crippled," regularly provided food for the families of men serving in the Union army. He was repeatedly arrested and threatened with hanging, each time promising to stop supporting Unionist families. But he never kept that promise. As he later testified, "I fed them all the time as I had done before."[40]

In Virginia's Floyd County, home guards threatened to hang Jacob Moses for harboring his dissident brother Jefferson and son-in-law David Spangler. They kidnapped the nine-year-old son of a deserter when his family refused to reveal the father's whereabouts. They looted the farm of an old couple named Wilson when they refused to turn over their three deserter sons. The guard threatened to shoot William Dillon for aiding deserters among his family and friends. Dillon called their bluff, proclaiming that "he would [as] soon die that way as any way." The guardsmen backed down.[41]

Dillon was lucky. Confederate home guards did not always bluff. Guardsmen in northern Alabama warned Bird Norris to enlist or be shot as a traitor. Norris refused, saying he would rather be shot than join the "stinking Rebel army." The guard killed him and threw his body in a ditch. Solomon Curtis of Winston County, head of a well-known Unionist family, lost three sons to the home guard. Joel Jackson Curtis was killed for refusing to enlist in the Confederate army. His brother, George Washington Curtis, joined the Union army and was shot to death for it while home on leave. Another brother, Thomas Pink Curtis, Winston County's probate judge, got two gunshots through the right eye for his Union sympathies.[42]

From surviving records, it is often difficult to distinguish between home guards, local or state militiamen, conscript companies, partisan rangers, guerrilla outfits, or simple bushwhackers. It was sometimes just as difficult for contemporaries to tell the difference. Often lumped together as "home guard" units, many wore civilian clothes and operated with or without official sanction. Some who claimed Confederate authority actually had little if any. Confederate guerrilla William Quantrill, ranging mostly in Missouri, regularly ignored orders from his superiors and went his own way. As one biographer noted, Quantrill killed for the love of killing. His pleasure in doing so was expressed as "a sort of gay, nervous chuckle. Sometimes this strange giggle would be heard right after he had killed a man. The guerrillas themselves found it rather eerie and even a little frightening."[43]

Another vicious killer was Champ Ferguson, leader of a Rebel guerrilla outfit that operated along the Kentucky-Tennessee border on the Cumberland plateau. At times acting as a scout for John Hunt Morgan's Confederate cavalry, Ferguson spent most of his time carrying out a terrorist campaign against pro-Union civilians. His first documented murder came in November 1861 when, without a word of warning, he shot a man in his sickbed. In April 1862, Ferguson shot an unarmed boy of sixteen, then finished him off with a knife. Ferguson and his gang later tortured three suspected Union men to death after taking them prisoner and looting their homes. In 1864, the Confederate government tried to curb men like Ferguson and Quantrill by revoking its Partisan Ranger Act, passed two years earlier. But that perfunctory move did little to stop the home-front bloodletting. By that time, and long since, the Confederacy's brutal inner civil war had become as much a part of the larger conflict as anything on the battlefield.[44]

One of the most brutal attacks in northern Alabama came after J.R. Rowell and his family, who lived near the line of Walker and Winston counties, were harassed by the home guard because Rowell refused to enlist. Rowell soon grew tired of the intimidation and decided to do some intimidating of his own. As the guardsmen passed along a nearby road, Rowell fired his musket at them and fled through the woods. Though none of the guardsmen were injured, they determined not to give him a second chance. They captured Rowell before he could reload, then debated what might be the most painful means of killing him. They finally suspended Rowell upside down from a tree limb, drove splinters of lighter pine into his flesh, set the splinters afire, and watched as flames engulfed the man and burned him to death.[45]

It was hardly uncommon for home guards to take such fiendish delight in dispatching their victims. Five such victims were James Taylor, Samuel Tatum, Alfred Kite, Alexander Dugger, and David Shuffield. In March 1863, these men from Carter County, Tennessee, who all refused service in the Confederate army, were making their way north when a band of conscript hunters and Johnson County home guards caught up with them at the Watauga River. The Rebels killed Taylor and Tatum on the spot. Guardsmen hanged the remaining three from a nearby tree in such a way that the weight of their bodies slowly

Some home guards took fiendish delight in dispatching their victims. Captain Roby Brown and his guardsmen caught five deserters, and shot two outright. They lynched the other three. According to one contemporary, as the men slowly strangled, Brown "had a complete frolic around them while they were struggling in all the agonies of a terrible death. He knocked them with his gun, and would then dance up to them, and turn them around violently, telling them to 'face their partner.'" Illustration from Ellis, *Thrilling Adventures*.

choked them to death. One of the guards, Captain Roby Brown, took special delight in the spectacle, according to a contemporary account. As the victims gasped for air—their tongues turning black and their eyes bulging out—Brown "had a complete frolic around them while they were struggling in all the agonies of a terrible death. He knocked them with his gun, and would then dance up to them, and turn them around violently, telling them to 'face their partner.'"[46]

The home-guard units that patrolled Tennessee's Carter, Johnson, and Sullivan counties were among the South's most brutal. They would, wrote one contemporary, rather shoot Union men than squirrels—they "loved to see them jump." So frequent were their murders at one killing ground on the Carter-Sullivan line that locals called it the boneyard. John Smith met his end there when the home guard shot him for refusing to volunteer. Henry Archer was killed there as well after pleas from his wife, with a young child in her arms, were made in vain. So was John Blevins, whom the home guard suspected of "bushwhacking." Without charge or trial, they dragged Blevins to the boneyard. "I have never shot at a man in all my life," Blevins insisted, "and I have never knowingly wronged any person; therefore, if you kill me, you will kill an innocent man."

"Well, then," retorted one of the guards, "if you have told us the truth, you need not be afraid to die!" They shot him three times in the chest and left his body where it fell.[47]

Levi Guy was another Johnson County man who learned about home-guard cruelties the hard way. According to one neighbor, the seventy-year-old man "scarcely knew what either side of the contending parties was fighting about." Still, he had two sons in the Union army. That was all the excuse local home guardsmen needed to kill him. One morning while the old man was eating breakfast with his family, the guard pounded on his door, tied his hands behind his back, and led him off. Guy's daughter tried to follow but, according to one contemporary account, guardsmen "caught hold of her very roughly and whipped her until the blood ran from her arms and back profusely, and then drove her back to the house." The guard then hanged Levi Guy from a tree about half a mile from his home.[48]

Another victim of home-guard summary execution was George M. Kierce, a sixty-year-old farmer in south Georgia's Worth County. Kierce often allowed deserters and layouts to hide on his property. In November 1862, he and his thirteen-year-old son John disappeared. Some locals said they had fled to the North. Others thought they had gone to Florida. Most, however, were sure they had been murdered. According to court records, Justice of the Peace Hudson Tabor had issued warrants against George and John Kierce the day before they vanished. Deputy Sheriff Lewis Simmons arrested Kierce and his son and was escorting them to Judge Tabor when they were stopped by George Green, the local conscript officer, and a band of thirteen home-guard riders. Green took custody of the Kierces, then told his men to "continue their search for said deserters as it would be a more easy matter now to take them." That was the last time anyone admitted to seeing Kierce and his son alive. Weeks later, a family member finally discovered their bodies sunken in nearby Abram's Creek. Their throats had been cut, the boy's almost to the point of decapitation, and their clothes were filled with gravel to weigh them down.[49]

Desertion was usually even more dangerous for its perpetrators than for their protectors. Of those sentenced to death by court-martial during the war, two-thirds were deserters. Many did not get even the formality of a trial. Samuel Henderson Frier of Irwin County, Georgia, like the rest of his family, had opposed secession. Too poor to hire a substitute, he joined the Confederate army under threat of conscription in May 1862. Frier deserted later that year in Virginia and made his way back home, telling his family that he had never been able to reconcile himself to killing. "Thou shalt not kill" was the Good Book's teaching. It was a creed he would follow for the rest of his life. He would not have long to hold it. A few months later, Frier was ambushed by Confederate home guards who shot him dead without warning. Frier's widow, two young children, and other family and friends laid him to rest in Irwin County's Brushy Creek Primitive Baptist cemetery.[50]

Bob Anderson of Louisiana was another unfortunate deserter for whom a hearing was denied. Jack Maddox, at the time a neighborhood slave, recalled Anderson's gruesome mutilation decades after the war.

> Goin' home I stopped by Mrs. Anderson's place. She had a boy named Bob who deserted and was hidin' at home. Some 'federate soldiers come and say they'll burn the house down lessen he comes out. So he came out and they tied him with a rope and the other end to a saddle and went off with him trottin' 'hind the hoss. His mammy s[e]nt me followin' in the wagon. I followed thirteen mile. After a few miles I seen where he fell down and the drag signs on the ground. Then when I come to Hornage Creek I seen they'd gone through the water. I went across and after a while I found him. But you couldn't tell any of the front side of him. They'd drug the face off him. I took him home.[51]

"Hung Women Till Nearly Dead"

The results of home-guard encounters with deserters were not always so one-sided. In February 1863, Captain John West of North Carolina's Yadkin County home guard went after a group of deserters and draft dodgers hiding in a schoolhouse. The men had planned to head for Union lines in Kentucky as soon as the weather cleared, but West's men caught up to them first. As West spread his force around the building, one of the guardsmen, without orders, fired and killed a conscript. More shots rang out from the guardsmen before West could get them under control. Not knowing that one of the besieged men was already dead, West walked up to the schoolhouse with his shotgun in hand, pounded on the door, threw it open, and yelled, "Men, surrender!" One of the conscripts responded with a muzzle blast that tore half his head off. Conscripts quickly poured out of the building, firing as they came. The guard returned fire. When the shooting finally stopped, West and one his guardsmen were dead, along with two of the conscripts. More lay wounded on both sides. Several of the conscripts got away and headed for Kentucky.[52]

That winter in neighboring Madison County, guardsmen took a less direct approach. They determined to draw local draft resisters out of hiding by cutting their families off from the state's salt distribution. The move amounted to a sentence of death by starvation since meat could not be cured or preserved without salt. So on January 8, a band of fifty deserters and draft resisters from Shelton Laurel raided the county seat of Marshall and took what salt and other provisions they needed. Within days, hundreds of Confederates were scouring through the Laurel Valley. As historian Phillip Shaw Paludan put it in his book about the incident, aptly entitled *Victims: A True Story of the Civil War*, "it was the fortunate women and old people who had their men taken from them."

> Those unfortunate enough to be relatives of suspects that the troops could not find were whipped and tortured and hanged until almost dead and then let down again for more questioning. Eighty-five-year-old Mrs. Unus Riddle was whipped, hanged temporarily, and robbed. Seventy-year-old Sally Moore was whipped with hickory rods until the blood ran down her back. Another woman, the mother of an infant child, was tied in the snow to a tree and her baby placed in the doorway of their cabin. Unless she talked, the soldiers told her, they would leave them both there. Sarah and Mary Shelton, wives of two suspected Marshall raiders, were whipped and suspended by ropes around their necks. A young mentally retarded girl named Martha White was beaten and tied by the neck all day to a tree.

The Confederates rounded up fifteen men and boys, no more than five of whom had participated in the Marshall raid. Two managed to escape during their first night of captivity. The remaining prisoners, ranging in age from thirteen to sixty-five, were marched out of Shelton Laurel the next morning, presumably to imprisonment with or without trial. They had gone only a short distance when their captors led them off the road and ordered five to their knees. The prisoners quickly realized that they were about to be murdered. As they begged for their lives, some of the soldiers refused to fire. "Fire or you will take their place," warned the detachment commander. They fired, or at least enough of them did so to complete the executions. Then five more captives were forced to the ground. A volley exploded and four of the five lay dead. The fifth, a thirteen-year-old boy named David Shelton, had enough life left in him to plead for mercy. "You have killed my old father and my three brothers; you have shot me in both arms—I forgive you all this—I can get well. Let me go home to my mother and sisters." Hardly had David spoken before another volley rang out and he was shot dead. Moments later, the remaining three prisoners followed him to eternity. A day later, relatives found the victims buried in a shallow mass grave. Wild hogs had rooted up one of the bodies and eaten much of its head away.[53]

In Montgomery County, North Carolina, Rebel home guards regularly harassed and assaulted women whom they suspected of aiding draft evaders and deserters. The same was true in Wilkes County, where the home guard "hung women till nearly dead, (some of them pregnant,) to make them tell on deserters." Adam Brewer of Moore County, leader of one such home-guard unit, ordered his men to shoot three women who had thwarted his attempt to capture a seventeen-year-old deserter. They were saved only by the refusal of Brewer's men to fire. Some women were not so fortunate. Pro-Confederates in Cooke County, Texas, lynched a soldier's wife in front of her three young children. Her crime had been to publicly express hope that the Federals would soon overrun the state so her husband could stay home with his family. In the vicinity of Cleveland, Tennessee, Confederate guerrillas shot a woman for holding similar views. Near Bull's Gap, Confederate soldiers hanged several Union women who refused to reveal their husbands' whereabouts. They shot another for no more than "making a too free use of her tongue."[54]

Family and friends regularly aided groups of deserters and draft dodgers. It was dangerous work. Home-guard units hunting for men evading service could be brutal, even deadly. One woman wrote to North Carolina's governor complaining of guardsmen rounding up women and "boxing their jaws and knocking them about as if they ware Bruts" in an effort to force information on their men's whereabouts. Two women had their hands held under a fence rail while a soldier sat on it. Some who refused to talk were killed. Illustration from Ellis, *Thrilling Adventures*.

Phebe Cook of North Carolina complained to Governor Vance of the treatment state militia troops meted out to women suspected of helping their men avoid service. She wrote of officers rounding up women and "boxing their jaws and nocking them about as if they ware Bruts" in an effort to force confessions from them and information on their men's whereabouts. Two North Carolina women who refused to tell where their husbands were hiding had their hands held under a fence rail while a soldier sat with his full weight on it.[55]

The wife of William Owen, leader of a North Carolina deserter band, experienced a similar torture. When she refused to tell a Rebel home guard where her husband was, its commander, Colonel Alfred

Pike, slapped her. According to Pike, his men then "tied her thumbs together behind her back & suspended her with a cord tied to her two thumbs thus fastened behind her to a limb so that her toes could just touch the ground. . . . I think [then] she told some truth, but after a while, I thought she commenced lying again & I . . . put her thumbs under a corner of a fence, [and] she soon became quiet and behaved very respectfully." When criticized for his behavior, this southern gentleman was unashamed and unrepentant. Pike insisted that he would leave the Confederacy "before I will live in a country in which I cannot treat such people in this manner."[56]

In spite of the dangers, southern women continued to resist. Tabitha Brown and Adeline Bolin of Randolph County, North Carolina, told Captain W.R. McMasters that his place would be torched if he did not release James and Joseph Brown. McMasters brushed their warning aside as an idle threat. That night, "unknown persons" torched his barn. One contemporary recalled a Missouri woman who "stood between her husband and a Secesh with a loaded gun." When it came to protecting their families, he wrote, "the gentler sex are anything but gentle."[57]

A group of Florida women made that plain when Confederate horsemen came after their deserter husbands. In a letter to his wife, their commanding officer told of general anti-Confederate sentiment, organized resistance, and women rising in defense of their men.

Corpl Smith returned from the East side of the St Johns [River] last night and gives a gloomy picture of affairs on that side, and an incident happened to him, that will illustrate the feelings on that side. He rode up to the house of one of my Deserters about daylight but the man was not at home, he then went on a few miles to another's home and there they saw both the men at work in the field, but the deserters saw them when they were about ½ mile from them and ran for the swamp close by, Corpl Smith and party charged their horses as fast as they could, and the women (about a dozen) came out with hoes and axes and tryed to cut Smith off, but all the party were good horsemen but Smith and passed safely but his horse took fright and threw him in a bunch of palmettoes and the women shouted theres one of the d—d rascals off. Smith got up and the women blew the horn to let others know and told Smith if he would stay 15 minutes they would catch h—l, using all the time the most profane language they could think of. Some of the party would have gotten the deserters but they . . . got to the swamp before they could be overtaken, some of the party fired at them but missed. Smith says they have regular spies and that no party can go through the country without being found out by these persons on the watch.[58]

Popular support and plenty of hiding places made it difficult for Confederate authorities to bring in deserters. One deserter band set up camp on an island in the Chattahoochee River just north of Columbus, Georgia. Family and friends kept them supplied until the end of the war. In northern Alabama, Melissa Turbyfill and her daughters aided her husband and almost twenty other layouts hiding

In spite of the dangers, southern women took an active role in protecting their men from Confederate authorities. One group of Florida women, armed with hoes and axes, went after a Confederate patrol that was pursuing their deserter husbands. Tabitha Brown and Adeline Bolin of Randolph County, North Carolina, told Captain W.R. McMasters that his property would be torched if he did not release James and Joseph Brown. McMasters brushed their warning aside as an idle threat. That night, "unknown persons" set his barn afire. One contemporary recalled a Missouri woman who "stood between her husband and a Secesh with a loaded gun." When it came to protecting their families, he wrote, "the gentler sex are anything but gentle." Illustration from Aughey, *Tupelo*.

in the area. The women carried food to them, washed their clothes, and gave them "timely warning of the approach of the rebels." Margaret Shoe of Alabama's Cherokee County "smuggled provisions" to her brother and brother-in-law. The two men were "often hunted and watched so closely that neither of them could slip in home to get anything to eat for fear of being caught."[59]

In North Carolina's Montgomery County, two sisters, Sarah Moore and Caroline Hulin, took food and supplies to their husbands, who were hiding in the surrounding woods dodging the draft. In Dale County, Alabama, two deserters lived in a cave near their homes during the war's last two years. Said one local resident, they "were peaceable, and did not disturb any one." At one point, a military patrol discovered their hideout and found cotton cards and spinning wheels that they used to help clothe their families. The deserters themselves were never found. Few ever were. When patrols were nearby, women had various ways of calling for help or warning their husbands to stay in hiding—blowing horns or whistles, ringing bells, or hanging out quilts of different colors or patterns to warn of danger.[60]

Such help was most often local. But if Confederate pressure got too intense, and if there was time enough, there were underground railroads out of the South with guides and safe houses along the way. The Reverend John Aughey wrote that many men "who would not muster nor be enrolled as conscripts resolved to escape to the Federal lines." He recalled "skillful guides who could course it from point to point through the densest forests, with the unerring instinct of the panther."[61] He knew what he was talking about. Aughey himself used such guides and safe houses during his escape from Tupelo, Mississippi, in 1862. Great care had to be used in identifying those willing to help. A few days after his jailbreak—tired, hungry, and still wearing his prison leg irons—Aughey spotted a likely-looking farmhouse.

I remained near it till I was satisfied there were no negroes held by that family. I then went boldly up, knocked, gained admittance, and asked for some water, which was given to me. The lady of the house, scrutinizing me closely, asked me if I were from Tupelo. I replied in the affirmative. She then inquired my name. I gave her my Christian name, John Hill, suppressing the surname. Her husband was sitting near, a man of Herculean frame; and as the wife's inquisitiveness was beginning to alarm me, I turned to him and said: "My friend, you are a man of great physical powers, and at this time you ought to be in the army. The Yankees are overrunning all our country, and the service of every man is needed." His wife replied that he was not in the army, nor would he go into it, unless he was forced to go. They had been told that the cavalry would be after him in a few days, to take him as a conscript; but she considered the conscript law base and tyrannical. Overjoyed at the utterance of such sentiments as these, I then revealed my true character. I told them that I had recently made my escape from Tupelo, where I was doomed to execution on the gallows, and that I was now flying from prison and from death. I then exhibited the iron bands upon my ankles. Both promised all the aid in their power.

The couple fed Aughey, gave him a new suit of clothes, helped remove his leg irons, and led him to a Union friend's home a half mile away. Aughey was passed from one safe house to another, escorted by sympathizers from point to point, until he finally reached Union army pickets at Rienzi, Mississippi, just south of Corinth.[62]

"Secret Meetings"

Aughey mentioned few names in his 1863 memoir, writing that he did not want to "compromise the safety of my Union friends who rendered me assistance, and who are still within the rebel lines." Nor did he want to put in danger friends with whom he had conspired to resist Confederate authority. There were plenty of them to be concerned about. Soon after the Confederate Congress adopted conscription, he and other like-minded neighbors had banded together for mutual advice and support.

> Knowing that in a multitude of counsellors there is wisdom, we held secret meetings, in order to devise the best method of resisting the law. We met at night, and had our counter-signs to prevent detection. Often our wives, sisters, and daughters met with us. Our meeting-place was some ravine, or secluded glen, as far as possible from the haunts of the secessionists; all were armed; even the ladies had revolvers, and could use them too. The crime of treason [against the United States] we were resolved not to commit.[63]

Aughey's group was one of many secret societies—large and small, active and passive—that sprang up across the South to oppose the war. As early as April 1862 came reports from Louisiana telling of secret societies and clubs in Natchitoches and Sabine parishes dedicated to restoring the Union. In Montgomery, Alabama, there was a Closet Fellowship that held secret meetings on Commerce Street at Israel Robert's hardware store and George Cowles's dry goods store on Market Street. Its members passed around northern newspapers, talked about the war's progress, and condemned the treason of pro-Confederate neighbors. There was also Atlanta's Union Circle, whose members worked to undermine Confederate authority and sometimes aided escaping federal prisoners of war. Also assisting federal escapees was a Union Association in Charleston, South Carolina, said to be fourteen hundred strong. Two Union officers imprisoned in the city who made good their escape later wrote that they could not have done so without help from Association members.[64]

The first such society known to be sizable and well organized was the Peace and Constitutional Society, founded in the fall of 1861 in Arkansas's Ozark Mountains. By the end of that year, the society numbered seventeen hundred. It had secret signs and passwords to identify members, each of whom took an oath to encourage desertion from the Confederate army and enlistment in the Union army. A piece of yellow cloth posted on or near a cabin marked the residents as society members. They identified each other at night with the call of a wolf's howl answered by a hooting sound like that of an owl. Of a sample of nearly two hundred members, historian Ted Worley discovered that the vast majority were native southerners and relatively poor. None held any slaves.

The society's effectiveness as an organized resistance movement was at least partially diminished within months of its founding when Confederates arrested over one hundred of the society's leading members. Under threat of execution, some revealed its secrets and divulged the names of other members. Still, the strength of anti-Confederate sympathies among Ozark residents ensured that the Peace and Constitutional Society's mission would continue in spite of its organizational breakdown.[65]

The same was true for the Peace Party, or Union League, in Texas. Centered around Cooke County in the northern part of the state, it had secret signs, handshakes, and passwords. And its members swore allegiance to the Union. There were also accusations that its members, said to number in the thousands, were stockpiling arms and ammunition. In October 1862, local officials began rounding up suspected Union men in and around Gainesville, the county seat. They quickly threw together a vigilante "citizens court" to give their proceedings at least the appearance of judicial decorum. But there was no question that executions would soon follow. The court was comprised mainly of men who followed or feared James G. Bourland, the local provost marshal.

Bourland was a rabid anti-Union man described by those who knew him as "a good fighter and a good hater." But at age sixty-one, he had no stomach for fighting on the battlefield. When conscription came, this planter and former state senator had himself appointed provost marshal. It was a job he relished. Bourland's aggressive draft efforts accounted in part for the strong membership of the Peace Party. Now Bourland held the fate of Peace Party members in his hands through his citizens court. Over the next few days, on weak or trumped-up evidence, the court ordered at least forty-four men executed in what came to be known as the Great Hanging at Gainesville. Bourland was later called "the Hangman of Texas."[66]

Among his victims was John M. Crisp, a Cooke County blacksmith and deacon in the Church of Christ. Crisp admitted that he was an initiated member of the Peace Party and that he had initiated others. But he insisted that he had never committed any act of aggression against the Confederacy. There was no evidence that he had. Still, the vigilantes found him guilty and sentenced him to hang. Crisp barely had time to scribble down a will leaving his modest possessions to his wife and three children before he was hauled out to the hanging tree.[67]

Gainesville was not the end of Texas-style justice. In February 1863, pro-Confederates slaughtered 180 peace men in central Texas for no other crime, wrote one Texan, than "loving the flag of Washington." A Hays County refugee recalled that vigilantes would shoot "Union men to see which way they would fall," slice open the throats "of loyal men, that they might listen to the music of the death rattle," and lynch "crowds of faithful citizens just to observe the varieties of the death gasp." The man compared what he had witnessed to France's Reign of Terror after the French Revolution.[68]

Persecution of Texas dissenters continued throughout the war. Very often, it was a persecution based on class. Such was the split between slaveholders and nonslaveholders in parts of the state that the violence amounted to open class warfare. In *Brushmen and Vigilantes*, authors David Pickering and Judy Falls point out that in the Sulphur Forks region of northeast Texas, "many of the vigilantes were wealthy men or their middle-class followers while records for the victims show that most of them had little wealth."[69]

The most widespread of the South's antiwar organizations was the Peace Society, dedicated to ending the conflict with or without southern independence. Little is known of the society's early days. It probably was formed in northern Alabama or eastern Tennessee in 1862. From there its influence spread throughout the Deep South. Historian Walter Fleming estimated that by 1863, at least half the men left in Alabama were associated with the Peace Society. In northern Alabama especially, the Peace Society was reported by one contemporary to be "open, bold, and defiant."[70]

Though its membership numbered in the thousands and it counted many more as sympathizers, the Peace Society was only loosely organized. One contemporary wrote from Opelika, Alabama, that the Peace Society had "no regular times or places of meeting, and has no

Organizations like the Peace Society and the Heroes of America operated throughout the South. Composed mostly of those who wanted nothing more than an end to the war, Unionists were often at the heart of these organizations and remained their driving force throughout. During their secretive meetings, they pledged to encourage desertion, protect each other, and hold firm in their allegiance to the Union. Illustration from *Harper's Weekly*.

organized 'lodges' or 'communities.' Men who have studied the obligations, signs, &c., and who can communicate them well are styled 'eminent,' and pass through the country giving the 'degree' to all whom they regard as fit subjects." Those inducted into the society promised always to aid other members and their families. They also promised never to "cut, carve, mark, scratch, show, &c., upon anything, movable or immovable, under the whole canopy of heaven, whereby any of the secrets of this order might become legible or intelligible."[71]

Members recognized each other by a variety of complicated signs, which differed from one region to another. One of the most complex was a handshake and greeting popular in central Alabama. It was, according to one report, "given by taking hold of the hand as usual in shaking hands, only the thumb is turned with the side instead of the ball to the back of the hand." The following dialogue, which each member committed to memory, would then commence.

> What is that?
> A grip.
> A grip of what?
> A constitutional peace grip.
> Has it a name?
> It has.
> Will you give it to me?
> I did not so receive it, neither can I so impart it.
> How will you impart it?
> I will letter it to you.
> Letter it and begin.
> Begin you.
> No, you begin.
> Begin you.

Then, starting with any letter but the first, they spelled the word P-E-A-C-E by calling out letters alternately to each other.[72]

Other signs of recognition included a salute with the right hand closed and the thumb pointed backward over the shoulder, throwing a stick to the right using both hands, and tapping on the toe of the right foot three times with a stick or switch, then waving it to the right. In a crowd, a society member made himself known by three slaps on the right leg. One might also use the phrase, "I dreamed that the boys are all coming home." A distress signal was given by using the expression "Oh! Washington!" or "by extending the right hand horizontally and then bringing it down by three distinct motions." Repeating the word "Washington" four times could get a member of the Peace Society released from jail within twenty-four hours if his guard happened to be a brother member.[73]

The society's activities included spreading dissent among soldiers as well as civilians. Apparently the organization had considerable success. James Longstreet, Lee's senior corps commander, said that "the large and increasing number of desertions, particularly amongst the Georgia troops, induces me to believe that some such outside influence must be operating upon our men." In October 1863, a Savannah man wrote that troops in southeast Georgia were demanding peace and would soon turn to mutiny or desertion if they did not get it. A few months later, an insurrection plot was discovered among troops at the Rose Dew Island batteries, south of Savannah. Encouraged by local citizens connected with the Peace Society, the soldiers took an oath never to fight the Yankees, to desert at the earliest opportunity, and to encourage others to do the same. Members of the Peace Society claimed credit for mass desertions that contributed to Confederate defeats at Vicksburg and Missionary Ridge.[74]

Another peace organization, the Order of the Heroes of America, encouraged desertions as well by writing soldiers in the field, urging them to come home, and promising protection if they would. The Heroes of America, also called the Heroes of 1776 or the Red Strings (after the identification they wore), formed in the north central section of North Carolina and spread through the western part of the state and into the hill country of South Carolina, eastern Tennessee, and southwestern Virginia. Like its counterparts elsewhere, the Heroes had secret passwords, handshakes, obligations, and oaths. Its members swore to protect deserters and prisoners of war, to aid federal spy operations, and to do whatever they could to undermine the Confederacy.[75]

The Heroes began holding peace rallies in earnest shortly after the July 1863 Confederate defeats at Gettysburg and Vicksburg. In Wake County, North Carolina, they held two that summer, condemning Jefferson Davis and demanding an end to the war. At a Heroes meeting in Surry County, members called for maintaining "the Constitution as it is and the Union as it was." By fall, the Heroes were pressing for peace throughout the southern Appalachians and adjacent regions. Their message was especially well received in southwestern Virginia. No more than a quarter of the region's voters had ever favored secession. A Confederate officer sent there to hunt deserters lamented that southwest Virginians, most of them slaveless farmers, had "little knowledge and less sympathy with the troubles of the slaveholders, and as a class were opposed to secession." That was certainly the case in Wise County, where local Unionists were in regular contact with federal troops at nearby Pikeville, Kentucky. They kept their Union allies informed of Rebel movements and provided them with lists of area pro-Confederates. Beside each name was a note on how they were to be treated, based on their secessionist activities, when the Federals eventually took control of the region. Some were to take an oath to

Anti-Confederates organized a network of underground railroads to shuttle escaping Unionists to federal lines. They laid out routes, established safe houses, and used conductors to guide refugees on their way. One such guide, Daniel Ellis of Carter County, Tennessee, piloted over four thousand people out of the Confederacy. Late in the war, Ellis was made a captain in the Union army. He is shown here in his federal uniform. In 1867, Ellis published a memoir of his wartime experiences. Illustration from Ellis, *Thrilling Adventures*.

the United States and be released. Some were slated for imprisonment. Others were marked for execution.[76]

In addition to acting as informants for Union forces, the Heroes of
America organized an underground railroad to shuttle escaping
Unionists through the mountains to federal lines. Some had run afoul
of Confederate authorities. Others simply wanted to get out of the
South and away from the war. All across the mountain South, antiwar
activists assisted southern dissenters heading for Union territory.
They guided refugees from Alabama, Georgia, and the Carolinas
safely through the hills to the Federals in Tennessee. One such guide,
Daniel Ellis, was said to have piloted over four thousand people out of
the Confederacy. In western Virginia's Shenandoah Valley, antiwar
Mennonites set up their own underground railroad. Using their
church and homes as safe houses, they ferried hundreds of refugees
and deserters out of the Confederacy. In north Georgia's Union
County, Austin Mason organized a chain of safe houses to shelter prisoners and deserters as they fled north through the mountains.[77]

"Union Men to the Core"

Men like Mason were hardly unusual. Anti-Confederate activists
throughout the South established an extensive network of safe houses,
guides, and secret signals to aid refugees, deserters, draft dodgers, and
Union men wishing to enlist with the Federals. In southeast Alabama
and southwest Georgia, residents of the Wiregrass region helped deserters and draft dodgers make their way south to the Union forces in
Florida. Ezekiel Bird of southern Alabama's Monroe County helped
several area Union men escape south to enlist with the "First Floridy"
federal regiment with the aid of his brother-in-law in Holmes County,
Florida. Bird later told how he sent "Tom McMillan and Dick McMil-
lian of the neighborhood of Burnt Corn in this county to go, [as well
as] Benjamin Martin, Jasper and Oliver Braxton, my brothers-in-law,"
into Florida, giving them directions to safe houses along the way.[78]

A similar network of Unionist safe houses ran north and west from
Virginia's Shenandoah Valley. Another "sort of 'underground railroad'
system," as one contemporary described it, stretched from northern
Alabama through Chattanooga and the Sequatchie Valley to Possum
Creek, Kentucky, a distance of almost three hundred miles. Over

routes like these and many more, men called "pilots"—such as Bill Looney of Winston County, Alabama, Daniel Ellis of Carter County, Tennessee, and Henry Colson of Lee County, Virginia—guided tens of thousands to Union lines. Southerners even helped Union prisoners of war make their escapes. One day in late 1864, J.B. Norman of southwest Georgia's Colquitt County came across two Yankee escapees from Andersonville on his property. He fed the men and put them up for the night. The next morning he served them steak, then pointed them toward Florida.[79]

W.H. Shelton, an officer with the First New York Artillery, was captured in battle and imprisoned at Camp Sorghum, South Carolina, in September 1864. He escaped in December but was caught and temporarily confined in the Greenville jail. But the jailer happened to be a Union sympathizer. He released Shelton and gave him directions to Union lines, along with the names of people willing to aid him. After a journey over the mountains, with the help of Unionist families along the way, Shelton arrived safely in Union-occupied Knoxville, Tennessee.[80]

Those requiring the services of the South's Unionists were most grateful. A Wisconsin colonel trying to reach Sherman's army in Chattanooga later wrote that they were "generous, hospitable, brave, and Union men to the core; men who would suffer privations, and death itself, rather than array themselves in strife against the Stars and Stripes, the emblem of the country they loved. . . . under their homespun jackets beat hearts pure as gold, and stout as oaks."[81]

Union men were not alone in their efforts to help escaping prisoners. Some of the most daring allies captured Yankees had were the South's Union women. In Atlanta, Emily Farnsworth, Cyrena Stone, and other women of the city's Union Circle slipped prisoners cash and other contraband to ease their escape. Lieutenant Alonzo Cooper, who escaped from a prison camp in Columbia, South Carolina, was given shelter by a woman near Walhalla who, as Cooper later wrote, "was quite bitter towards the Confederacy on account of her son having been conscripted and her being left alone, with no one to work her farm or care for her children. She was too poor to hire the work done, and was obliged to do all that was done towards supporting herself and the children." In South Carolina's Pickens District, escaping prisoner Lieutenant Hanibal Johnson of the Third Maine Infantry came upon the cabin of a woman named Prince, who was glad to help anyone opposed to the Confederacy. Her husband had opposed secession, then was forced into service by the draft and killed in battle. Now his widow operated a station along an underground railroad smuggling anti-Confederates to Union territory. She led Johnson to a hideout in the Appalachian foothills occupied by deserters and layouts who then guided him through the mountains to Union lines in Tennessee.[82]

Women in the southern Appalachians frequently gave escaping Yankees room and board, pointed them toward safe routes through the mountains, and served as guides to Union lines. In Flat Rock, North Carolina, three sisters of the Hollinger family, two of them married to Confederate soldiers, regularly moved fugitives through the lines to Union-held Tennessee. Escaping Union Captain Madison Drake got help in North Carolina from a like-minded woman who found him and several companions hidden in a ravine. She "boldly advanced" toward the group and demanded to know who they were. She warned them, "you must not use deceit or you will be shot down where you stand. A dozen true rifles are now leveled at you, and if I raise my hand you will fall dead at my feet." The woman was relieved to learn that they were Yankee soldiers trying to make it to the Union lines in Tennessee and that they were no threat to her husband, a deserter from the Confederate army. She took the men to her cabin, fed them, and gave them directions to federal forces. Drake later recalled that they had "never met such a woman . . . certainly the bravest of her sex."[83]

Like other Union escapees, Drake and his comrades found themselves beholden to former enemies as well. Gangs of deserters and layouts, which were common in the mountains, occasionally shared their hideouts, their knowledge of the landscape, and what rations they had with Yankees on the run. Drake's admiration and appreciation of such men came through clearly in his recollections: "Here we were, four Yankee officers, in the heart of the enemy's country, in a mountain fastness, surrounded by some of the men whom we had encountered in battle's stern array at Bull Run, Roanoke, Newbern, Fredericksburg, and on other ensanguined fields, who now were keeping watch and ward over our lives, which they regarded as precious in their sight—willing to shed their blood in our defense."[84]

Much to his surprise, Drake also discovered friends among Rebel soldiers still on duty. At one point during their journey, Drake's startled group came across a Confederate officer who accused them of being "d—n Yankees." But before they could bolt, he assured the fugitives that they had nothing to fear from him. The officer told of having three sons killed in battle and a fourth dying of fever in a Delaware prison. He was sick of war and wanted nothing more to do with it. The officer wished Drake and his companions well, then continued on his way.[85]

In the Virginia mountains, there were spies, or scouts as they were called, giving aid to the Federals. In the spring of 1862, Confederates at Lebanon in Russell County were attacked by federal troops guided through the mountains by local Unionists. In Florida, Governor Milton complained that deserters from the Confederate army were "in constant communication with the enemy" and would "pilot . . . [them] in any raid which may be attempted." Civilians, too, were causing problems for Florida Confederates. One Rebel cavalryman reported in April 1862 that "at least three-fourths of the people on the Saint Johns River and east of it are aiding and abeting the enemy." One federal officer recalled that "negroes and poor whites . . . are very willing to communicate all the information they are in possession of." Even in the Confederacy's capital city of Richmond, Virginia, there was a thriving network of Unionists active in helping Yankee captives get out of prison and slip through the lines. They also functioned as a spy ring, giving escapees valuable information to take with them.[86]

One of the most effective Richmond spies was a middle-aged spinster named Elizabeth Van Lew, or Crazy Bet, as she was known locally. A member of one of Virginia's wealthiest families, Van Lew cultivated her reputation for mental instability by dressing strangely and wandering city streets singing nonsense songs. At one point, she was seen in an outfit of "buckskin leggings, a one-piece skirt and waist of cotton, topped off with a huge calico sunbonnet." Adding to her unorthodox reputation were her long-standing antislavery views. She had freed the family slaves, made sure they were reunited with their spouses, and made her home a station on the Underground Railroad. But her unaware neighbors saw her as a harmless eccentric, gracious but too unbalanced to be a threat.

As one of the richest women in town, Van Lew played hostess in her palatial home to some of the Confederacy's most prominent figures. She relayed by secret code any information she gathered to the Federals, using slaves and free blacks eager to help as couriers. It was a nerve-racking existence. As one report put it, "there was not a moment during those four years when Lizzie Van Lew could hear a step behind

One of the most effective spies for the Union was Richmond's Elizabeth Van Lew, or Crazy Bet, as she was known locally. A member of one of Virginia's wealthiest families, Van Lew cultivated a reputation for mental instability by dressing strangely and wandering city streets singing nonsense songs. Adding to her unorthodox reputation were her long-standing antislavery views. She had freed the family slaves, made sure they were reunited with their spouses, and made her home a station on the Underground Railroad. But her un-aware neighbors saw her as a harmless eccentric, too unbalanced to be a threat. Photo from the National Park Service.

her on the street without expecting to have somebody tap her on the shoulder and say, 'You are my prisoner.'" But no one ever did. When the Union army finally entered Richmond, her home was among the first to display the Stars and Stripes.[87]

Social conventions of the day that downplayed women's capabilities also made them some of the war's most effective spies. Mary Gordon and Carrie King spied for the Union army in Georgia. Anna Campbell in northern Alabama rode seventy miles in thirty-six hours with intelligence for the Federals. In Tennessee, Lucy Williams rode through heavy rain to warn the Yankees of General John Hunt Morgan's planned attack. Acting on her word, they struck first and killed Morgan in the fray.[88]

Pauline Cushman, a New Orleans–born actress, established a reputation as a staunch secessionist by toasting Jefferson Davis onstage in Louisville, Kentucky, then set out on a campaign of counterespionage. Working with the Union's Army of the Cumberland, Cushman wormed her way into the confidence of Nashville secessionists, all the while reporting their activities to the Yankees. She acted as a federal courier too, and her exploits ranged from Kentucky and Tennessee through the northern tiers of Mississippi, Alabama, and Georgia. She was finally caught in the spring of 1863 near Shelbyville, Tennessee, with drawings she had taken from a Rebel army engineer. Cushman escaped, was recaptured, then rescued in a Union surprise attack. The Federals gave her an honorary commission, and she spent the rest of the war touring the North and lecturing on her exploits as the Little Major.[89]

In the spring of 1862, Rebel authorities caught three Mississippi women carrying important documents to the Union army at Shiloh. Mississippi was home also to Levi Naron of Choctaw County, one of the most effective Union spies in the West. Naron joined the Union Secret Service in 1862 and, wrote one appreciative federal officer, "rendered valuable services in that capacity." Union General Grenville Dodge made Naron—or Chickasaw, as he was covertly known—his chief of scouts, a position he held for over a year. Dodge wrote of Naron: "Daring, bold, and shrewd, he rendered me most valuable services by keeping me informed of the movements of the enemy in Tennessee, Alabama, Mississippi and Georgia, and by operating against the enemies' outposts."[90]

In Georgia, James George Brown of Murray County led a network of native pro-Union spies who operated throughout the northern part of the state. Further south, in late 1864, James C. McBurney of Macon, who had previously guided a federal raid through Alabama and Georgia, provided William T. Sherman with information on resources and railroads during his March to the Sea. Georgians' spying for the Union was hardly the worst of it. Earlier that year, Governor Joe Brown had issued a call to all militia members and government employees, ordering them to rally in Atlanta and help fight off the Yankees. Soon after, word came from Dawson County that the local surveyor, Elias Darnel, "instead of obeying your proclamation went about organizing a federal home guard to assist the enemy."[91]

Two personae of Pauline Cushman, a New Orleans–born actress who held an honorary commission in the Union army and served as a courier and spy for the Federals headquarterd in Nashville. On the pretext of looking for her brother, a Confederate soldier, Cushman easily moved between the lines. She wore a number of disguises during her service, including a soldier's uniform. Confederates arrested Cushman near Shelbyville, Tennessee, and sentenced her to death by hanging. She escaped, was recaptured, then rescued in a Union surprise attack. Her cover as a spy now useless, Cushman spent the next several years lecturing on her exploits as the Little Major. She is shown here in civilian dress and in the uniform she wore on stage. Photo in uniform from the Brooklyn Public Library, New York. Photo in civilian dress from the Library of Congress.

In eastern Tennessee's Fentress County, one of the most active Unionist home-guard units was led by David Beatty, widely known as "Tinker Dave." He had tried early on to stay out of the war. Then in January 1862, local Confederates ransacked his farm and warned him to choose sides or leave the county. Many of Beatty's neighbors got the same treatment. They ignored the warning, but as Beatty later recalled, Confederate partisans "kept running in on us every few weeks . . . killing and driving people off." Beatty was soon organizing the area's anti-Confederates into a Unionist guard to patrol Fentress and Overton counties, fighting a series of pitched battles with area Confederates in the process. Late that year, Beatty's men became even more aggressive as Federals starting supplying them with munitions during their advance into Tennessee.[92]

One of the South's most notorious anti-Confederate partisan bands was led by a Unionist named King. Operating in southeastern Kentucky, King and his men terrorized anyone who openly supported the Confederacy. One of King's more brutal acts came in late 1862, after the Battle of Perryville. Three wounded Rebel soldiers, too weak to travel, were left by their comrades to recuperate with a sympathetic family near the town of London. King and five of his men showed up, dragged the men out of bed, and hanged them from a nearby tree with telegraph wire.[93]

In Georgia's Pickens County, 125 men formed a Union home guard to protect themselves from Confederate partisans, to raid pro-Confederate plantations, and to assist the advancing Federals. One Yankee officer was sure that several hundred more men in neighboring counties could be called to arms for the Union. In August 1864, the Federals did just that. Hoping to form not simply a home guard but a regular fighting force, they recruited about 300 north Georgia men. Some were sent directly to the Fifth Tennessee Mounted Infantry. Others formed an independent company operating in Fannin County attached to the Fifth Tennessee. The rest were enrolled as the First Georgia State Troops Volunteer Battalion. Though well armed, the First Georgia was ill trained and never much use to the Federals in regular combat. But the men of the First Georgia fought a running guerrilla war that kept Confederate loyalists busy who might otherwise have been battling the Federals.[94]

"A Greater Sacrifice for the Union"

There were other, better-trained Georgians willing to put their skills to use for the Union. Thomas A. Watson of Fannin County, William Fife of Harris County, Cornelius Dawson of Clinch County, and Andrew T. Harris of Murray County—all Confederate deserters—were among thousands of white Georgians who joined federal units. In total, about three hundred thousand southern whites joined the Union armies, a number almost equaling that of all of the Federals killed during the war. Among them were forty-four-year-old farmer Wesley Cornutt and his teenage son David of Ashe County, North Carolina, who served with the Union's Thirteenth Tennessee Cavalry. Another was Aaron Phillips, a farmhand who deserted from the Forty-second Virginia. Henry Rikard of Franklin County, Alabama, fled with several cousins to Iuka, Mississippi, where they all enlisted in the Sixty-fourth Illinois Infantry. Thirty Unionists from western Tennessee joined the Fifty-second Indiana at Fort Pillow. Others who volunteered for federal service included survivors of the Nueces Massacre in Texas.[95]

David R. Snelling of Baldwin County, Georgia, had deeply personal reasons for his Union stand. David's father, William, a man of modest means, died of fever when David was five. His mother, Elizabeth Lester Snelling, whose wealthy family had never approved of her marrying a poor man, was given only a small plot of land adjoining the large plantations her brothers owned. When Elizabeth died a few years later, young David was taken in by his uncle, David Lester. While Lester sent his own sons off to school, he put David to work in the fields along with the slaves. Treated much as a slave himself, David came to detest slavery. Threatened with conscription in the spring of 1862, David joined the Confederate army. That summer, he deserted and joined the Federals. Two years later, as a lieutenant in Sherman's cavalry escort during the March to the Sea, David went out of his way to lead a raid against his uncle's plantation a few miles from the state capital of Milledgeville. His troops seized as many provisions as they could carry and destroyed the cotton gin.[96]

Though most Confederate soldiers were nonslaveholders and poorer than their slaveholding neighbors, white southerners who served the Union were most often poorer still. In the North Fork district of western North Carolina's Ashe County, a comparison of thirty-four Union and forty-two Confederate volunteers shows that holdings in real and personal property among Confederates were more than twice that of their Union counterparts. In eastern North Carolina, the difference was even more dramatic. In Washington County, which supplied nearly equal numbers of troops to the Union and the Confederacy, Union soldiers were fourteen times poorer than

David Snelling joined the Confederate army under threat of conscription in May 1862. He deserted that summer and signed up with the Federals. Two years later, as a lieutenant in General William T. Sherman's cavalry escort during the March to the Sea, Snelling went out of his way to lead a raid against his uncle's plantation in Baldwin County, Georgia. It was southerners themselves who did much of the damage during Sherman's March. Members of the Union's First Alabama Cavalry, recruited from poor farmers in the northern part of the state who blamed black-belt planters for secession, relished the opportunity to sack plantations during Sherman's March. Snelling was one of three hundred thousand white southerners who served in the Union military. Photo from the Russell Library, Georgia College and State University.

those in the Confederate army. Such figures reflect a class-based Unionism that made itself felt all across the South. It was reflected too among members of the Union's First Alabama Cavalry, recruited from poor farmers in the northern part of the state, who relished the opportunity to sack plantations during Sherman's March to the Sea.[97]

"The poor hate the rich," wrote James Henry Hammond to a friend, "& make war on them every where." Many were happy to do so under the Stars and Stripes. Operating out of Mexico, the First Regiment of Union Troops plundered Texas ranches all along the Rio Grande. Cotton was the special target of Union raiders in Nueces County. Some were Hispanics who, like their Anglo comrades, saw the war as a chance to right old political and economic wrongs done them by wealthy Texans, most of whom supported the Confederacy.[98]

In Arkansas, the First Arkansas Cavalry Volunteers (U.S.), fought running battles with Confederate guerrilla bands. Back East, the First North Carolina Union Volunteers (U.S.) raided plantations along the state's tidewater region and fought off local Confederate troops sent to stop them. In one engagement, wrote a federal officer, the "loyal North Carolinians were fast and fierce in the pursuit of their rebel neighbors. The chase was given up only when the enemy was completely put to flight." Just as fierce were the Mississippi Mounted Rifles, all natives of the state, who aided federal raids into northern Mississippi and helped beat back Confederate General Nathan Bedford Forrest's April 1864 attack on Memphis.[99]

These southerners who fought for the Union, in the opinion of north Alabamian P.D. Hall, "made a greater sacrifice for the Union than the men of the North."

> Consider the loyal men of the South, especially as far south as Alabama, what they had to endure for their country. They were exposed and in danger every minute of their lives. They were shot sitting by their firesides or walking on the road; they had to leave their families to the abuse of the enemy; had to keep themselves closely concealed like the vermin in the woods until they could make escape through the lines, and then had to share the same hardships of soldiers life that the comrades of the North bore.[100]

For those who fell into enemy hands, the danger was even greater. Confederates sometimes expressed more rage toward their Unionist neighbors than the Yankees. When Rebels in Lenoir County, North Carolina, captured twenty-two local deserters turned Union soldiers, the men were not treated as prisoners of war. After a quick trial of questionable legality, they were hanged as traitors.[101]

Still, men like P.D. Hall came forward in droves to face such dangers. Hall served with the First Alabama Cavalry (U.S.), formed in January 1863 at Corinth, Mississippi, from among the thousands of Alabamians pouring into Union-held territory. Charles Christopher Sheats, a schoolteacher and member of the Alabama legislature, was one of the Union army's chief recruiters. During a visit to Blount County, Sheats delivered a fiery speech denouncing secession as "fiendish villainy." Within three days, 150 local men signed up for service in the Union army.[102]

In Florida, the Union's East Gulf Blockading Squadron recruited native anti-Confederates for service in the Second Florida Cavalry, based at Cedar Key. One of the unit's first members was Milledge Brannen. Born in Columbia County and living in the Tampa Bay area when the war broke out, Brannen was a former Confederate soldier who had become disillusioned with the Confederate cause. Brannen deserted and went home, became active among anti-Confederate refugees, then joined the Union's Second Florida Cavalry. From their coastal base, the men raided inland against plantations, railroads, and Confederate supplies. In May 1864, the Second Florida was instrumental to the federal occupation of Tampa.[103]

Like Brannen, Joseph Sanders of Dale County, Alabama, was a former Confederate who had deserted. Early in the war, Sanders enlisted with Company C of the Thirty-first Georgia, a company composed largely of men from the southeast Alabama counties of Barbour, Henry, Dale, and Coffee. Sanders was so admired by his comrades that they elected him one of their company sergeants. He fought with the Thirty-first Georgia, part of Stonewall Jackson's Corps, through the early Virginia campaigns. By all accounts, "there was not a braver man than he in the unit." Still, Sanders at length decided that the Confederate cause was not his. He fled south to Florida's Gulf Coast and sought refuge with Union forces. Soon after, the Federals granted him a lieutenant's commission in their First Florida Cavalry.

One of Sanders's first missions found him leading the advance guard of a federal raid into southern Alabama. With Lieutenant Colonel Andrew B. Spurling in command, 450 men of the Second Maine and First Florida cavalries headed north, following the rail line that led from Pensacola to Montgomery. Only eleven miles out of camp, they began picking up sentries from a Confederate cavalry unit. By the time their raid was over, the Federals had captured 38 prisoners, 47 horses, 3 mules, and 75 rifles. In his report on the expedition, Spurling spoke highly of Sanders's performance: "It would hardly be doing justice did I not make special mention of Lieut. Joseph G. Sanders, Company F, First Florida Cavalry. He is a worthy officer, and deserves high praise for his meritorious conduct. He was at all times in command of the advance guard, and much of the success is due to the prompt and faithful manner in which all orders were executed."

Not long after this raid, Sanders was placed on detached duty and took charge of a force composed mainly of local Union men from the Wiregrass. For the rest of the war, Sanders and his men conducted a series of raids throughout southeast Alabama. They seized horses and military supplies, plundered well-stocked plantations, and skirmished with Confederate forces. At one point, they raided the town of Elba in Coffee County and burned down the courthouse.[104]

In Arkansas and Missouri, the Ozark uplands were prime recruiting ground for Union companies of "Mountain Feds." Among the most

Among the most active of the Ozark "Mountain Feds," independent companies of local Unionists operating under authority of the Union army, were Williams's Raiders. The unit formed around the Williams clan of Arkansas's Conway and Van Buren counties and was led by fifty-one-year-old Thomas Jefferson (Jeff) Williams, pictured here in 1862. Williams and his neighbors were small farmers who at first wanted nothing to do with the war. But when Confederate draft officers came calling on his sons, Williams joined the Federals and went to war against the Confederacy. Photo from the Central Arkansas Library System.

active were Williams's Raiders, formed around the Williams clan of Arkansas's Conway and Van Buren counties and led by fifty-one-year-old Thomas Jefferson (Jeff) Williams. Williams and his neighbors were small farmers who at first wanted nothing to do with the war. But when Confederate draft officers came calling, Williams—along with his four sons, three sons-in-law, two brothers, a brother-in-law, four nephews, and twenty-five other men—struck out for federal lines in Missouri. They formed the heart of Company B, First Arkansas Infantry Battalion, electing Jeff Williams their captain and his son Nathan a second lieutenant.

In 1863, after the Federals entered northern Arkansas, they authorized Williams to form an independent company of local Unionists to fight back Confederate home guards in the region. For the next two years, Williams's Raiders fought with considerable success against Confederates trying to regain control in their corner of the Ozarks. But on February 12, 1865, Rebel guerrillas surrounded the Williams cabin, killed Jeff Williams with a volley of buckshot, and beat the Williams women. Williams's pregnant daughter-in-law, Sarah Jane, lost her baby after the Rebels hit her in the belly with their gun stocks. That night Sarah Jane's husband, Leroy, enraged at the killing of his father and unborn child, hunted down the Rebels and shot eight of them to death. The next day, joined by other Williams men and about seventy soldiers of the Third Arkansas Cavalry (U.S.), Leroy went after the rest. They tracked the Rebel gang to Clinton, twenty miles to the north, where they killed at least one of its members. Five more were taken prisoner in Quitman. Before the killing stopped, Leroy alone shot as many as sixteen men.[105]

"Destroying Angels"

Unlike Jeff Williams, Joseph Sanders, and their comrades, the vast majority of active dissidents and deserters never attached themselves to the Union army. Instead, they formed hundreds of armed bands, often called "layout" or "tory" gangs, to fight off Confederate authority. Some were committed Unionists. Others simply struggled to keep conscript and impressment companies at bay. Most were nonslaveholders who wanted no part of a rich man's war. But they were prepared to fight back when the Confederacy forced war upon them.

One such group of men in southern Mississippi's Jones County was led by Newton Knight, a slaveless farmer who deserted the Confederate army soon after conscription began. Upset that wealthy men could avoid the draft, Knight went home and took up with others of his community who felt the same way. "We stayed out in the woods minding our own business," Knight said, "until the Confederate Army began sending raiders after us with bloodhounds. . . . Then we saw we had to fight." And fight they did. For the rest of the war, Knight and his men, numbering around five hundred, drove off Confederate agents, ambushed army patrols, and looted government depots, distributing the food stored there to the poor. So successfully did they subvert Confederate control of the county that some called it the Free State of Jones.[106]

In Decatur, Mississippi, a Shiloh veteran went home and refused to return to the army unless it paid him for the mule he had lost in the battle. No funds were forthcoming. So he formed a band of area deserters and draft dodgers that became, as one resident complained, "so strong that the community in which they live have to submit to any demand they make." They organized a warning system of horns and trumpets, and dodged or fought off anyone sent to capture them. "Unless something is done soon," wrote a frightened pro-Confederate, "we will be in as bad or worse condition than Jones County."[107]

The spring of 1863 found a band of twenty-five deserters ranging over Mississippi's Simpson County. When the sheriff arrested several of them, their friends broke them out of jail. That whole part of southern Mississippi was, in fact, largely controlled by deserters and resisters who killed or drove off anyone connected with the Confederacy. In spring 1864, Major James Hamilton, quartermaster for taxation in Mississippi, wrote his superiors that in the state's Seventh District, covering most of southern Mississippi, deserters had "overrun and taken possession of the country." Hamilton's agent in Jones County had been driven off, and Hamilton had heard nothing more from him. In Covington County, deserters made the tax collector cease operations and distribute what he had on hand to their families. Deserters raided the quartermaster depot in Perry County and destroyed the stores there. Under the circumstances, Hamilton could no longer continue tax collection in that region.[108]

It was the same across vast sections of the South. Most famous are the partisan struggles in Kentucky and Missouri, but the Deep South was almost as violently divided against itself. By the summer of 1863, there were ten thousand deserters and conscripts in the Alabama hill country formed into armed bands. Some did so to fend off Confederate authorities, killing officers sent to arrest them. Others went on the offensive. In Randolph County, about four hundred deserters organized and carried out "a systematic warfare upon conscript officers." Still others in or near the Black Belt targeted planters and their property. "Destroying Angels" and "Prowling Brigades" swept out of their piney-woods strongholds to burn cotton, gin houses, and any supplies they could not carry away.[109] In March 1864, a petition reached the governor's desk with news of anti-Confederates in the southeastern Alabama counties of Henry and Dale.

> These bands now number in both counties upwards of 300 men and are generally well armed and stand in bold defiance of all law and authority. . . . They have murdered, within the last twelve months, four good and loyal citizens; they have stripped several plantations of mules and horses and burnt to the ground several cribs of corn.[110]

Seeking safety in numbers, deserters and draft evaders began banding together early on. By summer 1862, there were layout gangs in Calhoun County, Florida, just west of Tallahassee, who had "armed and organized themselves to resist those who may attempt their arrest." In September, forty men of southwest Georgia's Marion County "secured and provisioned a house and arranged it in the manner of a military castle." Though Confederate troops tried repeatedly to force them out, they had little success against these men, determined as they were to "resist to the last extremity." Illustration from Ellis, *Thrilling Adventures*.

In Louisiana, James Madison Wells, though a man of means himself, denounced the Confederacy as a rich man's government and organized a guerrilla campaign against it. From his Bear Wallow stronghold in Rapides Parish, Wells led deserters and other resisters in raids against Confederate supply lines and depots. Further south, in the state's Cajun parishes, bands of anti-Confederates did the same. One group that ranged west of Washington Parish, known locally as the Clan, numbered more than three hundred. Commanded by a Cajun named Carrier, it drove off home guards and forced plunder from all who opposed them. A woman from Bayou Chicot wrote to Governor Moore of local guerrillas there: "We could not fare worse were we surrounded by a band of Lincoln's mercenary hirelings." Confederate Lieutenant John Sibley wrote in his diary that one band of "marauders" had "declared vengeance against Confederate soldiers. . . . After killing five members of the Home Guard, they almost inhumanly beat their faces to pieces with the breach of their guns so no friend would know them again."[111]

In Texas's Rio Grande county of Zapata, local Hispanics denounced the Confederacy, formed a band of pro-Union partisans, and plundered the property of loyal Confederates. In Bandera County, just west of San Antonio, residents became so upset with the inequitable tax system that they formed a pro-Union militia, declined to pay their taxes, and swore to kill anyone who tried to make them do so. At the state's northern extreme, near Bonham, several hundred anti-Confederates established three large camps close enough that the entire force could assemble within two hours. They patrolled the region so effectively that no one could approach without their knowing of it. In the central Texas county of Bell, deserters led by Lige Bivens fortified themselves in a cave known as Camp Safety. From there they mounted raids against the area's pro-Confederates. According to an 1863 report, two thousand other Texas deserters "fortified themselves near the Red River, and defied the Confederacy. At last account they had been established . . . eight months, and were constantly receiving accession of discontented rebels and desperadoes."[112]

An Arkansas band of anti-Confederates operated out of Greasy Cove, a mountain pass at the head of the Little Missouri River. Made up of "deserters, disaffected, and turbulent characters," as one newspaper called them, they swept through the countryside harassing Confederate loyalists and challenging Confederate authority. So did anti-Confederates in east Tennessee, a region where open rebellion against the Confederacy was common from the start. As early as the fall of 1861, bands of native Unionists disrupted Confederate operations by spying for the Federals, cutting telegraph lines, and burning railroad bridges. The next spring, Unionists in Scott and Morgan counties staged a coup. They forcibly took control of all county offices, disbanded the Confederate home guard, and put in its place a force made up of local Union men.[113]

After pro-Confederates from neighboring North Carolina mounted a series of raids against Unionists in and around the Smoky Mountain town of Cades Cove, Tennessee, the area's Union men formed their own militia. Led by Russell Gregory, pastor of a local Primitive Baptist church, they established a network of sentries along the roads to warn of approaching danger. In the spring of 1864, raiders invaded Cades Cove once again to steal livestock and provisions. They plundered several farms, taking all they could carry, but never made it back to North Carolina with their booty. Near the state line, Gregory's militiamen felled trees across the roads and ambushed the Rebel partisans, forcing them to scatter and leave their loot behind.[114]

When her Unionist husband, Keith, joined the Confederate army to avoid conscription, Malinda Pritchard Blalock of North Carolina cut her hair short, passed herself off as his brother "Sam," and joined the army too. They both intended to desert, but Keith rolled in poison oak and got a medical discharge. "Sam" was discharged as well. When enrolling officers tried to conscript Keith, he and Malinda fled to Grandfather Mountain and formed an anti-Confederate guerrilla outfit. Malinda is shown here holding a photograph of Keith. Both survived the war and lived long after. Photo from the Southern Historical Collection, University of North Carolina at Chapel Hill.

Anti-Confederates, deserters, and resisters in the North Carolina mountains also formed defensive militias and set up warning networks. Wilkes County was home to a band of five hundred deserters, organized as a guerrilla force, who openly challenged Confederates to come and take them. Wilkes County's Trap Hill gang was especially aggressive in harassing local pro-Confederates. In Cherokee County, about one hundred layouts formed a resistance force that disarmed Confederate soldiers and terrorized Confederate loyalists.[115]

The husband-and-wife team of Keith and Malinda Pritchard Blalock led a gang of anti-Confederates entrenched on North Carolina's Grandfather Mountain. Faced with conscription earlier in the war, Keith had joined the Confederate army and planned to desert to Union lines at the first opportunity. His young wife, Malinda, could not bear the thought of being parted from him. So she cut her hair short and disguised herself as a man, enlisting with her husband as his brother "Sam" Blalock. Their plan to escape went awry after their unit was put on garrison duty at Kinston, North Carolina, nowhere near Union lines. So Keith rolled around naked in poison oak and got himself a medical discharge. "Sam" got a discharge too when she revealed herself to be a woman.

After Keith recovered back home, Confederate enrolling officers tried to draft him. This time, he and Malinda rounded up all the weapons they could carry and fled up the slopes of Grandfather Mountain. Others threatened with conscription soon joined them and formed a layout gang that survived on the fish, game, and wild berries that were abundant on the mountain. When the Blalock gang fired on a pursuing conscript company, wounding one of the soldiers, Confederate authorities put a price on Keith Blalock's head. The couple eventually fled to Tennessee, where Keith joined a Union guerrilla outfit that frequently ranged into North Carolina gathering intelligence for the federal army.[116]

South Carolina's hill country, too, saw its share of resistance. Centered in Greenville, Pickens, and Spartanburg counties, deserter bands had designated assembly areas and a "well-arranged system of signals" to warn of trouble on the way. "Every woman and child," according to one report, was "a watch and a guard for them." Deserters commandeered and fortified an island in the Broad River. They also built fortified positions at Jones Gap, Hogback Mountain, Table Rock, Caesars Head, and Potts Camp. Near Gowensville, they built a heavy log fort, "loopholed and prepared for defense." Deserter bands went on the offensive, too. A force of more than five hundred controlled a region bordering North Carolina. Operating in groups of between ten and thirty, they chased off conscript companies, raided supply depots, and looted and burned the property of anyone who openly supported the Confederacy.[117]

Much the same was true in southwestern Virginia, where J.E. Joyner noted large numbers of deserters with weapons, which they vowed to use "against the Confederacy if there is any attempt to arrest them." Montgomery, Floyd, and Giles counties especially were "infested by armed bands of deserters." Local Unionists, too, aroused by Confederate home-guard depredations, formed armed militias. One such unit, headed by "Captain" Charles Huff of Floyd County, regularly backed up local deserters and ambushed home-guard patrols. The job was made easier by Joseph Phares, a double agent who kept Huff informed of the guard's plans while feeding its officers disinformation.[118]

Though their motives were not always the same, the one thing nearly all armed resisters had in common was that they were men of modest means. In eastern Tennessee, for example, Unionist guerrillas were mainly small farmers, artisans, and laborers. By contrast, their pro-Confederate counterparts held three times as much real estate and twice as much personal property. The rise of such class warfare was the very thing that slaveholders had tried to avoid for so long and that had, in large part, led most to push for secession in the first place. "Ironically," as historian Charles Bolton points out, "by engineering disunion, slaveowners fostered the growth of the kind of organizations they had long feared: class-based groups that pitted nonslaveholders against the interests of slaveowners."[119]

Nowhere was that more evident than in the low country of North Carolina. Planters in the region were terrified to learn that, as one wrote, Unionists among the lower classes had "gone so far as to declare [that they] will take the property from the rich men & divide it among the poor men."[120] It was no idle threat. From near the war's beginning, bands of Unionists had been raiding coastal plantations. Formed initially to protect themselves from conscription and Confederate raiders, their objectives eventually expanded to include driving planters from their land and dividing it among themselves.

In the spring and summer of 1862, a pro-Union newspaper in the port town of New Bern reported the formation of Unionist militias in Washington, Tyrrell, Martin, Bertie, Hertford, Gates, Chowan, Perquimans, Pasquotank, and Camden counties, "not only for self-protection against rebel guerillas, but for the purpose of expatriating all the rebel families from their limits." Further west, in the central piedmont region of North Carolina, class antagonism was also a strong motive for resistance. Many members of the Heroes of America were poor men who, as one contemporary recalled, were "induced to join the organization by the promise of a division here after among them of the property of the loyal Southern citizens."[121]

Plantations were also the targets of deserter and layout gangs in Georgia's cotton belt. "These scoundrels," as a Milledgeville paper called them, "seek the fairest, fattest and most quiet portion of our territory for the theatre of their depredations. They pounce suddenly upon the prosperous plantations, and sweep them of their best laboring stock, and such stores of meat, grain and forage as they can carry off."[122] In south Georgia's Coffee County, a band of layouts headed by "Old Man" Bill Wall plundered livestock and produce on lands belonging to Ben Pearson. When Pearson threatened retaliation, he found a grave dug outside his front door. He finally offered Wall a reward and amnesty if the Old Man would help local authorities lay a trap for his men. Something of a poor-man's poet, Wall could not resist poking fun at Pearson's assumption that he might do such a thing.

If it is my choice to stay at home,
and the woods in beauty roam;
Pluck the flowers in early spring,
and hear the little songsters sing!

Why, then, should I, for the sake of gain,
leave my conscience with a stain.
A traitor! who could hear the name
with no respect for age or fame;

Who, for the sake of a little gold,
would have his friends in bondage sold?
I would rather take the lash
than betray them for Confederate trash.

You say they kill your sheep and cows,
You say they take your hoss and your plows,
You say they took your potatoes away,
You say they dug your grave one day.
All this may be true;
It makes me sorry for you.

Yet, sir, if I, these men betray
and they were all taken away,
And they did not in the battlefield fall,
They would then come back and kill
"Old Man Bill Wall"[123]

"Resist to the Last Extremity"

As Wall's example suggests, the Confederacy's keystone state of Georgia was one of the most divided in the South. Anti-Confederate gangs like Wall's operated in every part of the state. Some areas were so hostile to the Confederacy that army patrols dared not enter them. The pine barrens tract of southeast Georgia was a favorite hideout for those trying to avoid Confederate entanglements. Soldier Camp Island in the region's Okefenokee Swamp was home to as many as a thousand deserters. In southwest Georgia, a Fort Gaines man begged Governor Brown to send cavalry for protection against deserters and layout gangs. So did pro-Confederates in northwest Georgia's Dade and Walker counties. All across the state, from the mountains to the Piedmont to the Wiregrass, there raged an inner civil war so violent that the editor of Milledgeville's *Confederate Union* wrote, "We are fighting each other harder than we ever fought the enemy."[124]

From the upland county of Gilmer came news in July 1862 of "tories and traitors who have taken up their abode in the mountains." That same month, a letter arrived on the governor's desk from Fannin County, just north of Gilmer, warning that "a very large majority of the people now here perhaps two thirds are disloyal." Anti-

Conscript companies sent to round up deserters and draft dodgers ran into increasingly stiff resistance. Hundreds of layout and deserter gangs went on the offensive, harassing home-guard companies, attacking government supply wagons, and raiding local plantations. They eliminated Confederate authority in large parts of the South. So violent did the South's inner conflict become by 1863 that one southern newspaper editor wrote: "We are fighting each other harder than we ever fought the enemy." Illustration from Devens, *Pictorial Book of Anecdotes and Incidents.*

Confederates became so aggressive in Fannin that one man called it a "general uprising among our Torys of this County." September 1862 found Lumpkin County overrun by tories and deserters, robbing pro-Confederates of guns, money, clothes, and provisions. One Confederate sympathizer wrote that "the Union men—Tories—are very abusive indeed and says they will do as they please." The *Dahlonega Signal* estimated that one of Lumpkin County's tory bands, led by "the notorious Jeff Anderson," numbered between one and two hundred.[125]

One of the earliest formed and most active bands of Union men in north Georgia was led by Horatio Hennion. A northerner by birth, Hennion moved to White County's Mossy Creek community in his early twenties and married a local girl. The other men in his band of at least two dozen were natives of Georgia and the Carolinas. All were nonslaveholders. Some were tenants or day laborers who owned no land. Those who did own land held no more than a few hundred dollars' worth of real estate and personal property.

Hennion was working as a wagon maker in Gainesville when secession came. From the start, he made no secret of his support for the Union. After war broke out, Hennion remained openly anti-Confederate even as other local Unionists were falling silent. Threats to his life forced him and his family back to Mossy Creek. There he hoped to live in peace. Then, in the summer of 1861, pro-Confederates tried to kill him. He fled to North Carolina but soon returned and organized a band of anti-Confederates that included men from White County and neighboring Hall County. They fought running battles with Confederate conscript companies, rescuing one of their members from the White County jail after a draft officer arrested him. Hennion's band became even more effective when he signed "an agreement of mutual protection" with deserters hiding out in the region.[126]

Soon after he got word of events in the mountains, Governor Brown issued a proclamation aimed at the "very considerable number of deserters and stragglers" and those who aided them. Brown knew "that numbers of these deserters, encouraged by disloyal citizens in the mountains of Northeastern Georgia, have associated themselves together with arms in their hands and are now in rebellion against the authority of this State and the Confederate States." He issued a proclamation "commanding all persons . . . to return to their respective commands immediately." Brown also warned "all disloyal citizens to cease to harbor deserters or encourage desertion . . . as the law against treason will be strictly enforced against all who subject themselves to its penalties."

Brown's warning had little effect, and in late January 1863 he took action. He sent a mounted force under Colonel George Washington Lee, commandant of Atlanta, and Captain E.M. Galt to Dahlonega with orders to "secure the arrest of deserters and restore the public tranquility." By early February, around six hundred deserters had been rounded up and marched back to the army. Fifty-three civilian Unionists were arrested and sent to Atlanta, among them the tory leader Jeff Anderson. But only a month later, Confederate loyalists in Lumpkin County were begging Governor Brown for more troops. In June, the *Athens Southern Watchman* reported that "some of those who were forced into the army by the cavalry last winter have returned with Government arms and ammunition in their hands and are creating serious apprehensions of future troubles." Already anti-Confederates led by a Hall County man calling himself Major Finger had attacked a small ironworks in White County. They burned the coal, stole the tools, and broke the forge hammer. In Fannin County, tories attacked a group of Confederates sent to arrest deserters, killing one man and wounding at least two others.

Fannin County was hit again in August 1863, when tories led by Soloman Bryan disarmed county residents loyal to the Confederacy. According to one pro-Confederate, they "robbed our people of every single gun and all the ammunition." Similar confrontations took place all over the Georgia up-country. A Union County man informed the governor that the "mountains are filling with deserters and disloyal men," and begged him to send arms and ammunition. Brown sought help from the Richmond government, telling Jefferson Davis that "tories and deserters in North Eastern Georgia are now disarming the loyal people and committing many outrages." He got no response. Brown finally sent a state force that arrested "quite a number of deserters, stragglers, marauders," but the effort did little to combat the rise of anti-Confederate resistance. One Gilmer County Confederate wrote that "the Tories with their squirrel rifles, pick off our men from behind rocks and trees and all manner of hiding places. In this way they have killed six or eight of our soldiers." J.J. Findley of Dahlonega reported that "the District is overrun with Deserters, Tories, and Rogues . . . and that the condition of things is worse in that region than ever."[127]

Resistance was just as fierce in the lower part of the state. In September 1862, forty men of southwest Georgia's Marion County "secured and provisioned a house and arranged it in the manner of a military castle." Armed and provisioned for the long haul, they swore not only to prevent their own capture but also to protect anyone who sought sanctuary in their fortress. Though Confederate and state military officials tried repeatedly to force them out, they had little success against these men, determined as they were to "resist to the last extremity." Captain Caleb Camfield, stationed at Bainbridge with a detachment of cavalrymen, had no better luck. He finally retreated after fierce battles with layout gangs in south Georgia and north Florida.[128]

Anti-Confederates in the region were often backed by federal forces operating along the Florida coast. In February 1863, John Harvey, representing a group of five hundred Wiregrass deserters and draft evaders, met with Lieutenant George Welch of the USS *Amanda* to discuss placing his friends under federal protection. Armed only with shotguns, they had been skirmishing with conscript companies for some time, and their ammunition was running low. They preferred to be taken into protective custody as refugees, and, reported Welch, said "that they would follow me or any other leader to any peril they are ordered to rather than leave their families." Welch was sympathetic but declined, saying he did not have enough manpower to guarantee safe passage for the men and their families from that deep in enemy territory. However, as Unionist strength in the region increased, the Federals did begin running ammunition and other supplies to the area's anti-Confederate partisans.[129]

As early as the summer of 1862, there were newspaper reports of layout gangs in Calhoun County, Florida, just west of Tallahassee, who had "armed and organized themselves to resist those who may attempt their arrest." They were already in contact with the blockading fleet and receiving arms from them. At one point, they even hatched a plot to kidnap Governor Milton and turn him over to the Federals. A pro-Confederate citizen learned of the scheme and warned Milton, who stayed in Tallahassee to avoid capture.[130]

Just east of the state capital, deserter bands regularly raided plantations in Jefferson and Madison counties. Along Florida's western Gulf Coast, armed and organized deserters and layouts were abundant in Lafayette, Walton, Levy, and Washington counties. In southwestern Florida between Tampa and Fort Myers, they ranged virtually unchallenged. On Florida's Atlantic coast, the counties of Volusia, Duval, Putnam, and St. John's saw running battles between anti-Confederate bands and soldiers trying to bring them in.[131]

William Strickland's band of Wiregrass anti-Confederates was among the most active of Florida's deserter/layout gangs. Born in south Georgia's Lowndes County around 1835, Strickland migrated to Florida's Big Bend county of Taylor, where he began raising cattle. A year after the war broke out, he enlisted with the Confederacy's Second Florida Cavalry. In December of 1862, Strickland got word that his wife was seriously ill. Though his unit was stationed in Jefferson County, just across the Aucilla River from his home in Taylor, Strickland's superiors refused to grant him a furlough. He went home anyway and stayed for four months. When he returned in the spring, he was court-martialed as a deserter.

Strickland deserted again and joined with other deserters and draft evaders living on Snyder's Island in the relative safety of Taylor County's Gulf Coast marshlands. There they raised crops, tended cattle, and visited family from time to time. Unable to mount an assault through the marshes, Confederate forces rounded up the men's families and imprisoned them at Camp Smith near Tallahassee. Enraged at the arrests, Strickland and his comrades went on the offensive. They drew up an organizational constitution, established an alliance with the federal Gulf Coast naval squadron, and went to war against the Confederacy as the Independent Union Rangers of Taylor County.[132]

By 1864, virtually all Confederate authority in Taylor County had been eliminated. The sheriff had fled, and his replacement, Edward Jordon, was about to do the same if he could not get help. In a February letter to his superiors, Jordon told of receiving "a message from a Squad of Persons that call themselves Union men. I have thought it best to desist . . . until there is a force in the county to check them, if not I shall have to leave."[133]

"Traitors and Lawless Negroes"

Among the most eager and effective allies men like Strickland had were local slaves. They hid deserters and draft evaders traveling through the region, funneled plantation supplies to their bands, and often joined with them in their war against the planters and the Confederacy. A worried Confederate officer wrote in August 1864 that "many deserters . . . are collected in the swamps and fastnesses of Taylor, LaFayette, Levy and other counties, and have organized, with runaway negroes, bands for the purpose of committing depredations upon the plantations and crops of loyal citizens and running off their slaves. These depredatory bands have even threatened the cities of Tallahassee, Madison, and Marianna." That same month came word that a band of "500 Union men, deserters, and negroes were . . . raiding towards Gainesville."[134]

Such alliances had been forming for some time. As early as April 1862, a Confederate general urged Florida's governor to declare martial law in Nassau, Duval, Clay, Putnam, St. John's, and Volusia counties "as a measure of absolute necessity, as they contain a nest of traitors and lawless negroes." So did many other parts of the South. In North Carolina, a Randolph County woman wrote that "our negroes are nearly all in league with the deserters." From Wilmington came warnings of interracial bands raiding between Fayetteville and Lumberton. St. Landry Parish in Louisiana was home to a united anti-Confederate band of whites and blacks. In north Georgia, former slaves who had liberated themselves joined Jeff Anderson's band of raiders operating in the mountains around Dahlonega.[135]

So numerous were interracial bands in the Wiregrass region of southeast Alabama that the governor called it "the common retreat of deserters from our army, tories, and runaway negroes." Slaves who did not run away could be just as dangerous to slaveholders as those who did. Those belonging to Columbus Holley of Dale County, in the heart of Alabama's Wiregrass country, made that clear. Holley was known to pass any knowledge he had of area deserters on to authorities. John Ward, leader of a local deserter gang, hatched a plan to kill him for it. Holley's slaves were eager to help. On the designated evening, two of them met Ward at a rendezvous point not far from the plantation, lifted him from his horse, and carried him on their shoulders to Holley's bedroom window. With one shot, Ward killed Holley as he slept. The slaves then carried Ward back to his horse, and he made a clean getaway. Because Ward's feet never touched the ground, there was no scent for the bloodhounds to follow. The only tracks near the house were those of the slaves, but no one thought of that as unusual. Their footprints were all over the plantation. Besides, the slaves owned no guns. And they kept the secret to themselves. The mystery of Holley's murder remained unsolved until years after the war, when Ward finally confessed on his deathbed.[136]

Slaveholder fears of lower-class cooperation across racial lines had been on the rise throughout the late antebellum era. Those fears helped drive them to establish a Confederate slaveholders' republic in which they hoped resistance might be more easily controlled. Far from making control easier, though, secession gave rise to new opportunities for resistance, especially among the slaves.

4

"Yes, We All Shall Be Free"

"I can just barely remember my mother." That was what Tom Robinson, born into slavery on a North Carolina plantation, told an interviewer for the 1930s Federal Writers Project. He was only ten years old when sold away from his mother shortly before the war started. "But I do remember how she used to take us children and kneel down in front of the fireplace and pray. She'd pray that the time would come when everybody could worship the Lord under their own vine and fig tree—all of them free. It's come to me lots of times since. There she was a'praying, and on other plantations women was a'praying. All over the country the same prayer was being prayed."[1]

Secession and war served only to make such prayers more expectant and intense—and to make slaves more rebellious. Despite efforts to conceal the war's implications from them, slaves had many ways of learning about what its outcome could mean for them. Years after the war, Hattie Nettles of Opelika, Alabama, remembered climbing a fence as a young girl to watch Confederate soldiers pass by. She did not know where they were going at first, but it was not long before she found out. Mary Gladdy, a Georgia freedwoman, recalled "the whisperings among the slaves—their talking of the possibility of freedom." Anne Maddox heard a great deal of talk about Abraham Lincoln from older slaves on her Alabama plantation. So did Louis Meadows, who was well aware that Jefferson Davis intended to keep him and his friends enslaved. "That was why," Meadows said, "everybody hoped Master Lincoln would conquer."[2]

Throughout the war, slaves met in secret to hold prayer meetings for freedom. According to Mary Gladdy, those on her plantation gathered in their cabins two or three nights a week for such meetings. They placed large pots against the doors to keep their voices muffled. "Then," she said, "the slaves would sing, pray, and relate experiences all night long. Their great, soul-hungering desire was freedom." Those few slaves who could read kept up with events through pilfered newspapers and spread the word to their neighbors. As news of Confederate reversals became more frequent, excitement among the slaves grew. Young Ella Hawkins of Georgia heard the older slaves whispering among themselves, "Us is gonna be free! Jes as sho's anything. God has heard our prayers; us is gonna be free!" When a white minister preached that slavery was ordained by God and prayed aloud for Him to drive the Yankees back, one Georgia slave prayed silently to herself, "Oh, Lord, please send the Yankees on."[3]

In her reminiscences of the war years, Susie King Taylor wrote vividly of the excitement among her Savannah neighbors: "Oh, how those people prayed for freedom! I remember, one night, my grandmother went out into the suburbs of the city to a church meeting, and they were fervently singing this old hymn,—"

> Yes, we all shall be free,
> Yes, we all shall be free,
> Yes, we all shall be free,
> When the Lord shall appear,—

Suddenly local lawmen burst in and arrested the entire congregation for "planning freedom." They further accused the slaves of singing "the Lord" instead of "Yankee," as King recalled, "to blind any one who might be listening."[4]

Enslaved blacks were not simply waiting for either God or the Yankees to give them freedom. They were taking it for themselves. Though Lincoln's Emancipation Proclamation is often referred to as having "freed the slaves," it only grudgingly recognized what blacks had themselves already forced on Lincoln's government. The document, as Professor Ira Berlin points out, "heralded not the dawn of universal liberty but the compromised and piecemeal arrival of an

Susie King Taylor escaped from Savannah with other members of her family in April 1862. She took refuge on the South Carolina coast with a newly formed Union regiment made up of former slaves. Taylor served the regiment for the rest of the war by washing, cooking, nursing, and teaching (she had secretly learned to read and write while enslaved). Though one of many thousands of black women to serve with Union regiments, she was the only one to leave a published memoir of her wartime experience. Photo from Taylor, *Reminiscences*.

undefined freedom. Indeed, the proclamation's flat prose, ridiculed as having the moral grandeur of a bill of lading, suggests that the true authorship of African American freedom lies elsewhere—not at the top of American society but at the bottom." Union General John Logan admitted as much when he wrote of the slaves and their resistance efforts: "It is not done by the army, but they are freeing themselves."[5]

Slaveholder Laura Comer illustrated Logan's point when she wrote in her diary: "The servants are so indolent and obstinate it is a trial to have anything to do with them." Slaves resisted slavery by feigning ignorance or illness, sabotaging plantation equipment, and roaming freely in defiance of the law. A Confederate officer in Charleston complained that "gangs of negroes" who should have been at work on fortifications were "idle" on city streets. One disturbed white passenger on a southwest Georgia rail line was astonished to see "crowds of slaves in gayest attire" getting on and off the trains "at every country stopping place." In Houston, Texas, a newspaper editor wrote with worried amazement that blacks were refusing to step aside for whites on city streets and sidewalks.[6]

As for forced labor, what work slaves did was done with measured effort. Some refused to work at all. A Georgia plantation mistress wrote of one of her slaves: "Nancy has been very impertinent. . . . She said she would not be hired out by the month, neither would she go out to get work." Another Georgia woman wrote to her husband: "We are doing as best we know, or as good as we can get the Servants to do; they learn to feel very independent." In Louisiana, one slaveholder told another that his slaves would not even pretend to work. From New Orleans, a newspaper correspondent wrote in September 1862: "There is no doubt that the negroes, for more than fifty miles up the river, are in a state of insubordination. . . . The slaves refuse obedience and cannot be compelled to labor." So resistant were slaves becoming to enslavement that a South Carolina woman wrote in 1863: "If this war lasts two year longer, African Slavery will have ceased in these states."[7]

Such a situation hardly squared with the "faithful slave" image, though slaveholders continued to press it publicly. But what they would not say in public they had to admit among themselves. So pervasive and open was slave resistance that many slaveholders seemed resigned to it. In South Carolina, a plantation mistress wrote to her mother that slaves knew the war provided opportunities for them that "must be taken advantage of. . . . Times and slaves, have changed." Catherine Edmondston wrote from her North Carolina plantation: "As to the idea of a *faithful servant, it is all a fiction*." In a letter to a friend, one Alabama slaveholder admitted that "the 'faithful slave' is about played out."[8]

"I Fear the Blacks More Than I Do the Yankees"

Tension between slaves and slaveholders hung over the South like a storm cloud whose lightning could strike anywhere at any time—and slaveholders knew it. Despite their public insistence that slaves were generally content, slaveholders knew better than anyone besides the slaves themselves that discontent was the norm. That was certainly clear to Jane Eubanks of Columbia County, Georgia, who wrote to Governor Brown about needing men assigned to control local slaves. There were four hundred slaves in her vicinity and few white men to keep them subdued. In December 1863, Mrs. John Green of Burke County wrote to Brown about the lack of white men in her area, most of them forced away by the draft. She urged Brown to create a police force for the protection of Georgia's "planting interest." Green insisted that Brown must "see to it, that [the planter] class of citizens are protected."[9]

Eubanks and Green were hardly alone in worrying about the possibility of slave rebellion. "It is dreadful to dwell on insurrections," wrote a South Carolina slaveholding widow. Still, she could not ignore the risk. "Many an hour have I laid awake in my life thinking of our danger . . . we know not what moment we may be hacked to death in the most cruel manner by our slaves." The danger for some slaveholders was real enough. Early in the war, another widowed Carolina slaveholder was smothered to death by her slaves. When she heard of the murder, Ada Bacot wrote of her own slaves: "I fear twould take very little to make them put me out of the way." Mrs. A. Ingraham of Vicksburg shared Bacot's concerns: "I fear the blacks more than I do the Yankees." A Virginia woman felt that having slaves was like having "enemies in our own households."[10]

Sensing a rise in violent tendencies among her slaves, Addie Harris of Alabama wrote: "I lay down at night & do not know what hour . . . my house may [be] broken open & myself & children murdered." Some slaveholders locked up their slaves in their cabins at night. Others shackled slaves with chains. In Georgia, slaveholders were calling on legislators for more slave patrols. The state assembly responded by reinforcing laws forbidding slaves to travel without a pass. It also canceled all exemptions from patrol duty. In frontline or urban areas, Confederate soldiers were diverted to augment slave patrols. In isolated rural regions, some slaveholders hired their own patrols.[11]

C.F. Howell of Jackson County, Mississippi, told his governor in August 1862 that no more men could be spared for military service. Those remaining were all needed to ride patrol over the local slaves. If the army drafted any more men from Jackson County, warned Howell, "we may as well give it to the negroes . . . now we have to patrol every night to keep them down."[12]

But slaves would not be kept down. Such was the force of slave resistance that patrols were losing their power of intimidation. One slave boy who outran patrollers made fun of them after he was safely behind his owner's fence. Some slaves went so far as to fight back.

They tied ropes or vines neck-high across a dark stretch of road just before the patrollers passed by. These traps were guaranteed to un-horse at least one rider. When a group of patrollers broke in on a prayer meeting near Columbus, Georgia, one slave stuck a shovel in the fireplace and threw hot coals all over them. Instantly the room "filled with smoke and the smell of burning clothes and white flesh." In the confusion, every slave got away.[13]

Try as they might, slaveholders had an increasingly difficult time controlling slaves. A Georgia plantation overseer complained by letter to his absentee employer that his slaves would not submit to physical punishment. One slave simply walked away when the overseer told him he was about to be whipped. "I wish you would . . . come down and let the matter be settle," the overseer wrote, "as I do not feel wil-ing to be run over by him." In Texas, a slave threatened with a beating by his owner "cursed the old man all to pieces, and walked off in the woods." He refused to come back until he was promised there would be no punishment. Another slave drew a knife on an overseer who tried to whip him. His owner locked him up and placed him on a bread-and-water diet. Such punishment did little to suppress rebel-lion. It only made slaves press even more persistently for freedom. "I am satisfied that his imprisonment has only tended to harden him," one overseer wrote soon after releasing an unruly slave. "I don't think he will ever reform."[14]

Besides being terribly painful, whipping was for slaves a key symbol of their lowly social status. It is hardly surprising, then, that resistance to whipping became one of the main ways slaves sought to demon-strate a measure of independence. Such resistance could be dangerous. Some planters were known to turn their dogs on slaves who refused to be whipped. Others, like a man on the Hines Holt plantation in Geor-gia, were shot for it. The slave had fought off six men who tried to hold him down.[15]

Despite such dangers, slaves gauged their chances and continued to resist. When a Tennessee slaveholder tried to whip a teenage slave, the youth threw him down, grabbed an ax, and ran off. In Choctaw County, Mississippi, slaves turned the tables on their master, Nat Best, subjecting him to five hundred lashes. One day while hoeing in the fields, a Georgia slave named Sylvia was told by an overseer to take her clothes off when she got to the end of a fence row. She was going to be whipped for not working fast enough. When the overseer reached for her, she grabbed a wooden rail and broke it across the man's arms. Another slave named Crecie, described as "a grown young woman and big and strong," was tied to a stump by an overseer named Sanders in preparation for whipping. He had two dogs with him in case Crecie resisted. When the first lick hit Crecie's back, she pulled up the stump and whipped Sanders and his dogs.[16]

Sanders was fortunate to escape Crecie's wrath with his life. Some were not so lucky. When one overseer began beating a young slave girl with a sapling tree, another slave grabbed an ax and killed him. It was with good reason that, as a Texas slaveholder wrote, "a great many of the people are actually afraid to whip the negroes." When one overseer whipped a slave, the victim's comrades made a rope from their cotton suspenders and hanged the overseer. *The Mobile Advertiser and Register* told of a slave who had poisoned his owner. Texas bondsmen killed an overseer known for "meanness over the slaves." In Virginia, a band of slaves armed with shotguns killed two planters returning to their homes. After Mississippi slaveholder Jim Rankin returned from the army "meaner than before," as one of his chattels told it, a slave "sneaked up in the darkness an' shot him three times." Rankin lingered in agony the rest of the night before he died the next morning. "He never knowed who done it," one slave recalled. "I was glad they shot him down."[17]

Few slaves actually tried to kill their owners, a fact that one student of the war years attributed to "civilized restraint." But from the beginning of the war, slaveholders feared that increasing insubordination might lead to a violent slave uprising. As early as May of 1861, an Alabama planter urged the men in his district to stay at home and save their families "from the horrors of insurrection." Southwest Georgia's *Albany Patriot* complained that area blacks would "congregate together contrary to law, *exhibit their weapons*, and no doubt devise their secret, but destructive plans."[18]

During the late spring and early summer of 1861, a rebellion hysteria swept across large parts of the South's plantation belt, southwest Georgia included. Slaveholders in the large plantation districts along the Chattahoochee and Flint rivers were especially distraught. Panic spread through Decatur County in June when one of the local slave patrols caught a slave named Israel away from his plantation without a pass. Israel's capture led the patrollers to believe that a general slave revolt involving slaves from plantations all over the county was about to break out. Rumors spread that blacks in the county seat of Bainbridge were collecting firearms and planning to "kill all of the men and old women and children and take the younger ones for their wives." Two suspected insurrection leaders were arrested. Local whites swore that they would be killed if they ever got out of jail. By midsummer, insurrection mania had died down, but slaveholder fears of rebellion remained constant. William Mansfield wrote Governor Brown that slaveholders in Stewart County were terrified of their slaves, fearing that local militiamen were not "prepared to quell any riots that might begin." A Fort Gaines man asked the governor for a company of cavalry to protect slaveholders in southwest Georgia from the general slave rebellion that he felt sure was coming.[19]

Throughout the war, rebellions and rumors of rebellions kept slaveholders constantly on alert. In Richmond, a black saloon waiter named Bob Richardson was thrown in Castle Thunder for plotting a slave uprising. Slaves in Monroe County, Arkansas, laid plans to rise up and kill local slaveholders. Several slaves were arrested. Three— two men and a girl—were hanged. In the area around Natchez, Mississippi, slaves on a number of plantations laid plans to kill their owners and set themselves free. When word leaked out, local whites hanged at least forty blacks and tortured many more. Sometimes authorities did not move quickly enough. Slaves in Yazoo City, Mississippi, did rise up, setting a fire that destroyed the courthouse and fourteen other buildings. A similarly dangerous plot was discovered near Troy, Alabama, in which a number of whites were implicated.[20]

"They Will Help the Negroes"

It was not uncommon to find whites involved with rebellious slaves. From the war's early months, so strong was anti-Confederate sentiment among southern whites that many were perfectly willing to work with blacks in undermining the government. December 1861 brought word from north Georgia's Gordon County to the governor's office of local Unionists holding secret meetings and organizing a military force to protect themselves from Confederate authorities. They swore to resist attempts to draft them into the Confederate army. And they swore to aid the Federals. Most troubling was that the Unionists "say in case of an insurrection they will help the Negroes."[21]

In July 1861, the *Columbus Sun* reported that a vigilance committee in southwest Georgia's Mitchell County had uncovered plans for a slave uprising to be led by several local whites. James Patillo, William McLendon, Samuel Edwards, Romulus Weeks, Stephen G.W. Wood, John C. Morgan, and Ephraim McLeod were all named as conspirators. According to the *Sun*, Patillo was to supply the slaves "with as much ammunition as he possibly could to butcher the good citizens of the county." Patillo, McLendon, Weeks, Morgan, and McLeod all got the lash for their crimes and were expelled from the county. Edwards and Wood escaped a whipping but were ordered never to set foot in Mitchell County again "under the penalty of death."[22]

In the spring of 1862, three white men in neighboring Calhoun County tried a similar scheme. Mindful of the previous year's failed attempt in Mitchell County, Harvell Scaggs, William Scaggs, and Giles Shoots, all citizens of Calhoun County, sought out federal help to back the venture. Traveling down to the Gulf Coast under pretense of making salt, the trio contacted Union blockaders. Soon they were running "superior new guns" to slaves in Calhoun County. The plot came to light in June, and the three men were sentenced "to receive a sound whipping, to be tarred all over, and then ordered to quit the State." Some thought the punishment much too light. A local editor asked, "Is it safe to the community to suffer such inhuman wretches, such dangerous animals, to go at large?" He suggested changing the sentence to life in prison or, better yet, execution.[23]

John Vickery and three slaves got just that when they tried to instigate a slave uprising in south Georgia's Brooks County. Vickery was a local white man of modest means for whom no evidence can be found of prior trouble with the law. In fact, Vickery is found on Brooks County jury lists in 1863. However, he next appears in the records on August 23, 1864, at the end of a hangman's rope. Details of events leading to his execution vary, but all sources agree that Vickery, with the assistance of local slaves, organized an insurrectionary force that intended to murder some of the county's wealthier planters.

After killing the planters and stealing whatever weapons they could find, the conspirators next planned to set the county seat of Quitman afire and seize the local rail depot. From there they would head south toward Madison, Florida, then seize and burn that town. Hoping to be reenforced by deserters and Union troops on the Gulf Coast, the men would return to Quitman, from where they could control the region.

Slaves plotted rebellion, sometimes with the help of whites. As early as July 1861, seven local whites in Mitchell County, Georgia, were found helping to plan a slave uprising. Next year in neighboring Calhoun County, three whites were discovered running guns to slaves in preparation for a revolt. Similar plots were discovered in Adams County, Mississippi, Taylor County, Florida, and Columbia, South Carolina—all involving whites. In Brooks County, Georgia, a local white man and three slaves were lynched for their part in a conspiracy. After such executions, the bodies were often left to rot where they hung as a warning example. Illustration from Ellis, *Thrilling Adventures*.

On the eve of the planned uprising, local authorities learned of its details from a slave arrested for theft. After forcing information out of other slaves, the Brooks County police patrol arrested Vickery and three of the leading slave co-conspirators.

It is hardly surprising that Vickery's plan involved Confederate deserters and Union troops from Florida. As early as January 1863, Confederates were warned that Dead Man's Bay on the Gulf Coast should be considered a prime target for a Union invasion. Dead Man's Bay was in Taylor County, a stronghold of Unionists and deserters who would be willing to help Union troops. The ground was firm, no natural obstructions blocked the roads between the bay and the interior, and there was a direct route from the bay to Madison, Florida. Just such a landing occurred one week prior to the planned Vickery uprising. Eight hundred Union troops disembarked at the mouth of the Aucilla River with another five hundred at Dead Man's Bay. It is possible these were the men that Vickery and his allies were to meet at Madison and lead back into south Georgia.

After Vickery's arrest, the Brooks County home guard determined to use the conspirators as warning examples against further plots. A home-guard court convened to try the case, although it had no authority to do so. Governor Brown had specified that either county inferior courts or state militia courts would try all cases resulting from police-patrol arrests. But Brooks County, for that day at least, was controlled by the home guard. Vickery and his three slave co-conspirators stood little chance of acquittal. After a mock trial, the court presented its findings: John Vickery—guilty of arson, inciting slaves to insurrection, and aiding slaves to flee to the Yankees; the slave Sam—guilty of insurrection and inducing slaves to insurrection; the slave Nelson—guilty of insurrection; and the slave George—guilty of insurrection. All were condemned to death by hanging. At six o'clock that evening the sentence was carried out on the courthouse square.[24]

Despite the dangers, many white southerners continued to help blacks when they could. A few did so for pity's sake, others for profit, and still others because they would take any chance to undermine planter rule. Robert Bezley of Atlanta was arrested in December 1862 for giving fraudulent passes to slaves. In Shelby, North Carolina, a white man was hanged for the same crime. A white stonecutter was found heading a slave insurrection plot in Columbia, South Carolina. Officials in Adams County, Mississippi, discovered a cache of guns stored by slaves in preparation for a rebellion. At least one white man was implicated in the affair.[25]

Some white farmers gave escaped slaves safe haven in exchange for work on their lands. Others gave them cash for stolen plantation supplies, no questions asked. A white merchant in Plymouth, North Carolina, worked out a deal with local slaves to buy goods stolen from their owners' plantations; the deal fell through when word of it leaked out. In some cases, blacks were such valuable trading partners that whites would take great risks to preserve the connections. In Granville

County, North Carolina, two whites helped a black man named Kearsey break out of jail so he could maintain the extensive trading network he controlled.[26]

Such cooperation, however, was by far the exception. Though most whites never wanted secession and eventually turned against the Confederacy, they remained committed to keeping the South a white man's country and to keeping blacks "in their place." That some whites were willing to help blacks usually said more about how they felt about slaveholders than slaves. Southern blacks were more often left to help each other or help themselves.[27]

One slave who had learned to write forged a pass and made his way from Richmond north to federal lines. Another slave journeyed five hundred miles, writing his own passes along the way. Some slaves did not have quite that far to go. In northern Missouri, the free state of Iowa was right next door. So common was it for slaves to cross the border during the war that many slaveholders either moved south or had their slaves "sold down the river." Joe Johnson was a Missouri slave who feared that fate. So he hid his family in a wagon, slipped past the slave patrols, and kept going until he reached the Iowa border. For slaves in Texas, the route to freedom most often led south to Mexico. "In Mexico you could be free," recalled a former Texas slave. "They didn't care what color you was, black, white, yellow, or blue. Hundreds of slaves did go to Mexico and got on all right." Another freedman remembered that slave patrols constantly rode the Rio Grande during the war, but hundreds of slaves got through their lines and crossed the river.[28]

Slaves trapped farther east in the heart of Dixie had a much harder time making their way to free territory. That had always been true but was even more so during the war. With whites using greater vigilance, escaping slaves took greater risks. In South Carolina, William and Anne Summerson risked suffocation by having themselves packed in rice casks and shipped out of Charleston. In March 1864, several slaves struck out from Floyd County, Georgia, headed for Union lines in Tennessee. Slave catchers cornered two of the fugitives just short of the state line. Both were suffering from exposure and frostbite. One later died from the ordeal.[29]

Many escaping slaves found it simpler and safer to stay close to home. After a severe beating, one Georgia slave ran away and dug out a sizeable cave in which he took up residence. A short time later, under cover of night, he crept back to his old plantation, packed up his wife and two children, and took them back to his cave, where they all lived until the war's end.[30]

Fugitives often banded together for mutual support and protection. They sustained themselves by living off the land and making raids against local plantations—the very plantations on which they had labored without pay for years. In their view, it was time for back pay. S.S. Massey of Chattahoochee County, Georgia, complained to the governor that runaway slaves were "killing up the stock and stealing ever thing they can put their hands on." In Blakely, Georgia, the *Early County News* reported in March 1864 that there had been "more *stealing*, and *rascality generally*, going on in Blakely and Early County, for the past few months, than has ever been known . . . negroes are doing a great deal of this stealing, burning, &c."[31]

The Okefenokee Swamp served as a runaway haven in southeast Georgia. For slaves in the tidewater regions of North Carolina and Virginia, the Great Dismal Swamp offered a refuge. In the North Carolina swamp counties of Camden and Currituck, there was a band of fugitives numbering between five and six hundred who made frequent raids on area plantations and Confederate supply depots. Frightened planters urged authorities to stop the raiders, but rooting them out of their well-defended hideouts was dangerous work. Sometimes it was fatal. In October 1862, a patrol of three armed whites went into the backwoods of Surry County, Virginia, looking for an encampment of about one hundred fugitives. They found the camp but surely wished they had not. None were ever seen alive again.[32]

"Ready to Help Anybody Opposed to the Rebels"

Those slaves who did not escape gave aid to those who did. They funneled food and supplies to their fugitive friends and relatives, passed information to them, and provided a much needed support network. It would have been difficult if not impossible for many fugitive bands to operate effectively without such support. The same was true for bands of white deserters, draft evaders, and their families, who also depended on local slaves for support. Like so many other enslaved blacks, Jeff Rayford did whatever he could to help deserters hiding in the Pearl River swamp of Mississippi. As he told an interviewer years after the war, "I cooked and carried many a pan of food to these men." Another Mississippi freedman recalled carrying food to hideouts where women and children had taken up residence. In Jones County, Rachel Knight, a slave of both white and black ancestry, was a key ally of the deserter gang led by Newton Knight, her owner's grandson. She supplied food for the men and served as a spy in their operations against local Confederates.[33]

Any number of slaves helped their owners and owners' relatives avoid Confederate service. Riley Tirey, one of twelve slaves owned by Robert Guttery of Walker County, Alabama, told how he carried blankets and other supplies to Guttery, who was hiding in the woods, "to help him keep out of the way of the Rebel cavalry." Another Alabama slave, Benjamin Haynes, took provisions to his owner's son, who was "hid out to prevent his being conscripted." Though slaves' motives for rendering such aid were varied, among them was the knowledge that every effort made to help keep anyone out of Confederate service put them a step closer to freedom.[34]

Slaves also welcomed strangers who were trying to avoid Confederate service. Deserters traveling home through the plantation belt knew that slave cabins were their safest bet for food, shelter, and support. One deserter killed Georgia planter William McDonald when

Southern blacks undermined the Confederate war effort whenever they could. They gave refuge to deserters, carried food to deserter gangs and fugitive slaves, spied for the Union army, and aided those headed for Union lines. As a grateful former Union prisoner of war later wrote, "They were always ready to help anybody opposed to the Rebels. Union refugees, Confederate deserters, escaped prisoners—all received from them the same prompt and invariable kindness." Illustration from Browne, *Four Years in Secessia*.

the slaveholder discovered him hiding in his slave quarters. The slaves did not intervene. Nancy Johnson, enslaved on a Georgia plantation during the war, told how "some of the rebel soldiers deserted & came to our house & we fed them. They were opposed to the war & didn't own slaves & said they would die rather than fight. Those who were poor white people, who didn't own slaves were some of them Union people. I befriended them because they were on our side."[35]

Defining white Unionists as being on "our side" became easier for southern blacks as word of the Emancipation Proclamation, effective January 1, 1863, began to spread. Though it did not free all slaves, it did make eventual freedom a direct Union war aim. Like never before, blacks came to identify with the Union cause, with white southern Unionists, and with Union soldiers. But taught from birth to deal cautiously with whites, blacks did not always know what to make of their new allies' motives, nor did they trust them entirely. Still, with freedom and Union joined together, blacks were ready to join with whites in whatever effort might serve the interests of both. As an escaping Union prisoner of war put it, "They were always ready to help anybody opposed to the Rebels. Union refugees, Confederate deserters, escaped prisoners—all received from them the same prompt and invariable kindness."[36]

Once word of emancipation spread, most southern blacks went out of their way to help the Federals every chance they got. Black women in Savannah secretly gave food to Union prisoners. Susie King Taylor, a black Savannah native, wrote of the city's prison stockade as "an awful place. The Union soldiers were in it, worse than pigs, without any shelter from sun or storm, and the colored women would take food there at night and pass it to them through the holes in the fence. The soldiers were starving, and these women did all they could towards relieving those men, although they knew the penalty should they be caught giving them aid."[37]

Blacks also helped imprisoned anti-Confederates escape. Robert Webster, a mulatto barber in Atlanta, helped an aging Tennessee Unionist named William Clift break out of the city's military prison in December 1863. Clift had served as a courier for the Federals in his home state until he was arrested by his own son, Moses Clift, a Confederate cavalry officer. Webster supplied the old man with a rope to use in making his escape. Along their routes of escape, people like Clift could expect to find safe haven and escorts among the slaves.

Nancy Johnson told of a Yankee fugitive who showed up at her doorstep one evening. After keeping him hidden through the next day, she recalled, "my husband slipped him over to a man named Joel Hodges & he conveyed him off so that he got home."[38]

In February 1862, John Ennis, an officer captured at First Manassas, escaped from a South Carolina prison. Making his way north, he happened upon several blacks near Spartanburg who directed him to the cabin of a white Unionist. The man mapped out a route for Ennis across the mountains to Unionists in Tennessee. Henry Estabrooks, a Union prisoner escaping through Virginia, recalled that he could always find shelter at "negro-cabins." He remembered one couple who gave him "a small piece of miserable stuff called bread, and some sour syrup, which I ate ravenously. The food was not fit for swine; but it was the best they had, and I was very thankful for it." They promised Estabrooks a series of guides to escort him along his way, then hid him for the night in a stable loft under piles of straw.[39]

John Kellogg, a Union prisoner escaping through the Georgia mountains with the help of local blacks, was impressed by what he called the slave "telegraph line." Slaves near Carnesville told Kellogg and his comrades of Union troop movements, some at a distance of 150 miles, between Chattanooga and Atlanta. The information was essential to planning the safest route back to federal lines. Union prisoner James Gilmore, who slipped out of Richmond's Libby Prison and made it back to safety with the help of Virginia blacks, made his gratitude clear in a manuscript he authored shortly after the war. Gilmore's publisher, Edmund Kirke, was eager to get it into print. "It tells," Kirke said, "what the North does not as yet fully realize—the fact that in the very heart of the South are four millions of people—of strong, able-bodied, true-hearted people,—whose loyalty led them, while the heel of the 'chivalry' was on their necks, and a halter dangling before their eyes, to give their last crust, and their only suit of Sunday homespun, to the fleeing fugitive, simply because he wore the livery and fought the battles of the Union."[40]

On July 18, 1864, as a Union raiding party approached the outskirts of Auburn, Alabama, a group of local blacks hurried out to warn its commander, Colonel William Hamilton, of Rebels hidden among the thickets ahead. In a charge that "could be better heard than seen," Hamilton and his men rushed the surprised Confederates, who, as Hamilton reported, "broke on our first fire and scattered in every direction."[41]

"It is a matter of notoriety," lamented one high-ranking Confederate official, "in sections of the Confederacy where raids are frequent that the guides of the enemy are nearly always free negroes and slaves." Jim Williams, an escaped former slave from Carroll Parish, Louisiana, led federal troops through the canebrakes of his old haunts to ambush a small Confederate force.[42] In North Carolina, Colonel S.H. Mix of the Third New York Cavalry expressed appreciation to his guide in the form of a certificate, which read:

> Samuel Williams, colored man, served the United States Government, as guide to my regiment out of Newbern, N. C., in the direction of Trenton, on the morning of the 15th of May, and performed effective service for us at the imminent risk and peril of his life, guiding my men faithfully until his horse was shot down under him, and he was compelled to take refuge in a swamp.[43]

Harriet Tubman, famous for her prewar service on the Underground Railroad, headed a ring of spies and scouts who operated along the South Carolina coast. Mary Louveste, an employee at Virginia's Gosport Navy Yard, where the Confederacy's ironclad warship *Virginia* was under construction, smuggled out plans and other documents related to the new secret weapon. She carried the material to Washington, D.C., where she placed it in the hands of Union Secretary of the Navy Gideon Welles. "Mrs. Louveste encountered no small risk in bringing this information . . . and other facts," Welles recalled years later in support of her pension application. "I am aware of none more meritorious than this poor colored woman whose zeal and fidelity I remember and acknowledge with gratitude." There was even a black Union spy in the Confederate White House. Mary Elizabeth Bowser, an associate of Unionist Richmond socialite Elizabeth Van Lew, worked as a maid at the presidential residence. She funneled anything worthy of note to Van Lew, who passed the information on to the Federals at City Point.[44]

A black Virginia couple named Dabney proved to be one of the most innovative spy teams of the war. In early 1863, as Union and Confederate armies eyed each other across the Rappahannock River, they escaped enslavement and the husband found work as a cook and groom for the Federals stationed at the river. He became interested in the army's telegraph system and asked some of the soldiers how it

An enslaved Virginia couple named Dabney escaped in the spring of 1863 and devised one of the most effective intelligence systems of the war. The husband went to work for Federal troops on the Rappahannock River's north side while the wife served as laundress to Confederate officers encamped south of the river. She communicated Rebel troop movements to her husband by way of a clothesline, different colored shirts representing Confederate units and their positions. For weeks leading up the Battle of Chancellorsville, Confederates could not make a move without the Federals knowing about it, thanks to the Dabneys' "clothesline telegraph." Illustration from Wilson, *Black Phalanx*.

worked. Soon after, his wife went back across the lines to get a job doing laundry for a Confederate general. Within a short time, the husband began updating Union officers on Rebel troop movements. The officers were astonished at how accurate the information seemed to be and asked the man how he knew such things. He took them to a hill overlooking the river and pointed across to the headquarters of General Robert E. Lee.

That clothes-line tells me in half an hour just what goes on at Lee's headquarters. You see my wife over there; she washes for the officers, and cooks, and waits around, and as soon as she hears about any movement or anything going on, she comes down and moves the clothes on that line so I can understand it in a minute. That there gray shirt is Longstreet; and when she takes it off, it means he's gone down about Richmond. That white shirt means Hill; and when she moves it up to the west end of the line, Hill's corps has moved upstream. That red one is Stonewall. He's down on the right now, and if he moves, she will move that red shirt.

Blankets with pins at the bottom revealed deceptive troop movements intended to distract Union commanders. During the weeks leading up to the Battle of Chancellorsville, thanks to the Dabneys' clothesline telegraph, Confederates could not make a move without the Federals knowing about it.[45]

"Our Slaves Are Walking Off . . . Every Day"

Very often intelligence came from escaping slaves, who brought news of fortifications, military movements, and Confederate troop strength. One evening near Fortress Monroe, six Virginia slaves arrived behind federal lines with detailed information on Confederate deployments in the region. There were two earthworks guarding approaches to the Nansemond River "about one-half mile apart— the first about four miles from the mouth—both on the left bank. . . . Each mounts four guns, about 24-pounders. . . . The first is garrisoned by forty men of the Isle of Wight regiment, the second by eight. One gun in each fort will traverse; the chassis of the others are immovable." The men went on to give valuable information on major troop deployments: "The Isle of Wight regiment is at Smithfield. The Petersburg Cavalry Company is at Chuckatuck. There are thirteen regiments of South Carolina troops at the old brick church near Smithfield. . . . At Suffolk there are 10,000 Georgia troops."[46]

Sometimes escaping slaves brought more than information. In May 1862, Robert Smalls ran the side-wheel steamer *Planter* with its cargo of ammunition and artillery out of Charleston harbor and turned it over to the blockading Federals. Smalls was a skilled seaman whose owner had hired him out as assistant pilot on the ship. When he learned that General David Hunter, commanding the Federals at Beaufort, had effectively freed all the slaves in his area of operations, Smalls laid plans to escape. On the night of May 12, after his captain and white shipmates went ashore, Smalls and a few other black crewmen fired up the boilers and headed for a nearby wharf where they

In May 1862, Robert Smalls and several other slaves ran the transport steamboat *Planter*, with its cargo of ammunition and artillery, out of Charleston harbor and turned it over to the blockading Federals. Smalls was a skilled seaman whose owner had hired him out to serve as assistant pilot. As the *Planter* came alongside the USS *Onward*, Smalls stepped forward, took off his hat, and called out, "Good morning, sir! I've brought you some of the old United States guns, sir!" Photo from the U.S. Army Military History Institute.

picked up family members. They then headed down the harbor and past Fort Sumter. Guards at outposts along the way, and even those at Sumter, suspected nothing because Smalls knew all the proper signals. And in the darkness, no one ashore could tell that the crewmen waving to them were all black.

Once past Sumter, Smalls ordered full steam and made for the Federals, hoping they would see the old sheet he had hoisted as a white flag of truce. As Smalls approached the first Union vessel he sighted, someone yelled "All hands to quarters!" and the startled Yankees brought their guns to bear on the *Planter*. A member of the federal crew later recalled:

> Just as No. 3 port gun was being elevated, some one cried out, "I see something that looks like a white flag;" and true enough there was something flying on the steamer that would have been *white* by application of soap and water. As she neared us, we looked in vain for the face of a white man. When they discovered that we would not fire on them, there was a rush of contrabands out on her deck, some dancing, some singing, whistling, jumping; and others stood looking towards Fort Sumter, and muttering all sorts of maledictions against it, and '*de heart of de Souf*,' generally.

As the *Planter* came alongside, Smalls stepped forward, took off his hat, and called out, "Good morning, sir! I've brought you some of the old United States guns, sir!"[47]

More and more, in groups large and small, slaves made their way to Union lines. In what historian W.E.B. Du Bois called a general strike against the Confederacy, slaves by the tens of thousands simply walked away from enslavement and announced their freedom to the Union army. As early as summer of 1861, at least fifteen thousand slaves escaped to the Federals. A year later, in North Carolina alone, one Confederate general estimated that slaves worth at least a million dollars had run off. By summer 1862, at least thirty thousand slaves from South Carolina and Georgia had fled to the Union forces occupying those states' coastal regions.[48]

After the Federals took New Orleans and other parts of southern Louisiana in 1862, slaves flocked to their camps. One Union general reported that "they are now coming in by the hundreds nay thousands almost daily. . . . Many plantations are deserted along the coast."[49] A large planter in La Fourche Parish recorded the exodus in his diary.

> October 28, 1862: The negroes are in a very bad way in the neighborhood and I fear will all go off.
>
> October 30, 1862: Found our negroes completely demoralized some gone and some preparing to go. I fear we shall lose them all.
>
> October 31, 1862: The negroes . . . run off. It looks probable that they will all go.
>
> November 2, 1862: Our negroes . . . are still leaving, some every night. The plantation will probably be completely cleaned out in a week.
>
> November 5, 1862: This morning there was a rebellion among the negroes at Mrs. G. Pugh.[50]

Depriving the Confederacy of much-needed labor, escaping slaves made clear how devastating their attitudes and actions were to the Confederate war effort. So many slaves were escaping to the Federals by summer 1862 that Confederate General John Pemberton issued orders allowing only white soldiers to work near Union lines since slaves "could not be trusted to work so near the enemy." He also diverted troops to "prevent the escape of slaves and for protection of persons and property against insubordination of negroes."[51]

Such efforts did little to hold back the flood of refugees, especially after the Emancipation Proclamation took effect in January 1863. Mary Chestnut reflected the dread of many slaveholders when she confided to her diary: "If anything can reconcile me to the idea of a horrid failure after all to make good our independence of Yankees, it is Mr. Lincoln's proclamation freeing the negroes. . . . Three hundred of Mr. Walter Blake's negroes have gone to the Yankees." And the fur-ther Union armies advanced, the more slaves sought their promise of freedom. In 1863, escaping slaves set up camps all around Union posts in Arkansas. By 1864 there were huge refugee settlements at Fort Smith, Van Buren, Little Rock, and Pine Bluff. In December 1864, when Sherman's army moved through Georgia, a single column re-ported seventeen thousand blacks trailing behind.[52]

Even slaves from border slave states, where the proclamation did not apply, were leaving their owners in droves. Maryland's *Baltimore American* reported: "Our slaves are walking off . . . every day. . . . The slightest coercion to compel moderate labor, and they are seized with a desire to walk to a free State." Slaves in Missouri were doing the same, crossing into Kansas by the hundreds. One witness told how "they emigrate during the night, in squads or families, accompanied generally by a span of good mules and a lumber wagon with whatever portables they can seize upon."[53] On a single day in the area of Lex-ington, Missouri, one man recorded the flight in his diary:

> At sunrise this morning Mr Wallace cam over to see if we had lost our team or any thing last night. Told us all of his negros had gone, nine, taken his oxen and wagon. In a short time Mr Bellis cam by, said his waggon harness and hoarses wer stolen last night. I wen in town. Doc Hassell told me all his, two, negros wer gone, Judge Stratton lost all his (two). Brigadire General Vaughn lost two, Mr Parrner, Mr Packard, Mrs White and many others lost thare negros besides many teams wer stolen by them. Mr Musselman came in town and stated abought 80 negros passed his neighbourhood this morning on thare way to Kansas.[54]

Escaping slaves frequently offered their services as soldiers to the Union army, but at first all such offers from blacks—slave or free, South or North—were refused. Though differing with Confederates on the issue of disunion, Lincoln was largely united with them in his racist views. Blacks, he said, simply could not make good soldiers. "If we were to arm them," Lincoln said, "I fear that in a few weeks the arms would be in the hands of the rebels."[55]

Arming blacks would also imply a move toward citizenship for them. Northern upper classes had wanted the war primarily to maintain easy access to cotton-state resources. With the aid of middle- and lower-class nationalism, that was all they set out to do. Since slave labor produced most of the cotton, many feared that the end of slavery might mean the end of cheap cotton. So Lincoln promised that this war would be a white man's war, fought by and for white men. As far as the federal government was concerned, neither slavery nor blacks had any business in the affair. That suited the soldiers just fine, and they were not shy about letting their superiors know it. Within earshot of the White House, they marched into Virginia singing:

> To the flag we are pledged, all its foes we abhor.
> And we ain't for the nigger, but we are for the war.[56]

Field commanders got the message both from the troops and from their superiors. In the fall of 1861, as escaping slaves were filtering into Union camps, Major General Henry Halleck issued orders barring them from federal lines. It was not the army's role, Halleck wrote, "to decide upon the relation of master to man." As far as he and Lincoln were concerned, slaves, like stray cattle, were private property and were to be returned to their legal owners. General William Harney, commanding the Department of the West, dutifully ordered his troops to return runaways. So did Colonel D.S. Miles in Virginia, who ordered one of his subordinates to make sure that any escaped slaves were sent "back to the farm."[57]

Despite Lincoln's efforts not to make slavery a war issue, blacks themselves forced the question by refusing to stay put. The further south Lincoln's army advanced, the more self-emancipated blacks flooded Union lines. And it was impossible to re-enslave them. They simply would not submit to it. "What shall I do with my niggers?" asked the exasperated commander of Louisiana's Fort Macomb in 1862. The commander at Fort Saint Philip was just as perplexed: "I have no authority to feed them. . . . I cannot have them in the fort, and I know not what to do." One officer wrote in his diary that blacks were "coming into camp by the hundred and are a costly curse. They should

In 1861, Lincoln said flatly that he had "no purpose, directly or indirectly, to interfere with slavery in the States where it exists." When fugitives from slavery began flocking to Union lines, federal officers issued orders sending them "back to the farm." But they would not go there. Northern whites came to fear that if slavery were not abolished in the South, the North would soon be "overrun by escaped fugitives." By their own persistence, enslaved men and women forced emancipation on a reluctant administration and made the war a struggle against slavery. Photo from the Library of Congress.

be kept out or set at work, or freed or colonized or sunk or something." The post commander at Point Lookout, Maryland, complained in September 1862 that slaves were "continually crossing over from the Eastern shore of Va., and coming in from Md., all getting within our lines, by landing on the beech, until the number is greater than we know what to do with."[58] By the war's second year, it was becoming clear that this war for the Union was inevitably a war against slavery. Blacks were seeing to that whether whites wanted it or not.

There was pressure for emancipation on the northern home front too. Abolitionists had been lobbying for emancipation from the war's beginning with little success. But news of so many black refugees coming into Union lines sparked a new concern among white northerners. If the war ended with slavery intact, would the slaves go back to their former owners? Yankee troops had already tried and failed to force them back. George Boutwell, former governor of Massachusetts, warned in the summer of 1862 that if slavery were not abolished, the North would soon be "overrun by escaped fugitives." A New Bedford editor expressed the same fears in August, telling his readers that, far from encouraging black migration north, emancipation was the "only possible way to *avert* the threatened influx."[59]

His fears seemed to be confirmed a few weeks later when General John A. Dix reported to Secretary of War Edwin Stanton that contrabands in Virginia were suffering terribly. Poorly fed and clothed, crowded into shacks and tents, they were dying "by the hundreds and thousands." The army was simply not equipped to care for them all. So Dix asked permission to contact Governor John Andrew of Massachusetts as well as the governors of other northern states and arrange temporary asylum and employment for the refugees. When word of the plan reached Massachusetts, whites howled in protest. Opposition was especially fierce among Republicans, who accused Dix of saddling their party with the stigma of encouraging black migration to the North. Governor John Andrew, a longtime abolitionist, took the lead in arguing that black refugees must remain in the South. Within weeks of Dix's request, Andrew was in Washington telling administration officials face-to-face that Massachusetts would not be a haven for escaped slaves. Silence among white abolitionists confirmed the widespread hostility toward black refugees and went a long way toward defeating Dix's plan to resettle freedom-seeking blacks. "Massachusetts don't want them," declared the editor of Springfield's *Daily Republican*. "No free state wants them."[60]

Pushing for a policy of racial containment, northern whites from a broad range of political affiliations pressured Lincoln to keep blacks in the South. Republicans and War Democrats in Congress who supported ending slavery as a necessary war measure put pressure on Lincoln as well. Some even argued that escaping slaves ought to be enlisted and put on the front lines. Battle and desertion had depleted Union ranks, and few white volunteers were willing to replenish them. In the summer of 1862, Congress forced Lincoln's hand. It passed the Militia Act, authorizing black enlistment under white officers, and the Second Confiscation Act, freeing all slaves owned by pro-Confederate slaveholders. The Second Confiscation Act left in doubt the future of blacks in the United States since it also called for their deportation abroad, or colonization. But it left no doubt that Congressional Republicans meant to end slavery among the Rebels and keep black migration to the North in check.[61]

Though the act's intent was clear, its enforcement would be unwieldy. Determining the difference between those slaveholders who had engaged in disloyal acts and those who had not would be almost impossible. Moreover, Lincoln feared that to enforce the act might cause more white soldiers to desert. Emancipation might even push the remaining loyal slave states—Missouri, Kentucky, and Maryland—out of the Union. "I would do it," Lincoln confessed late that summer, "if I were not afraid that half the officers would fling down their arms and three more states would rise."[62]

Lincoln also worried that an emancipation announcement coming after a string of military defeats in the summer of 1862 would make his government look weak and desperate. But the Battle of Antietam changed that. On September 22, just days after the Army of the Potomac turned back a Rebel advance near the western Maryland village of Sharpsburg, Lincoln issued his preliminary Emancipation Proclamation. Effective January 1, 1863, slaves held in areas still in rebellion against the United States would be free. The Proclamation was a tentative document that freed only slaves it could not immediately reach; slaves in the "loyal" slaveholding states and parts of Confederate states already under Union control were not affected. It was "a necessary war measure," Lincoln wrote, meant primarily to undermine the rebellion. And it encouraged black "colonization," Lincoln's ultimate solution to the "negro question." But to ease enforcement, it went further than the Second Confiscation Act in promising freedom to all slaves held in rebellious regions, not just those held by rebellious slaveowners. Most importantly, it turned the Union army into a force for liberation and called on blacks themselves to join that force.[63]

"Liberty Is What We Want"

The Emancipation Proclamation had its intended effect on African American men. Eager to enlist, they poured into recruiting offices across the North and flocked to Union lines across the South. Frederick Douglass was among the most enthusiastic supporters of black enlistment. "The iron gate of our prison stands half open," he told African Americans as he urged them to arms. "One gallant rush . . . will fling it wide." Two of Douglass's sons joined that rush, along with more than two hundred thousand other black men who served in the Union's land and naval forces. Over 80 percent of them were from the southern states. Nearly all of those had been slaves. But no longer. "Once let the black man get upon his person the brass letters, 'U.S.,'" Douglass proclaimed, "let him get an eagle on his buttons and a musket on his shoulder and bullets in his pocket, and there is no power on earth which can deny that he has earned the right to citizenship." Prince Rivers, a self-emancipated sergeant in the First South Carolina Volunteers, made clear what that meant to him: "Now we sogers are men—men de first time in our lives."[64]

Despite the enthusiasm of men like Rivers, there were some former slaves who were reluctant to exchange one kind of servitude for another, much less fight for the Union. Recruiters in Kansas sometimes had difficulty finding volunteers among refugee slaves. In South Carolina, Union General David Hunter so often resorted to heavy-handed coercion in trying to get recruits for his first black regiment that some of the conscripts quickly deserted. When blacks enlisted, they did so for their own reasons. "Liberty is what we want and nothing shorter," wrote an anonymous black soldier in Louisiana. "We care nothing about the union. we have been in it Slaves for over two hundred And fifty years."[65] At a "war meeting" of former slaves on Geor-

Members of the 107th Regiment, United States Colored Troops, organized at Louisville, Kentucky, and photographed here at Fort Corcoran, Virginia. Over two hundred thousand African Americans served with the Union's land and naval forces during the Civil War. More than three-fourths of them were southerners, most formerly enslaved. Late in the war, Lincoln confessed that the Union could not have been preserved without their service. "Any different policy in regard to the colored man," Lincoln wrote, "deprives us of his help. . . . Keep it and you can save the Union. Throw it away, and the Union goes with it." Photo from the Library of Congress.

gia's St. Simons Island, a northern correspondent witnessed several speakers, including one black man, trying to draw new recruits.

> They were asked to enlist for pay, rations and uniform, to fight for their country, for freedom and so forth, but not a man stirred. But when it was asked them to fight for themselves, to enlist to protect their wives and children from being sold away from them, and told of the little homes which they might secure to themselves and their families in after years, they all rose to their feet, the men cam forward and said "I'll go," and the women shouted, and the old men said "Amen."[66]

Sidney Joyner enlisted with the Second North Carolina Regiment, United States Colored Troops (USCT) for the express purpose of marching south and freeing his wife and child from bondage in Louisiana. In September of 1863, members of the Louisiana Native Guards, USCT, got permission to go on recruiting detail. They had more on their minds than recruiting soldiers. With signed passes in hand, they swept through southern Louisiana freeing slaves and taking them back to New Orleans. When slaveholders protested that they were loyal Unionists in Union-held territory and that the Emancipation Proclamation did not apply there, the soldiers leveled their rifles and threatened to shoot anyone who stood in their way. At one plantation in St. Bernard Parish, five soldiers marched on their old master's house and freed their wives.[67]

The slaveholder was fortunate that he suffered only the loss of a few slaves. He might have suffered much worse, and some did. Sam Miller was one of several former slaves who, as soldiers in a Union raiding party operating along the Georgia coast, burned down the mansion of his former owner, Captain William Brailsford. Sam, who earlier had been whipped severely by Brailsford, said after the raid, "I feel a heap more of a man." William Harris of the First Regiment, USCT, gave his former master a lashing so violent that "blood flew at every stroke." Harris then turned the whip over to three female slaves who "took turns in settling some old scores." Fortunately for slaveholders, such retribution was the exception rather than the rule. Most black soldiers were far more concerned with ending slavery than taking revenge on slaveholders. When slaveholders fell under the control of former slaves, violence rarely came of it.[68]

Major William Holden learned that firsthand, much to his relief. Henry, a former slave of his who had run off to join the Union army after Holden whipped him, came marching back one day leading a dozen more black soldiers. As a young slave who witnessed the homecoming later recalled:

> Now ole Major was sitting in his favorite chair on the porch when he saw Henry coming with those soldiers and he like to fell, he was that scairt. . . . poor ole Major thought Henry remembered that whipping. But Henry drew the men up in front of ole Major and he said, 'This is my master, Major Holden. Honor him, men.' And the men took off their caps and cheered old Major. And he nearly like to fell again— such a great big burden was off his shoulders then.

The soldiers took their seats at Holden's dining-room table, where his wife served them a roast chicken feast. For a former slave, to be served at his old master's table, something that would ever have seemed impossible, brought a satisfaction that few but those once held in bondage could understand. For Henry, it was an image he could forever hold in his mind as a sign that his freedom was real.[69]

The image of what that freedom might ultimately mean was not an easy one for whites to form, even those serving alongside blacks. Most white Union soldiers came to abolitionism grudgingly. Some refused to call themselves abolitionists at all. "I am no abolitionist," insisted a Fifty-fifth Ohio enlistee, "in fact dispise the word." But he came to feel that "as long as slavery exists . . . there will be no permanent peace for America. . . . Hence I am in favor of killing slavery." An Indiana sergeant wrote to his wife that although he could not care less for blacks, he would support the Emancipation Proclamation "if it will only bring the war to an end any sooner . . . anything to beat the South."[70]

Jacob Allen, a young abolitionist in the Union army, knew how his comrades felt about blacks and worried that their new antislavery feelings might not last. "Though these men wish to abolish slavery," he wrote to noted abolitionist William Lloyd Garrison, "it is not from any motive outside of their own selfishness; and is there not a possibility that at some not very distant day, these old rank prejudices, that are now lulled to sleep by selfish motives, may again possess these men and work evil?"[71] Frederick Douglass was worried too. What the government could do, it could undo. Might emancipation be in danger if the political winds turned against it? Barely a month after the proclamation took effect, Douglass voiced his concern before an assembly in New York.

> Much as I value the present apparent hostility to Slavery at the North, I plainly see that it is less the outgrowth of high and intelligent moral conviction against Slavery, as such, than because of the trouble its friends have brought upon the country. I would have Slavery hated for that and more. A man that hates Slavery for what it does to the white man, stands ready to embrace it the moment its injuries are confined to the black man, and he ceases to feel those injuries in his own person.[72]

For the moment, though, the greater threat to blacks was the Confederate government. On January 5, 1863, four days after Lincoln signed the Emancipation Proclamation, Jefferson Davis issued an enslavement proclamation under the heading "An Address to the People of the Free States." White northerners, he charged, had "degraded" themselves by allying with blacks. His government, on the other hand, would maintain white dignity by robbing all blacks of their freedom. As of February 22, 1863, Davis declared, "all free Negroes in the Southern Confederacy shall be placed on the slave status, and deemed to be chattels, they and their issue forever." Any black Union soldiers captured in combat would be subject to enslavement and their white officers subject to execution as leaders of servile insurrection.[73]

That was, of course, assuming that black regiments would ever see combat. So strong was prejudice against their abilities among most Union generals that it seemed as if black soldiers might never be used for any but menial tasks. "I won't trust niggers to fight," insisted General William T. Sherman. "Can they improvise bridges, sorties, flank movements, etc., like the white man?" he asked. "I say no." Blacks should, he said, "be used for some side purposes and not be brigaded with our white men." Many other officers felt the same way. They used black soldiers as a labor force for building fortifications, hauling carts, or digging latrines—anything that might rob them of an opportunity to earn the respect that came with service in combat. In some regiments, the colonel was "Ole Massa." Squads were "work gangs" and their officers "nigger drivers." The soldiers may as well have been slaves.[74]

"Remember Fort Pillow"

There were some white officers in black regiments committed to earning respect for their men, and they pushed hard for combat assignments. They made the most of their opportunities when they came. On May 27, 1863, the Louisiana Native Guards, composed for the most part of recently freed blacks, participated in an assault against Confederate fortifications on the Mississippi River at Port Hudson, twenty-five miles north of Baton Rouge. In an after-action report, one of the Guard's white lieutenants admitted that he had entertained some fears as to his men's "pluck"—"but I have now none," he added. "Valiantly did the heroic descendants of Africa move forward cool as if Marshaled for dress parade, under a most murderous fire from the enemies guns . . . these men did not swerve, or show cowardice. I have been in several engagements, and I never before beheld such coolness and daring. Their gallantry entitles them to a special praise. And I already observe, the sneers of others are being tempered into eulogy." Even Colonel Charles Paine, until then a determined opponent of using blacks in combat, had to admit that "the darkies fought well."[75]

A few days later, on June 7, two regiments of former slaves fended off attacking Rebels at Milliken's Bend, a federal stronghold on the

On June 7, 1863, two regiments of former slaves fended off attacking Confederates at Milliken's Bend, a federal stronghold on the Mississippi River just north of Vicksburg. One Union official reported that "the sentiment in regard to the employment of negro troops has been revolutionized by the bravery of the blacks in the recent Battle of Milliken's Bend. Prominent officers, who used in private to sneer at the idea, are now heartily in favor of it." Blacks received grudging admiration even from Confederates. One Rebel soldier wrote after the battle that his black foes fought "with considerable obstinacy, while the white or true Yankee portion ran like whipped curs." Illustration from *Harper's Weekly*.

Mississippi River just north of Vicksburg. "I never more wish to hear the expression, 'the niggers won't fight,'" wrote Union Captain M.M. Miller after the battle. One official reported to the War Department that "the sentiment in regard to the employment of negro troops has been revolutionized by the bravery of the blacks in the recent Battle of Milliken's Bend. Prominent officers, who used in private to sneer at the idea, are now heartily in favor of it."[76]

The notion that blacks lacked the discipline for soldiering was dealt a further blow on July 16 when the Fifty-fourth Massachusetts fought off a Rebel charge on James Island just south of Charleston, South Carolina. The regiment suffered nine killed, thirteen wounded, and seventeen missing in action—but it held fast. An even tougher test came two days later when the Fifty-fourth spearheaded an assault on Fort Wagner, which guarded the southern approach to Charleston harbor. Though the effort to take Wagner failed, it was not from a lack of trying. Six hundred men of the Fifty-fourth went in on the assault. Forty percent of them were captured, killed, or wounded. One of the most severely injured was Sergeant William Carney, who had retrieved a U.S. flag and carried it back with him despite wounds to his head, chest, right leg, and arm. He became the first of twenty-three black soldiers awarded the Congressional Medal of Honor during the war.[77]

Blacks sometimes received grudging admiration even from Confederates. After the engagement at Milliken's Bend, one Rebel soldier wrote that his black foes fought "with considerable obstinacy, while the white or true Yankee portion ran like whipped curs." Such observations provide evidence that the respect soldiers often displayed across the lines could be displayed toward black soldiers as well. One Yankee wrote of his surprise when Confederates agreed to a picket-line truce with black soldiers facing them. "The rebels and our colored soldiers now converse together on apparently very friendly terms, and exchange such luxuries as apples, tobacco, and hard tack, by throwing them to each other. It was hardly deemed possible that the enemy could be induced to refrain from firing on black troops wherever they could be seen."[78]

But Rebel commanders usually wanted their men to kill as many black troops as possible, at times including those who could have been taken prisoner. Despite the government's official policy that captured blacks were to be enslaved, the unofficial policy of many Confederate officers was that blacks in uniform should be shot on sight, even those trying to surrender. Still, some Rebels balked at such barbarism. At Milliken's Bend, they took blacks as prisoners rather than murder them in cold blood. One officer recalled hearing his men shout during the battle that surrendering blacks should be spared. When General Edmund Kirby Smith heard that so many blacks had been captured alive, he told one of his commanders: "I hope this may not be so, and that your subordinates who may have been in command of capturing parties may have recognized the propriety of giving no quarter to armed negroes and their officers." Rebel deserters later testified that three days after the battle, they saw black prisoners executed.[79]

Such atrocities took place in numerous engagements. Shortly after the Port Hudson battle, Confederate cavalry captured twenty-two black Union soldiers and killed them all. A Rebel lieutenant boasted of killing thirteen himself. In Arkansas, at the Battle of Poison Springs, eyewitnesses reported black prisoners of war being "murdered on the spot." The same occurred at the Battle of Saltville in Virginia. When Fort Williams fell to the Rebels in North Carolina, a Union lieutenant recalled that "the negro soldiers who had surrendered were drawn up in line at the breastworks and shot down as they stood." During the Battle of the Crater outside Petersburg, Virginia, attacking Confederates ran their bayonets through wounded black soldiers.[80]

At Tennessee's Fort Pillow, a federal outpost manned primarily by former slaves along with white southern Unionists, Rebel troopers under General Nathan Bedford Forrest forced their way in, then ruthlessly cut down their prisoners. Confederate Sergeant Achilles Clark vividly recalled the massacre: "The slaughter was awful. Words cannot describe the scene. The poor deluded negroes would run up to our men fall upon their knees and with uplifted hands scream for mercy but they were ordered to their feet then shot down. The white men fared but little better. Their fort turned out to be a great slaughter pen. Blood, human blood stood about in pools and brains could have been gathered up in any quantity." A few Confederate officers, and Clark himself, tried to stop the killing but got no support from Forrest. After the massacre, an enthused Forrest called Fort Pillow a clear demonstration that "negro soldiers cannot cope with Southerners."[81]

Following the Battle of Olustee, west of Jacksonville, Florida, victorious Confederates roamed among the wounded Federals, shooting every black soldier they could find. When William Penniman of the Fourth Georgia Cavalry rode up to ask what the men were doing, an officer replied, "Shooting niggers, Sir." Penniman protested that it was shameful to murder wounded prisoners, but the killings continued. One Georgia soldier later recalled: "How our boys did walk into the niggers, they would beg and pray but it did no good." The next day, Penniman rode over the battlefield. "The results," he said, "of the previous night became all to[o] apparent. Negroes, and plenty of them, whom I had seen lying all over the field wounded, and as far as I could see, many of them moving around from place to place, now . . . all were dead. If a negro had a shot in the shin, another was sure to be in the head."[82]

Ultimately, the take-no-prisoners policy worked more against Confederates than for them. When word of the murders spread, black soldiers began to fight with a fiery rage that astonished friend and foe alike. The Rebels, recalled one Union officer, "fear them more than they would fear Indians." A white cavalryman from Maine wrote home after one engagement that he saw black troops shooting Confederates who were trying to surrender. "The officers had hard work to stop them from killing all the prisoners," he recalled. "When one of them would beg for his life the niggers would say remember Port Hudson." After a company of black cavalrymen surrounded a band of Confederate guerrillas, someone shouted "Remember Ft. Pillow." The blacks captured seventeen prisoners, then shot them dead. A white officer in one black regiment wrote home to his wife that some of his men had killed five captured Confederates. "Had it not been for Ft Pillow," he lamented, "those 5 men might be alive now. . . . It looks hard but we cannot blame these men much."[83]

Indeed, few of their comrades faulted black soldiers for giving no quarter to men that they believed would give them none. The general rule was kill or be killed. Even for those blacks who survived initial captivity, life as a prisoner of war was always brutal and often brief. Private Joseph Howard of the 110th Regiment, USCT, wrote of his experience: "We were kept at hard labor and inhumanely treated. . . . If we lagged or faltered or misunderstood an order we were whipped and abused. . . . For the slightest causes we were subjected to the lash [and] we were very poorly provided for with food." Medical care for black prisoners was even more poorly provided. Often they could not get any at all. An inmate at Andersonville witnessed the treatment of one black captive who fell into Rebel hands after the Battle of Olustee: "One fellow had a hand shot off and some deranged brutes had cut off his ears and nose. The doctors refused to dress his wounds or even amputate his shattered arm; he was naked in the prison and finally died from his numerous wounds." Blacks held in Confederate prison camps died at a rate of 35 percent, more than twice the average for white captives.[84]

"Fearlessly and Boldly"

Despite their hard feelings on the matter, Confederate officers could not help but be impressed with the effectiveness of black soldiers. It was they and their men, after all, who had been on the receiving end of black fighting skill. After Port Hudson, Milliken's Bend, and Fort Wagner, some Confederates began to consider putting that skill to work for the Confederacy. A few had seen its potential from the start. As early as July 1861, General Richard Ewell told Jefferson Davis that there was only one way the Confederacy could secure its independence—"Emancipating the slaves and arming them." As the war dragged on, more officers came to agree with Ewell. By late 1863, perhaps half the army had deserted. If a way could not be found to fill the ranks, the war was all but lost.

Irish-born General Patrick Cleburne, commanding a division in the Army of Tennessee, urged filling empty ranks with black troops. In January 1864, he pointed out that "for many years, ever since the agitation of the subject of slavery commenced, the negro has been dreaming of freedom. . . . To attain it, he will tempt dangers and difficulties not exceeded by the bravest soldiers." Already blacks were fighting "bravely," as Cleburne stressed, for their freedom in the Union cause. Why not use that bravery to Confederate advantage?[85]

Southern slaveholders were overwhelmingly opposed to placing weapons in the hands of their slaves. They feared not only the loss of their "property" but also what slave conscription would mean for the future of the Confederacy and slavery itself. Howell Cobb summed up such concerns when he insisted that "you cannot make soldiers of slaves. . . . The day you make soldiers of them is the beginning of the end of the revolution."[86]

Aside from threats to the Confederacy's cornerstone institution, there was the question of whether giving guns to slaves would make them Confederates. It was an unlikely assumption. To Georgia's

Columbus Times editor, J.W. Warren, the idea seemed ridiculous. He was certain that slaves would never fight for the Confederacy even if they were freed. Warren's great fear was that blacks would join the Yankees as soon as they reached the front lines. If the slaves were armed, he warned, "We will ourselves, take the best in the country, drill and train them, and then hand them over—ready made warriors—to the enemy."[87]

Slaves themselves confirmed that notion. "Only let them give us arms," said one slave, "and we will show them who we will fight for." Another slave was more direct: "*My* master wouldn't be wuff [worth] much ef I was a soldier." Slaves saw that talk of the Confederacy arming them was the desperate act of a failed government in any case. "The slaves know too well what it means," said an elderly black woman. The Confederates would "never put muskets in the slaves' hands if they were not afeared that their cause was gone up. They are going to be whipped; they are whipped now."[88]

With a quarter million of its men dead and two-thirds of its soldiers absent by late 1864, the Confederacy was indeed gone up. But its leaders were not yet prepared to admit it. Grasping at an illusory last straw, in January 1865 General Robert E. Lee wrote to a friend that although he considered "the relation of master and slave . . . the best that can exist between the white and black races while intermingled as at present in this country," slaves had already been freed and used by Lincoln to crush the Confederacy. Why should the Confederacy not use them in its own defense? He urged the Confederate Congress to authorize slave enlistments immediately and adopt a plan for "gradual and general emancipation" following the war.[89]

Lee's men had mixed views on the matter. A month after the commanding general penned his sentiments, a North Carolina sergeant wrote that men in his company were deserting over talk of freeing blacks and putting them in the army. He too was considering it. "I did not volunteer my services to fight for a free negroes country," he insisted. But a Louisiana sergeant took a more practical view: "If we continue to lose ground as we have for the last 12 months, we will soon be defeated, and then slavery will be gone any way, and I think we should give up slavery and gain our independence." General John B. Gordon polled his corps outside Petersburg and found that most of its 8,600 officers and men favored enlisting blacks even if it meant emancipating them. Howell Cobb suspected that the men supported black enlistment mainly because they thought it might better their chances of getting a furlough or discharge.[90]

Still, there were those who refused to support making blacks soldiers for any reason, though they were no less eager to get home. Grant Taylor wrote home to his wife: "To think we have been fighting four years to prevent the slaves from being freed, now to turn round and free them to enable us to carry on the war. The thing is outrageous. . . . I say if the worst comes to the worst let it come and stop the war at once and let us come home."[91] One way or another—with or without black enlistment, with or without victory—soldiers just wanted to go home.

On March 13, 1865, at the urging of General Lee and President Davis, the Confederate Congress finally authorized recruitment of up to three hundred thousand slaves. The legislation made no mention of freedom for those who agreed to serve, insisting that both the states and slaveholders must consent to any alteration in the legal standing of slave soldiers. But in his General Order No. 14 implementing the program, Davis went a step further, stating that "no slave will be accepted as a recruit unless with his own consent and with the approbation of his master by a written instrument conferring . . . the rights of a freedman." It was not quite an Emancipation Proclamation. But it was a startling statement from the man who had for four years presided over a slaveholders' republic. And it was a frank admission that blacks had long since become, as one southern editor put it, "a sort of balance power in this contest, and that the side which succeeds in enlisting the feelings and in securing the active operation and services of the four millions of blacks, must ultimately triumph."[92]

The observation contained a great deal of truth, but the Confederacy came to realize it far too late. No more than a few dozen blacks were ever enlisted under its banner. Sixty from Richmond's Jackson Hospital came under fire at Petersburg on March 11, 1865, as members of the Jackson Battalion, composed of three companies of white convalescents and two companies of black hospital workers. That was two days before the Confederate Congress authorized black enlistments. On very rare occasions throughout the war, blacks such as those at Jackson Hospital had been pressed into combat service, often with guns at their backs and their families held hostage in slavery. But no black units ever saw combat as Congressionally authorized Confederate soldiers. No regiments of Confederate States Colored

Troops were ever formed. By contrast, over two hundred thousand blacks had joined Union forces by March 1865. Hundreds of thousands more were already free. They needed no favors from a near-dead Confederacy to secure that freedom. They were taking full measure of it themselves, especially black Union soldiers. One spoke with pride about how he had, "for once in his life . . . walked fearlessly and boldly through the streets of [a] southern city! And he did this without being required to take off his cap at every step, or to give all the side-walks to those lordly princes of the sunny south, the planters' sons!"[93]

5

"Now the Wolf Has Come"

For the South's other "persons of color," the southern Indians, both those in the southern states and in Indian Territory (now Oklahoma), loyalties were often more difficult to sort out. Many tried to steer a neutral course. But caught as they were "between two fires," southern Indians were usually forced to weigh their options and, often against their better judgement, choose sides.

In South Carolina's tiny Catawba band, numbering just fifty-five, almost every adult male at one time or another served in the Confederate army. Long since stripped of their own land, most Catawbas were day laborers working plantation lands that had once belonged to their ancestors. The enlistment bounty of $50 was very attractive for these impoverished and dependent men. They were too few to form a company of their own, and there were no "colored" units in the Confederate army for them to join, so they fought alongside their white neighbors in several South Carolina regiments of the Army of Northern Virginia. These were among the Civil War's few racially integrated units.[1]

Some southern Indians, more isolated and less dependent on the whites, were more successful in avoiding military entanglements. The Florida Seminoles, left to themselves nearly two decades earlier after fending off efforts to root them out, deftly maintained neutrality while allowing both the Union and the Confederacy to court them. In exchange for gifts and supplies, they shrewdly held out the possibility of an alliance without ever committing to either side.[2]

Others tried to remain neutral with less success. In Virginia's tidewater region, descendants of the once powerful Powhatans—the Pamunkey, Mattaponi, Chickahominy, Gingaskin, Nansemond, and Rappahannock Indians—had little love for the Virginians who had stripped them of nearly all their lands and stigmatized them as "free persons of color." With the war's outbreak, the Powhatans tended to remain at least nominally neutral. But when Union forces arrived in the spring of 1862, they found ready allies among the Powhatans. Many served the Federals as river pilots, land guides, and spies. They led gunboats and supply vessels as far as one hundred miles inland along the navigable waterways of eastern Virginia.[3]

The Lumbees of eastern North Carolina at first declared neutrality but became solidly pro-Union after Confederates began conscripting them to do forced labor, essentially enslaving them. Lumbee guerrilla bands took revenge by raiding local plantations, attacking Confederate supply depots, tearing up rail lines, and doing whatever else they could to disrupt Rebel operations. Most notable of the Lumbee bands was the one led by Henry Berry Lowry, whose exploits became the stuff of legend. Called The Robin Hood of Robeson County, Lowry became, in the words of one Lumbee scholar, "a folk hero to his people, a symbol of pride and manhood."[4]

The Confederacy also tried to conscript some Indians to serve as soldiers, though they proved to be no less resentful than those conscripted for forced labor. In the spring of 1863, Eastern Choctaws drafted into the First Choctaw Battalion, Mississippi Cavalry, deserted en masse to the Federals just before the Vicksburg Campaign got under way.[5]

In western North Carolina, some members of the Eastern Cherokee band expressed a willingness to serve with the Confederacy, but racism nearly kept them out of the ranks. William Thomas, an influential friend of the Cherokees, tried to get a state bill passed authorizing him to raise a Cherokee battalion. The legislature voted it down, citing fears that such a bill might confer citizenship on the Cherokees. In fact, the Cherokees were already citizens of North Carolina, though rarely treated as such, by virtue of previous treaty agreements. One of the bill's leading opponents quipped that he would as soon be seen alongside free blacks at a voting booth as to associate with

Called the Robin Hood of Robeson County, Henry Berry Lowry became a legendary folk hero among the Lumbee Indians of eastern North Carolina. The Lumbees at first declared neutrality. But when Confederate officials tried to conscript them for forced labor, men like Lowry formed guerrilla bands and went to war against the Confederacy. They raided plantations, attacked supply depots, and tore up rail lines. Among the Lumbee guerrillas, Lowry stood out as the most active and aggressive. Wrote one Lumbee educator: "While the name meant lawlessness and terror to the white community, it meant more truly a man who fought oppression to the Indians." Portrait from the North Carolina Department of Archives and History.

Cherokees. Undeterred by the setback, Thomas sought Jefferson Davis's permission to enlist Cherokees. Davis readily agreed, giving Thomas a colonel's commission and authorizing him to raise several battalions, one of which was made up entirely of Cherokees. From early 1862 through the war's end, Thomas's Legion of Cherokee Indians and Highlanders ranged through the mountains of western North Carolina and eastern Tennessee enforcing conscription, impressing supplies, and rooting out Union sympathizers.[6]

Many of those Union sympathizers were themselves Cherokee, deserters from Thomas's Legion among them. By 1863, Cherokee soldiers' families were feeling the effects of war. Hunger stalked the Cherokee district as corn meal, flour, and salt became almost impossible to get. In February 1864, Thomas wrote to his superiors that his soldiers' families were "now in a starving condition" and begged assistance for them. Already they were reduced to eating weeds and tree bark. This situation, Thomas warned, "if not arrested will produce much disloyalty to the South." It did. As with so many other Rebel soldiers, hard times turned hundreds of Cherokees against the Confederacy. Some deserted and moved their families out of the region. Others switched sides and joined the Federals. One group of Cherokees aided Union Colonel George Kirk during his raid through the Carolina mountains in June 1864. From then until the war's close, they served in Kirk's Third North Carolina Mounted Infantry Volunteers.[7]

"Our Wish Is for Peace"

Further west, peoples of the Indian Territory, often called the Nations because it was occupied by several Indian nations, were also divided in their views about which side to support. Most had no great love for white southerners. It was they, after all, who now occupied the home-lands from which most Indian Territory residents had been removed just a generation earlier. On the other hand, it was the hated govern-ment in Washington that had forced their removal from the East. If the Rebels could make good their independence from Washington, perhaps the Indians could, too. Supporting the Confederacy might be a first step toward reestablishing sovereign nationhood for themselves. Besides, Indian Territory was slave territory, and some of the Nations' most influential chiefs were slaveholders. But nonslaveholders, with a majority of close to 90 percent, were inclined to shy away from the Confederacy. Still, they also had issues with the Federals. For years, corrupt Indian agents appointed from Washington had swindled the Indians out of supplies, annuities, and anything else they could get their hands on. Some in Washington set their sights on Indian land as well. For years, Republican leaders had openly supported settling whites in Indian Territory despite treaties guaranteeing Indian land rights. Now Republicans controlled Washington, and many Indians feared another forced removal if they remained in the Union.[8]

The climax came in early 1861 when Washington withheld annuity payments due under treaty obligations for fear that the funds might fall into Rebel hands. Furthermore, to consolidate their forces in the East, federal troops evacuated their garrisons in the Nations. Without military protection, newly appointed U.S. Indian agents refused to en-ter the Indian Territory. It seemed to the Indians that Washington had abandoned them. Some feared a Confederate invasion; others thought the time was right to make a bid for independence. Whatever their motives, and most were mixed, the Choctaws were first to act. Their council authorized its chief to assure the seceded states that their "nat-ural affections, education, institutions, and interests" were with the Confederacy. Then the Chickasaw council issued its own Declaration of Independence and made clear its support for Confederate independence as well.[9]

Richmond seized the opportunity and sent Albert Pike, a well-known Arkansas editor and attorney, to negotiate alliance treaties in Indian Territory. By July, the Choctaw and Chickasaw councils were firmly in the Confederate camp. The two nations signed treaties with Pike and organized a mounted rifle regiment for Confederate service. In exchange, they got better terms than they had ever received from the United States. Under the new treaties, Richmond assumed all financial obligations of old agreements with the United States, guaranteed tribal land rights, promised the Nations self-government within their territorial boundaries, and let the Indians send delegates to the new Confederate Congress.[10]

Though Richmond's terms seemed more friendly than Washington's, whites could no more be trusted in the South than in the North. Pike had taken pains to portray himself as the Indians' benefactor and the Confederacy as their protector. But in a letter to Jefferson Davis, Pike spoke of the Indian Territory's agricultural fertility and its mineral resources, and of how the Confederacy could use them to its advantage with or without Indian consent. The "concessions" made to the Indians, Pike wrote, "are really far more for *our* benefit than for *theirs*; and that it is *we* . . . who are interested to have this country . . . opened to settlement and made into a State"—a state to be populated mainly by free whites and enslaved blacks.[11]

The Chickasaws and Choctaws were quickest to be lured in by Pike, largely because of geography. Both nations had lands bordering the Red River, the boundary they shared with Texas, and were more isolated from Union-held Kansas. Other tribes needed more convincing. John Ross, principal chief of the Cherokees, tried for months to steer a neutral course. In May 1861, Ross issued a Proclamation of Neutrality committing the Cherokees to a policy of "non-interference in the affairs of the people of the States and the observance of unswerving neutrality between them." He wrote to Confederate officials, "I am—the Cherokees are—your friends and the friends of your people, but we do not wish to be brought into the feuds between yourselves and your Northern Brethren. Our wish is for peace. Peace at home and Peace among you." Confederate Commissioner of Indian Affairs David Hubbard wrote asking Ross to reconsider, arguing that southerners had always been more honorable in their dealings with Indians than had northerners. To that claim Ross replied, "But few Indians now press their feet upon the banks of either the Ohio or Tennessee."[12]

Ross was supported in his opposition to a Confederate alliance by members of the Keetowah faction, made up mostly of nonslavehold- ing full-bloods who advocated traditional Cherokee ways. Also known as Pin Cherokees for the crossed pins they wore as insignia, the Kee- towahs generally held mixed-bloods and slavery in low regard, though Ross himself was a mixed-blood slaveholder of only one-eighth Cherokee ancestry. As the secession crisis engulfed the nation during the winter of 1860–61, about two-thirds of the Keetowahs formed a Loyal League to oppose any ties with the Confederacy.

Opposing the Keetowahs and Loyal League was the Blue Lodge, or Knights of the Golden Circle, composed mainly of mixed-bloods. The Knights were firmly proslavery, writing into their organizational constitution that "no person shall be a member . . . who is not a pro- slavery man." Though slavery was now the primary divisive issue, ani- mosities between the two factions went back to removal days, when most full-bloods refused to go voluntarily while the mixed-bloods were more willing to deal with their white cousins. Led by Stand Watie (ironically, at only one-quarter short of full-blood, more ethni- cally Cherokee than Ross), the Blue Lodge pressed for a Confederate alliance to help protect them "from the ravages of abolitionists." In early summer, with help from Confederate gunrunners, Watie unoffi- cially organized and armed a regiment of three hundred mixed-blood Cherokees for Confederate service. Watie himself was now a colonel in the Confederate army.[13]

By July, tempers within the Cherokee Nation had reached the boiling point. Ross and his allies were infuriated that Watie, without the council's permission, had violated the Neutrality Proclamation and placed Cherokees in Confederate service. That month, a com- pany of Watie supporters tried to raise a Confederate flag at Webber's Falls. When a mob of about 150 full-bloods assembled to stop the proceedings, violence appeared inevitable. Captain John Drew, who had once commanded a Cherokee home force, rushed in to negotiate a truce. Though Drew had connections to the Ross faction, he was generally respected by other Cherokees as well. Drew's reputation and diplomatic skills served to avoid bloodshed between his brethren that day.[14]

John Ross, principal chief of the Cherokees, tried to steer a neutral course. "I am—the Cherokees are—your friends," he told Confederate officials, "but we do not wish to be brought into the feuds between yourselves and your Northern Brethren. Our wish is for peace." But Union withdrawal from Indian Territory (now Oklahoma) in 1861 forced tribal leaders into Confederate alliances. When the Federals tried to return, many Indians switched sides, and the territory became a bloody killing ground. Photo from the National Anthropological Archives.

The alliance issue came to a head in August 1861 at a Cherokee national conference. John Ross presided. Watie was there as well, accompanied by over fifty armed members of his Confederate Cherokee regiment. Joseph Crawford, former federal agent to the Cherokees, attended to argue for a Cherokee alliance with the Confederacy. No U.S. agents were there to oppose him. By that time the Rebels had turned back a major Union advance at Bull Run. Only days earlier, on August 10, the Union had suffered defeat again at the Battle of Wilson's Creek in Missouri, just across the border from Cherokee lands in Indian Territory. Some of Watie's men, though not Watie himself, had helped beat back the Federals at Wilson's Creek and were credited with a pivotal role in the Rebel victory. It appeared that the Confederacy had all but secured its independence, and with the help of Cherokees at that.[15]

To most Cherokees assembled at Tahlequah, the path of wisdom seemed clear. Washington had abandoned them, and the Confederacy offered better terms. Already Indian Territory was bounded on three sides by the Confederacy, and hundreds of Cherokees under Watie were serving in the Confederate army. John Ross himself bowed to what seemed inevitable, pointing out that "the Indian Nations about us have severed their connection with the United States and joined the Confederate States. Our general interest is inseparable from theirs and it is not desirable that we should stand alone." His overriding objective was unity among the Cherokees as well as the Nations. "Union is strength," he wrote, "dissension is weakness, misery, ruin." The Keetowahs reluctantly agreed. On October 1, 1861, the Cherokees met with Albert Pike at Tahlequah and bound themselves to the Confederacy. As a demonstration of solidarity, Ross publicly shook hands with Stand Watie. Ross also offered for Confederate service the Cherokee home-guard regiment, manned primarily by full-blood Keetowahs under Ross's ally, Colonel John Drew.[16]

Also signing with the Confederacy at Tahlequah were bands of Osage, Quapaw, Seneca, and Shawnee Indians, all of them previously forced to settle in Indian Territory after expulsion from their homelands. Pike was in high spirits. Already he had secured treaties with most of the Indian Territory's western tribes, among them bands of Tonkawa, Caddo, Waco, Wichita, and Comanche. It seemed that all the Territory Nations, along with their various factions, would soon fall in line and support the Confederacy. The major remaining holdouts were a faction of Creeks, together with some of their close cousins, the Seminoles.[17]

"Sad at All the War Talk"

When the Creeks (or Muskogees in their own language) signed a treaty with Pike on July 10, 1861, and placed a Creek regiment in Confederate service, they had been among the first of the Nations to do so. However, that treaty was supported only by mixed-blood tribal leaders, among them Motey Kennard, Chilly McIntosh, and Daniel McIntosh. No full-blood chiefs, who generally opposed a Confederate alliance, had been present. They had been away at the Antelope Hills conference, a meeting of delegates from all the major nations in Indian Territory called to discuss their position toward war. When they returned, three of their chiefs discovered that their names had been forged on the Confederate alliance treaty.[18]

What divided the mixed- and full-bloods among the Creeks reflected divisions between those of other tribes. And their feud went all the way back to pre-removal days when mixed-bloods, especially the McIntosh, frequently betrayed their own people in favor of the whites. The full-blood Creek Chief Opothleyahola, an old but still energetic man of eighty in 1861, remembered well how the McIntosh and their mixed-blood allies had fought alongside whites against their brethren during the Creek War of 1813–14. He would never forget how William McIntosh helped General Andrew Jackson slaughter his kinsmen at the Battle of Horseshoe Bend. Nor would he forget how the McIntosh had bargained away Muskogee lands in the East for personal gain.[19]

There were also serious divisions among the Seminoles, most of whom were ethnically Muskogee. Pro-Confederate tribal leaders like John Jumper, an ordained minister, not only signed on with the Confederacy but also eagerly recruited Seminoles to enlist with the Creek regiment. But Billy Bowlegs and others among the more traditionalist chiefs rebuffed Pike's overtures and refused to take sides. They followed the lead of Opothleyahola, who had long counseled Indian neutrality. His heart, recalled a Creek resident of the Nations, "was sad at all the war talk. He visited the homes of his followers or any of the Indians and gave them encouragement to face all these things, but above all things to stay out of the war." At a council of the Nations, Opothleyahola urged his fellow Indians to hold themselves above "this white man's war." It came as a painful blow to him when Ross finally sided with the Confederacy. Still, the old chief refused to give in.[20]

At an August 1861 convention of anti-Confederate Creeks, Opothleyahola and other Creek leaders—among them Oktarharsars Harjo (better known as Sands), White Chief, and Bob Deer—declared the Confederate alliance treaty void and refused to recognize the authority of those chiefs who had signed it without National Council approval. They selected Sands to serve as acting principal chief and established a Creek government of their own.[21]

By September, more than seven thousand Indians—women and men, young and old, all forced to accept war or exile—gathered on the Little River near Opothleyahola's lands. Most were Creeks and Seminoles. There were antiwar Indians from other tribes, too, among them bands of Chickasaw, Kickapoo, Shawnee, Delaware, Wichita, and Comanche. They were doing well for the moment, but winter was coming, and the refugees needed help. That help was due them from the federal government, and Opothleyahola wrote to "the President our Great Father" reminding Lincoln of his treaty obligations.

> You said that in our new homes we should be defended from all interference from any people and that no white people in the whole world

should ever molest us . . . the land should be ours as long as the grass grew or waters run, and should we be injured by anybody you would come with your soldiers & punish them . . . now the wolf has come, men who are strangers tread our soil, our children are frightened & the mothers cannot sleep for fear. . . . When we made our Treaty at Washington you assured us that our children would laugh around our houses without fear & we believed you. . . . We do not hear from you & we send a letter, & we pray you to answer. Your children want to hear your word. . . . I well remember the treaty. My ears are open & my memory is good.[22]

Lincoln's ears were not 0open. Opothleyahola received no reply.

More antiwar Indians joined Opothleyahola over the next few months. November found nearly nine thousand of them encamped on the banks of Little River. There they planned to wait out the war. Though Opothleyahola refused to meet with Confederate officials, lest he be suspected of collusion, he did send word that he and his followers posed no danger to the Confederacy. That message was confirmed by Captain James McDaniel, a Confederate Cherokee, who advised leaving the neutrals in peace. Still, this nonaligned enclave in the heart of Indian Territory worried Confederate officials. Could it become a recruiting ground for the Federals? Already it was a haven for runaway slaves. Might those freedmen arm themselves and spread slave revolt among the Nations? There was no evidence of such a plan. But Colonel Douglas Cooper, commanding Confederate forces in Indian Territory, decided that the risk was too great. He called his Indian troops together for a campaign against the "Unionists" on Little River. With his Choctaw-Chickasaw and Creek-Seminole regiments, along with cavalry from Texas, Cooper set out promising either to compel Opothleyahola's submission or drive him and his people from the territory.[23]

Warned of Cooper's planned attack, the old chief and his followers broke camp and struck out for Kansas. It was an arduous journey. Cold and hunger took their toll, but it was the pursuing Confederates that made the trek most deadly. In late November, Cooper caught up with the refugees at Round Mountain, just northwest of Tulsa, and charged their camp. Opothleyahola's men ambushed the attackers, then set the prairie on fire to cover their retreat as they broke camp and headed north. Cooper stayed in hot pursuit. Reinforced by John Drew's mostly Keetowah Cherokee regiment, Cooper again sighted his prey on December 8 at Bird Creek. He ordered an assault for the next morning. During the night, though, nearly all of Drew's Cherokees deserted. Undeterred by this reduction in force, Cooper stuck to his plan, and on December 9 his remaining troops went in on the assault. Unexpectedly, out on Cooper's right, the Texans began taking heavy fire on their flank. It was a group of the missing Cherokees, over four hundred of them, who were now fighting for Opothleyahola and his refugees. The Texans reeled back but refused to break. Fighting continued, neither side giving way, until night made it impossible to tell friend from foe. Reluctantly, Cooper moved his men back to camp five miles from the battle site. Opothleyahola's men broke off as well and continued their flight to Kansas.[24]

Short on supplies, Cooper fell back to Fort Gibson near the Cherokee capital of Tahlequah. There he was met by a force of nearly 1,400 Texas and Arkansas cavalrymen, many of them veterans of Wilson's Creek, commanded by Colonel James McIntosh (no relation to Chilly or Daniel). He and Cooper together laid plans to pursue the refugees. But, still plagued by desertions among the Indians, mainly the Cherokees, Cooper's command had to be left behind. On December 22, McIntosh's force set out after Opothleyahola. Four days later, McIntosh and his men fell on the refugees at Shoal Creek (or Hominy Creek). Unable to beat back the battle-hardened veterans, the Indians scattered, leaving behind much of their livestock, wagons, and supplies. The Confederates rode after the panicked Indians, cutting down scores of them from behind with sabers or shooting them in the back. Stand Watie and his Cherokees, who had arrived on the field as combat was winding down, joined the pursuit.[25]

About four thousand survivors, less than half the refugees' original number, struggled on toward Kansas in scattered groups. Many had no wagons or livestock. Some were without food, and others walked over frozen ground with bare feet. Old people died. Children died. Babies were born and died of exposure. Warriors died defending their kin as Rebel cavalry continued to hound the fleeing Indians. On December 31, Texas troopers caught up with a small band of Creeks, Osages, and Cherokees. They killed the men and captured their families. What was left of John Drew's regiment attacked a group of their fellow Cherokees, killing one man and taking several prisoners. A detachment led by Colonel Cooper attacked refugee

Opothleyahola, the staunchly anti-Confederate Creek chief, seen here in younger days. He was eighty years old but still energetic when the war came. Nearly ten thousand anti-Confederate Indians, seeking safety in numbers, gathered around his home in the late summer and fall of 1861. Opotheyahola wrote to Lincoln asking for help but received no reply. Under threat of Confederate attack, he led his followers north to Kansas, harassed by Confederates all along the journey. Thousands were killed, and Opothelyahola was spent. He died shortly after reaching Kansas. Illustration from the University of Oklahoma Libraries.

Creeks encamped on the Arkansas River. One warrior was killed. Over twenty women and children were captured. Finally, harsh winds and freezing temperatures forced the Confederates to turn back. The refugees struggled on northward leaving trails of frozen bodies in their wake.[26]

In January 1862, the first of Opothleyahola's remaining followers staggered into Kansas, where they were finally able to set up camp in relative safety. But the effort to get there had cost them dearly. Soon after the Indians' arrival, a visiting federal agent reported on their journey to his superiors.

> Their march was undertaken with a scanty supply of clothing, subsistence, and cooking utensils, and entirely without tents, and during their progress they were reduced to such extremity as to be obliged to feed upon their ponies and dogs, while their scanty clothing was reduced to rags, and in some cases absolute nakedness was their condition. Let it be remembered that this retreat was in the midst of a winter of unusual severity for that country, with snow upon the prairie. Many of their ponies died of starvation. The women and children suffered severely from frozen limbs, as did also the men. Women gave birth to their offspring upon the naked snow, without shelter or covering, and

in some instances the new-born infants died for want of clothing, and those who survived to reach their present location with broken constitutions and utterly dispirited.

Among those whose health was destroyed by the ordeal was Opothleyahola. Sick with fever as he tried to make arrangements for supplying his people shortly after they got to Kansas, the old chief collapsed and died.[27]

"A Very Destitute Condition"

Though the campaign to drive out Opothleyahola's followers rid the Indian Territory of a major anti-Confederate element, its brutality served only to weaken Confederate support among the Indians. Hundreds of Cherokees had deserted to the Union side, and more were deserting every day. Most had been reluctant Confederates to begin with. One Texas Confederate serving in the Nations wrote: "I do not like to fight with the Indians very much, for you do not know at what moment they will turn over to the opposite side."[28]

During the winter of 1861–62, Colonel Cooper wrote to his superiors begging for reinforcements from Arkansas. The Indians were drifting away from their ranks so fast that Cooper feared anti-Confederate factions might gain control in the Nations if Arkansas troops were not sent in. Already civil war was breaking out that winter among the Cherokees. Trying to keep the peace among his people, John Ross offered amnesty to those who had deserted, even if they had gone to the Union side. The move infuriated Confederate Cherokees, especially those of Watie's regiment.

In February 1862, one of Watie's patrols caught a Cherokee named Arch Snail who had deserted Drew's regiment but later rejoined his unit. As the patrol was making its way back to camp, several of Snail's companions from Drew's regiment laid an ambush. Snail was killed in the ensuing melee. A short time later, a nephew of Watie's, Charles Webber, killed and scalped another returned deserter from Drew's regiment. Drew called the murder a "barbarous crime." Watie expressed regret, but justified his nephew by saying that the victim had once spoken with hostility toward "southern people and their institutions." John Ross reacted by trying to have the Confederacy promote his own nephew, Lieutenant Colonel William Ross of Drew's regiment, to brigadier general and place him in command of all Cherokee forces. The appointment would have given John Ross a more direct means of controlling Watie, but he got no response from Richmond.[29]

Growing divisions within the Cherokee nation reflected a wider conflict in Indian Territory. Bitterness lingered over the way many of their relatives in Opothleyahola's band had been treated, especially among the full-bloods. Most of the Indians, full-blood or not, were nonslaveholders who had followed their slaveholding chiefs into the Confederate camp with grave reservations. Now those reservations were turning to outright resistance.

To make matters worse for the Confederacy, Union forces in the region were on the move. On March 6, 1862, Federals heading south clashed with Confederates in Arkansas near Elkhorn Tavern, just east of Indian Territory. In the three-day Battle of Pea Ridge, pro-Confederate Indians fought alongside their Rebel allies in a failed attempt to turn back the Federals. After their defeat, Watie's men fell back to Fort Gibson, while most of Drew's regiment deserted to the Union side, further widening divisions among the Cherokees.[30]

Meanwhile a federal expeditionary force was forming in Kansas. It was made up of army regulars along with survivors of Opathleyahola's band and other anti-Confederate Indians who were still fleeing into Kansas. The Indian contingent was formed into two regiments. The First Kansas Indian Regiment contained eight companies of Creeks and two of Seminoles. The Second Kansas Indian Regiment was made up of Creeks, Cherokees, Choctaws, Chickasaws, and Osages.[31]

In late spring, an Osage scouting party came across a band of pro-Union Cherokees on their way north to Kansas. They brought news of a Union organization in the Nations, two thousand warriors strong, under the leadership of an Indian named Salmon. Salmon had sent the Cherokee band with a message to the Federals urging them to send help as soon as they could. Bolstered by the report, in late June, Union commanders in Kansas sent their expeditionary force on a campaign against Confederates in the Nations.[32]

On July 3 at Locust Grove, a small town in the Cherokee Nation, the expedition took a Rebel force by surprise and sent it flying back toward Tahlequah. Panic spread among pro-Confederates in the Cherokee capital as the expedition approached. Unionists welcomed their cousins among the Federals as returning liberators. Nearly all of

Drew's remaining regiment, six hundred Cherokees, deserted to the Federals. Drew himself was not present, having earlier written to his superiors claiming illness. The now-Union troops from Drew's Regiment assisted with the capture of nearby Fort Gibson and helped occupy Tahlequah itself. Many of the Union Cherokees took revenge on pro-Confederates, killing several and burning others out of their homes. Those Confederate Cherokees who could get away fled south to safety at Rebel outposts.[33]

Chief John Ross remained on his nearby Park Hill plantation with a guard of two hundred men, what was left of Drew's Regiment. Ross was inclined to surrender without bloodshed and knew that his guard favored joining the Federals. Still, he felt honor-bound to at least appear faithful to his Confederate alliance treaty. He worked out a deal with Union commanders under which he was declared a paroled prisoner of war and thereby released from any obligations to the Confederacy. His guard became part of the newly formed Third Kansas Indian Regiment.[34]

Despite their stunning success, the Federals were ill-equipped to follow up on their victory. With supplies running low and their forces in need of reorganization, Union commanders decided to head back to Kansas. On August 3, Ross and his family, along with one thousand other Cherokees who feared a looming Indian civil war, joined the expeditionary force on its march to Fort Leavenworth.[35]

As the refugees had feared, the leadership void left by Ross's capture made tensions among the Cherokees even worse. With Ross gone, pro-Confederate Cherokees met in late August, declared the office of principal chief vacant, and elected Stand Watie to fill the post. Among his first acts was a reaffirmation of the Cherokees's Confederate alliance. Anti-Confederate Cherokees, Ross ally Lewis Downing presiding, held their own council and declared Watie's election illegal, repudiated the Confederate alliance treaty, and abolished slavery. The Cherokee Nation now had two governments contending for legitimacy.[36]

Sporadic fighting between Union and Confederate Indians continued in the Nations. More Indians deserted to the Union side, including some of Stand Watie's men. Angry at the lack of support from Richmond and dissatisfied with Watie's leadership, which some thought was driving the Cherokees to ruin, there was talk among Watie's followers of imprisoning or even killing him. Watie defused the situation by granting a large number of furloughs.[37]

Born in Tennessee, Lewis Downing was taken to Indian Territory as a child on the Trail of Tears. He was a Baptist minister when the Civil War broke out. Like John Ross, Downing was a reluctant Confederate. For the sake of unity, he signed on as a chaplain with Drew's regiment of Confederate Cherokees in 1861. Comprised mainly of nonslaveholding Keetowahs, nearly all of the regiment's 1,200 men deserted within a year of its formation. Downing himself deserted in July 1862 and, like most other former members of Drew's Regiment, joined the Union army. Downing, pictured here in federal uniform, served as lieutenant colonel of the Third Kansas Indian Regiment. He also presided at the reformation of a Union-allied Cherokee government. Photo from the University of Oklahoma Libraries.

Then, in the summer of 1863, federal forces made another major thrust into Indian Territory. Driving down out of Kansas along the Grand River, Federals and their Indian allies under General James Blunt defeated Watie's force at Cabin Creek, then captured Fort Gibson and made it their base of operations. From there they planned further forays against Confederate-allied Indians. At the same time, a Confederate and Indian force under Colonel Cooper headed out from Fort Smith, Arkansas, to drive the Federals back. Cooper caught up with his quarry at Honey Springs on July 17, but Blunt's superior artillery drove the Confederates back. Sometimes called the "Gettysburg of the West," the Battle of Honey Springs, coming within weeks of both Gettysburg and Vicksburg, was the largest engagement of the war in Indian Territory and marked the end of Confederate dominance in the region.[38]

Blunt then turned east to take Fort Smith, driving terrified Confederates before him and leaving devastated Indians in his wake. Those fortunate enough not to be in Blunt's path feared that they soon would be, and they were eager to get out of his way. Blunt's campaign set off a mass migration among pro-Confederate Cherokees, Creeks, and Seminoles that was nearly as brutal as Opothleyahola's flight had been. It became known among survivors as "the stampede." Most fled south to unmolested areas of the Choctaw-Chickasaw country. Some went on into Texas.[39]

Because the previous year's refugees has been mostly anti-Confederate Creeks, the flight of pro-Confederate Creeks now left the Creek Nation almost entirely deserted. Thousands of them filed south in seemingly endless columns of displaced and dejected families. The Reverend Stephen Foreman, a longtime resident of Indian Territory, witnessed that parade of misery on a stop at the Chickasaw governor's home.

> A great many of the Creeks have also passed, on their way to some better camping place where water and grass are more abundant. Many of them are in a very destitute condition. All that they are with now is a pony, one [or] two pot vessels, and a few old dirty bed clothes and wearing apparel. If they ever had any more it is left behind at the mercy of their enemies. . . . Many who passed I was acquainted with and knew to be in good circumstances having an abundance of everything. Now their all is put into one or two small wagons.[40]

Refugee camps soon sprang up in southern Indian Territory along the Blue, Boggy, Kiamichi, Washita, and Red rivers. There were also camps in northern Texas at Bonham and Sherman. In all, the refugees numbered more than ten thousand. Roswell Lee, assistant superintendent of Indian Affairs, appealed to Richmond for help. So did Stand Watie, who insisted that annuities due the Cherokees be paid immediately. "Shall I continue to encourage them," Watie asked, "or shall I at once unveil to them the dread truth that our country is to be hopelessly abandoned, and they are to receive the reward of poverty and ruin for their unswerving fidelity to the Southern cause." In January 1864, the Confederate Congress appropriated $100,000 for relief of the refugees. Corrupt agents and contractors siphoned off much of the money. The rest was distributed in Confederate currency so devalued that many merchants would not accept it. As a result, the refugees continued to suffer and die.[41]

In addition to losing their homes, slaveholders among them were losing their slaves. Hundreds of slaves had fled the Nations with Opothleyahola's band. Others continued filtering into Kansas through 1862. Perry McIntosh escaped from his Creek owner in November

1862, intent on joining the Union army. He was captured in Maysville, Missouri, but increasingly slaves were making successful escapes. Then, in 1863, when the Emancipation Proclamation took effect, former slaves flooded up from the Nations as never before. Blunt's foray into Indian Territory encouraged even more escapees, adding many of them to his own force as Union soldiers.

Blunt's campaign was the last major effort either side made to drive their opponents out of Indian Territory. From mid-1863 through the war's end, Federals and Confederates alike maintained just enough forces in the region to hold what ground they had. Still, the Territory continued to be devastated by a guerrilla war that kept the Nations in turmoil. Much of the violence was driven by old tribal animosities. At the Wichita Agency in western Indian Territory, a band of nearly two hundred Union Indians, most of them Kickapoos, attacked their old enemies, the Tonkawas, and wiped out fully half the tribe— retribution for earlier cooperation with the Texans against them. Some of the violence sprang from conflicts within tribes, such as Stand Watie's attack on Union-held Tahlequah, during which he torched the Cherokee Council House, killed several Cherokees in Union service, captured Ross's son William, and burned John Ross's old home at Park Hill.[42]

The Nations were also terrorized by bands of outlaws, white and Indian, who flourished in the border regions by raiding Union and Confederate settlements alike. Among these raiders, the most feared in Indian Territory was William C. Quantrill's gang. Quantrill was originally commissioned by Confederate authorities to raise a force of partisans to raid Union border towns and to fight back Union guerrilla gangs, or Jayhawkers, from Kansas. But both Quantrill and his Jayhawker counterparts were just as likely to attack one side as the other. Most partisan bands, regardless of stated allegiance, were in fact raiders for profit who fought each other only when necessary to secure territory for plunder.[43]

Watie took pains to distance himself from such men. The Cherokee leader once wrote of Quantrill that he had "crossed the Arkansas river near the Creek Agency and killed eight men (Creeks) one of them shot a little boy and killed him. I have always been opposed to killing women and children although our enemies have done it." As Watie insisted in a letter to his wife, "I am not a murderer." Watie's efforts usually were focused against either Union-allied Indians or military storehouses and supply lines. Food was especially targeted. So hungry were Watie's men during the winter of 1863–64 that they named their outpost "Camp Starvation." One witness described the men as being in "a deplorable condition looking more like Siberian exiles than soldiers."[44]

Watie had long been disillusioned with the government in Richmond for its lack of help with supplies for his troops and their families. Confederate officials had made "no vigorous effort," he complained, to help him drive the Federals out of Indian Territory. A further complaint was that money appropriated by Congress for the Indians was being used elsewhere. He told of one case in which clothing "procured at great trouble and expense, to cover the nakedness of Indian troops" had been given to other Confederate forces. Watie noted that the enemy had "desolated the land and robbed the people, until scarcely a southern family is left east and north of the Arkansas River. . . . The promised protection of the Confederate government, owing, I am compelled to say, to the glaring inefficiency of its subordinate agents, has accomplished nothing; it has been a useless and expensive pageant. . . . the Indians will have at last to rely upon themselves alone."[45]

Instead of sending help, Confederate authorities made Watie a general, the only Indian to hold that rank on either side during the war. And they placed him in command of all Indian troops in the Nations, giving him even more men whom he could not feed. So Watie and his men were indeed forced to rely upon themselves. For most, the war became a struggle less for the Confederacy and more for survival. In June 1864, they captured the Union steamship *J.R. Williams* loaded with over $100,000 worth of supplies, including 150 barrels of flour and 16,000 pounds of bacon. Many of the Indians, especially the Creeks and Seminoles now under Watie's command, broke ranks and carried the supplies to their refugee families. The threat of further desertions forced even Waite to confront the war's changing nature. In September, after defeating a federal force at the Battle of Cabin Creek deep in Union-held Cherokee country, Watie's command captured 300 supply wagons loaded with food, clothing, blankets, and medicines, all valued at $1.5 million. Instead of following up their victory, however, Watie and his men made their way back to Confederate territory and distributed the supplies in the refugee camps.[46]

"The Wretchedness of Their Condition"

Indian refugees in Kansas were faring no better at the hands of federal agents. A few weeks after they began arriving in January 1862, an army officer wrote of the Indians:

> It is impossible for me to depict the wretchedness of their condition. Their only protection from the snow on which they lie is prairie grass, and from the wind and weather scraps and rags stretched upon switches; some of them had some personal clothing; most had but shreds and rags, which did not conceal their nakedness, and I saw seven, ranging in age from three to fifteen years, without one thread upon their bodies. . . . They greatly need medical assistance; many have their toes frozen off, others have their feet wounded by sharp ice or branches of trees lying on the snow; but few have shoes or moccasins. They suffer with inflammatory diseases of the chest, throat, and eyes. Those who come in the last get sick as soon as they eat. . . . Why the officers of the Indian Department are not doing something for them I cannot understand; common humanity demands that something be done, and done at once, to save them from total destruction.[47]

Frostbite was so rampant that over one hundred Indians had to have limbs amputated immediately.[48]

Three months later, with refugee numbers swollen to 7,600, conditions were little better. In late April, George Collamore, an investigator from the Office of Indian Affairs, was especially struck by the lack of adequate shelter: "Such coverings as I saw were made in the rudest manner, being composed of pieces of cloth, old quilts, handkerchiefs, aprons, etc., stretched upon sticks, and so limited were many of them in size that they were scarcely sufficient to cover the emaciated and dying forms beneath them." Under one of these shelters, Collamore found Opothleyahola's daughter "in the last stages of consumption." Nakedness was so common that Collamore was sure many of the men had given up their clothing to provide these crude shelters. And, not surprisingly, frostbite remained rampant. Collamore clearly recalled one "little Creek boy, about eight years old, with both feet taken off near the ankle." There were "others lying upon the ground whose frosted limbs rendered them unable to move."[49]

Food was just as scarce as shelter and just as abysmal. The entire weekly ration for each refugee was a pound of flour, a little salt, and a piece of bacon that Indians and agents alike described as "not fit for a dog to eat." The rancid meat had been shipped to the Indians from Fort Leavenworth after being condemned as "suitable only for soap grease." Those who ate the rotten pork became violently ill.[50]

The passing months brought Washington little closer to meeting its treaty obligations. As the winter of 1862–63 approached, the refugees were still "suffering for clothing and blankets." All they got in the way of shelter were condemned army tents. Archibald Coffin, directing physician for the refugees, complained in September 1863 of poor food leading to gastric disease and poor clothing and shelter leading to pneumonia. "It is no cause of surprise," he wrote, "if we find them falling victim to maladies that otherwise would not be regarded."[51]

Such conditions among the displaced Indians of Kansas were nothing new. In the spring of 1861, William Dole, the U.S. commissioner of Indian Affairs, sent Augustus Wattles on a tour of Kansas, mainly to report on how the Indians there might side in the upcoming Civil War. Wattles wrote back that Washington had nothing to fear from the Kansas Indians. They were in no condition to fight on either side. The Sac and Fox, driven from their Illinois homes a generation earlier and promised both reservation land and support through cash annuities, were in especially bad shape. "Nearly every family is out of provisions," wrote Wattles, "living scantily on one meal a day. Women and children look particularly thin." Most were practically naked. They had no houses, oxen, cows, farming tools, food, or clothing. The disturbed agent reported to Dole: "I have never seen so poor and so miserable a community of people before."[52]

Wattles blamed the destitution on corruption among government-licensed traders and contracted suppliers, who had been cheating the Indians, and the taxpayers, for years. When Wattles warned the corrupt businessmen of his planned report; they brushed him off. It was, they told him, an easy matter to buy influence in Washington. His report was no threat to their swindling enterprise. Certainly no report to Commissioner Dole was likely to make a difference. He was one of the chief swindlers.

"If I chose," wrote one of Dole's subordinates, "I could do something more than implicate. I could convict him of enough to dam him forever." Though Dole might have been implicated, conviction was unlikely. Dole, a close friend of Lincoln's, had known the president since their Illinois days. Dole was himself one of the most influential men in Illinois Republican politics. Lincoln had appointed him commissioner of Indian Affairs as a reward for past political favors, and now it was payday for Dole and his associates. He gave choice appointments in the Indian system to friends and relatives. He lined his own pockets by speculating in Indian land. During the war, he arranged to cheaply purchase Sac and Fox lands in Kansas that were supposed to be held in trust by the government, then sold them at inflated prices. Other Lincoln appointees, like Secretary of the Interior John Usher and Comptroller of the Currency Hugh McCulloch, also profited from corrupt Indian land deals. So did John G. Nicolay, Lincoln's personal secretary.[53]

Other Washington insiders, including members of Congress, cheated Indians through a kickback scheme called the Indian Ring. Politicians helped secure appointments for local Indian agents. The agents granted exclusive licenses and contracts for merchants to trade on the reservations. Then the merchants, who held effective monopolies, overcharged the Indians for shoddy goods and sent a portion of their ill-gotten gain back up the line. The overcharges usually ranged anywhere from 100 to 400 percent.

Senator Samuel C. Pomeroy, Republican of Kansas, was among the worst offenders. As financial agent of the New England Emigrant Aid Society in the 1850s, Pomeroy had culled out tens of thousands of acres for himself in Kansas, mostly at the expense of Potawatomies and Kickapoos. Pomeroy sold off most of the land, which made him one of the richest men in Kansas. He next entered politics, where he found it easy to continue his swindling ways. In July 1862, Pomeroy wrote to one partner in crime, W.W. Ross, describing a plan to skim annuities even before they went out to Indian agents. Pomeroy had arranged for J.K. Tappan of New York to hold an exclusive trade license with the Potawatomies. Tappan's orders would be charged directly against annuities. "This proceeding is recognized here at the [Interior] Department," Pomeroy assured Ross, "and is all right." Both men would get fully one quarter of the profits. "We have nothing to do, only to take our share of the profits at each payment."[54]

The Pomeroy scheme demonstrated not only how widespread corruption in the Union's Indian system was but also how obvious it was, especially to the Indians. That was a major reason that the Kansas refugees were so eager to get back home. Still, they needed the security Washington promised them under federal treaty. Fifteen hundred members of Opothleyahola's old band had tried to return home with the expeditionary force of 1862, but fled back to Kansas when the Federals withdrew.

Ross's Cherokees were also eager to go home. Ross himself met with Lincoln in September 1862 to protest the lack of federal protection, pointing out that the Cherokees had been forced to sign a treaty with the Confederacy only because federal troops had withdrawn from the Nations. Despite clear evidence to the contrary, Lincoln refused to admit any failure in protecting the Cherokees. But the president did promise to get them home and secure them there as soon as he could. Finally, in the spring of 1864, Ross and his people were given a federal escort into the Nations. But the escort did not stay, and Lincoln's promised protection never materialized. Constantly harassed by armed raiders (some of them Cherokees still loyal to the Confederacy), the returning Union Cherokees were never able to make a crop and suffered from hunger and illness through the rest of the war.[55]

The Kickapoos had had enough of Kansas too, but they did not wait for a federal escort to get out. In September 1864, seven hundred broke camp and headed for Mexico. At the war's outset, Mexico had invited the Kickapoos to settle there on condition that they help defend the country's northern border. It was an attractive offer. To the Kickapoos, an alliance with the Confederacy and their old enemies, the Texans, was out of the question. For years, the Texans had pushed them off their traditional hunting grounds. The Kickapoos had sometimes pushed back, but to little effect. Some of the Kickapoos accepted Mexico's invitation. Others fled to Kansas, counting on the federal government to meet its treaty obligations. That had been a mistake. Now the survivors were going to join their kinsmen in Mexico.[56]

The refugees first headed west toward the Texas Panhandle before turning south for Mexico. This long looping route would give Texas settlements a wide berth. The Kickapoos wanted no trouble. Despite their best efforts, trouble was about to find them. In late December, a detachment of about twenty Texas scouts picked up the Kickapoos' trail. At an abandoned campsite they discovered a fresh grave and, over the protests of a few, dug it up to see whom they were following. They unearthed the body of a young Kickapoo woman, smartly attired in buckskin and adorned with trinkets. Some scouts took the trinkets and wore them as souvenirs. Others warned that doing so might bring bad luck.

The scouts immediately sent back word of their find. Soon four hundred Confederate regulars under Captain Henry Fossett and Texas militiamen under Captain S.S. Totten were in pursuit. They caught sight of the Kickapoo encampment at Dove Creek on January 8, 1865. One of Fossett's officers suggested that they talk with the Indians to see if they were friendly. Fossett replied that "he recognized no friendly Indian on the Texas frontier." Fossett and Totten then ordered their mounted troops on a headlong charge over three miles of open ground. The surprised Kickapoos quickly rallied. After about thirty minutes of close fighting, the troopers retreated as quickly as they had appeared. That night, before the Kickapoos continued to Mexico, they buried fifteen warriors. The Texans had suffered twice that many casualties. As one scout recalled, of those who had plundered the young Kickapoo woman's grave, "every possessor of a trinket met death in the fight."[57]

Back in Indian Territory, the war was quickly winding down. Desertions among the Confederate Indian units under Stand Watie's command had rendered them useless as a fighting force. Most, at their families' behest, had already drifted back to the refugee camps and other areas of Confederate-held Indian Territory. Some had fled north to the Union side. Even Watie's wife Sarah, suffering from poor physical and mental health, begged her husband to resign his commission and come home. She longed "to feel free once in life again and feel no dread of war or any other trouble."[58]

Watie did not resign, hoping to retain what authority he had in the Nations. But by the spring of 1865, events were beyond his control. Remnants of Confederate armies in the east were surrendering, and on May 10 federal forces captured Jefferson Davis in Georgia as he tried to escape abroad. In the Nations, former allies were defecting in droves. Even the Choctaw Nation, long the most ardent of Confederate supporters among the Indians, had split and established two contending governments. In June, the staunchly pro-Confederate Choctaw council surrendered to federal agents, quickly followed by the Chickasaw council. Finally, on June 25, Stand Watie signed a document of surrender, becoming the last Confederate general to do so.[59]

Most Indians in the Nations had long since turned their backs on the Confederacy. Many, in defiance of their own tribal leaders, had from the beginning fought against it. More and more deserted to the Union side as the war continued, though the Union usually treated them with little regard. That lack of regard continued after the war, as reflected in the reconstruction treaties. Designed mainly to circumvent the old removal treaties, these new documents treated all Indians in the Nations as if they had been in rebellion against the United States. They forced the Nations to relinquish more land, concentrated even more tribes from Kansas and other states on what land the Indians had left, and provided Washington with a means of further land grabs in years to come.[60]

6

"Defeated . . . by the People at Home"

In the spring of 1864, editor E.H. Grouby of southwest Georgia's *Early County News* wrote, "We cannot help thinking this is the last year of the war. . . . We have now entirely too many little jackass upstarts filling positions in our government"—and avoiding conscription in the process. By October, Grouby was sure that those who still backed the Confederacy were mainly speculators who held "fat Government contracts," along with corrupt officials who were "not yet done fleecing the Government." He continued, "Their voice is still for war, war, war!"[1]

The voice of most common folk was for anything but war. During the following winter of 1864–65 citizens held antiwar meetings all over the South, at least those areas of the South still part of the Confederacy. Nowhere were such meetings more frequent or insistent than in Georgia. A Hart County meeting attended by "a large number" called on Governor Brown to arrange "a speedy peace." Citizens in Lumpkin County did the same. "All most to a man," wrote Lumpkin County resident James Findley, they were eager for peace. When Jackson County residents tried to hold an antiwar meeting, Confederate cavalry broke it up. Undeterred, protestors met again and drafted resolutions urging an end to the "bloody and destructive war." Asserting their "inalienable right of popular assemblage," Jasper County folk met at the courthouse to insist on an end to "the great sufferings of our people." Upson County citizens met at Thomaston and voted "to stop the war on any terms." According to one attendee, "some of the citizens go so far as to say that they will be glad to see Lincoln in possession of the state." One assembly in a rural district of Bibb County was especially aggressive in its demands. A crowd of about sixty voters, all but four of them antiwar men, met to elect local judges. After the balloting, one of the newly elected justices threatened to drive every Confederate official out of Macon and "pledged himself to raise 300 men in twenty-four hours for that purpose if required."[2]

There was at least one pro-war meeting in Georgia that winter. In February 1865, the *Augusta Chronicle and Sentinel* editor sarcastically wrote of "the 'great' war meeting—with a slim attendance, recently held in Coweta County." The paper noted that only five of those present had ever been in the army. The rest were exempts "occupying profitable bomb-proof positions—and of course wanted the war to go on." The editor hardly found that surprising. "They want our difficulties settled? Not a bit of it! . . . [T]hey would be obliged to come down to the level of common people. . . . This kind of patriotism is altogether too prevalent." The editor of Georgia's *Columbus Sun* agreed. It seemed to him that those most likely to advocate "fighting it out" were among the least likely to be in the army. "We know men of this stamp in Columbus."[3]

"A Government of Their Own"

By the winter of 1864–65, most common folk were too busy fighting off Confederates to worry about the Yankees. From its inception, the Confederacy had been fighting a two-front war: one against the North, another against disaffected and dissident southerners. With deserter and layout gangs, many allied with local blacks, controlling vast stretches of the countryside, one editor had written in 1863 that southerners were "fighting each other harder than we ever fought the enemy." Now the South's inner civil war was reaching its climax, and anti-Confederates were claiming more and more victories. A February peace meeting in Thomas County, Georgia, turned violent when the assembled antiwar men successfully beat back an assault by pro-Confederates. That same month in Irwin County, local Unionists and "a large number of deserters" convened an antiwar meeting at Irwinville. They adopted several peace resolutions, including one calling for the Confederacy's surrender. When a Rebel militia lieutenant tried to break up the meeting, Willis Bone, a longtime Unionist, knocked him down with a musket and led three cheers for Lincoln. The excited anti-Confederates then drove the lieutenant and every other supporter of the Richmond regime out of town. In effect, Irwin County seceded from the Confederacy that day.[4]

Other Georgia counties were threatening to do the same. Tatnall and Liberty men drew up formal resolutions declaring that they would rejoin the Union whether Georgia did or not. That sort of independent action had been going on for some time all across the South. Citizens of east central Mississippi's adjoining Newton and Kemper counties met in March 1863 and adopted resolutions expressing their willingness to rejoin the Union. In March 1864, Jackson County, Alabama, announced its allegiance to the Union and seceded from the

During the war's first year, Richmond began losing control of parts of the South to armed and organized anti-Confederates. By 1864, the territorial loss was widespread. In April of that year, deserter colonies in Marion County, Mississippi, and Washington Parish, Louisiana, formed "a government of their own in opposition to the Confederate Government." The *Natchez Courier* announced in July that "the county of Jones . . . has seceded from the State." In November, anti-Confederate Virginians centered in Montgomery and Floyd counties formed the State of Southwest Virginia and elected a governor, lieutenant governor, and "a brigadier-general of deserters." Illustration from *Frank Leslie's Illustrated Newspaper*.

Confederacy. That same month, voters in Arkansas approved a return to the Union by a margin of 12,177 to 266. In April, huge deserter colonies in Marion County, Mississippi, and Washington Parish, Louisiana, formed "a government of their own in opposition to the Confederate Government." In July, the *Natchez Courier* announced that "the county of Jones, State of Mississippi, has seceded from the State and formed a Government of their own, both military and civil." So did Mississippi's Attala County, declaring itself "the free state of Attala." In November, anti-Confederate Virginians centered in Montgomery and Floyd counties formed the State of Southwest Virginia and elected a governor, lieutenant governor, and "brigadier-general of deserters."[5]

That fall, Jefferson Davis got a disturbing letter from F. Kendall of Greenville, Georgia: "I assure you Sir that if the question were put to the people of this state whether to continue the war or return to the union, a large majority would vote for a return." State governors were getting the same message. In January 1865, one writer, who signed herself "A Poor Woman and Children," asked Governor Vance of North Carolina to "try and stop this cruel war." She wrote: "Here I am without one mouthfull to eat for myself and five children and God only knows where I will get somethin, now you know as well as you have a head that it is impossible to whip they yankees, therefor I beg you for God sake to try and make peace on some terms and let they rest of they poor men come home and try to make somthing to eat, my husband has been kiled, and if they all stay till they are dead, what in they name of God will become of us poor women and children. . . . fighting any longer is fighting against God."[6]

Another North Carolinian wrote to Governor Vance reminding him of what should have been obvious for some time: "This never was a war of the majority; with all its horrors it has been forced upon the people contrary to their will and wishes, and it is now perpetuated by the minority against the will of the majority. . . . what we want and need is *peace, blessed peace.*" A Randolph County citizen wrote to his local paper asking whether "the people, the bone and sinew of this once great country were ever legitimately consulted upon the subject of cecession." The implied answer, of course, was no.[7]

In February 1865, a poignant letter arrived in the office of Georgia's Governor Brown. J.T. Smith of Bibb County had sacrificed as much as anyone for the Confederacy. One son had been killed in battle. Another was maimed for life. Three more were still in the army, and all his property was gone. He urged Brown to "leave the sinking ship." Southern newspapers, he insisted, "all state falsehoods when they say that the armies are anxious still to fight. It is not true. The officers with high [salaries] and easy situations . . . get up meetings and pass resolutions to that effect without the knowledge and consent of nine tenths of the privates in the army. . . . They are going home as fast as they can get there. The country is full of deserters and almost every man in the community will feed them and keep them from being arrested. Stop it, my friend, stop it. All the enlightened world is against us, and God himself is against us!"[8]

One might have thought that planters, too, were against the Confederacy, judging by their lack of material support for it. With the Confederacy starving around them, planters still made sure that cotton dominated much of the South's landscape. In September 1864 alone, at least 440 bales were shipped out of Griffin, Georgia. Other cotton-belt towns reported similar shipments through that fall and into the winter. Sherman's men found about 25,000 cotton bales stockpiled in Savannah after they captured the city in December. When Columbus, Georgia, fell to Yankee troopers the next April, there were 125,000 bales packed in and around warehouses lining the wharves.[9]

While planters devoted prime farmland to cotton, hundreds of thousands of southerners continued to go hungry. In March 1865, a commissary agent wrote from Atlanta that "the suffering for food is absolutely heart rending." Knowing that poor women would break into his commissary and take what they wanted in any case, he had long since opened his doors to them. His office was, he said, "almost constantly thronged with women and children begging for bread. They do not ask for meat, but are satisfied with bread alone. During the late freezing weather, females walked as far as sixteen miles in the mud and ice, for the purpose of getting meal, which they would carry home upon their sholders." It was a pitiful sight, he wrote, to see them come in from the cold with their bonnets and shawls crusted with ice.[10]

Not all southerners were struggling so in the war's closing months, however. Finer foods were still available for those who could afford them. Blockade runners had long since given up importing basic necessities, preferring instead to smuggle items they knew would bring top dollar from those who could pay. In December 1864, T.J. Mac-Gare, owner of the Morgan Restaurant in Augusta, Georgia, put an ad in local papers aimed at "lovers of good living and drinking." A city editor who visited the establishment praised its "delicacies and luxuries" as well as its "excellent assortment of the finest kind of liquors." In January 1865, the Rialto Restaurant of Montgomery, Alabama, billed itself as serving "all the luxuries of the season." Another Montgomery establishment advertised the availability of real coffee instead of the cheaper substitutes for "those who consider price no object." As late as March, only weeks before the war's end, one lady wrote of a meal at the Cook House, a posh Columbus, Georgia, inn, where the table was so heavy with food that it "*actually groaned.*" There were sausages, roast pork, cold turkey, biscuits, hot rolls, cornbread, and cake. The next morning at breakfast there was real coffee with milk and sugar.[11]

With Confederate defeat on the battlefield assured and suffering at home more acute than ever, desertion continued to plague Rebel forces. Between October 1864 and early February 1865, records show 72,000 men deserting from armies east of the Mississippi River. The rapid drain of manpower is reflected in Lee's dispatches from the Army of Northern Virginia.

> November 18, 1864: Desertion is increasing . . . not withstanding all my efforts to stop it.
>
> January 27, 1865: I have the honor to call to your attention the alarming frequency of desertions.
>
> February 25, 1865: Hundreds of men are deserting nightly and I cannot keep the army together unless examples are made of such cases.
>
> March 27, 1865: The number of desertions from the 9th to the 18th . . . 1,061. . . . I do not know what can be done to put a stop to it.[12]

"They Are Determined to Get Out"

In April 1865, the last major Confederate armies surrendered. On May 10, Yankee troopers captured Jefferson Davis near Irwinville, Georgia, as he fled south in an effort to get out of the country and establish a Confederate government in exile. Other Rebel officials were soon in custody, and the Confederate nation ceased to be.

In a way, though, the Confederacy as a nation, with all the emotional attachments that the term suggests, never existed at all in the way popular imagination envisions it. Eminent Civil War historian E.

Merton Coulter observed that the Confederacy never became an "emotional reality" to most southern whites until long after the war was over—not until the Lost Cause mythology took hold. "The Confederacy," Coulter wrote, "was not blessed with a 'one for all and all for one' patriotism with which future generations of sentimental romancers were to endow it. Had it been so, this new-born nation might well have established its independence."[13]

From its beginnings, the Confederate cause lacked support from a majority of southerners. That, to a great extent, explains why it was lost. If a house divided against itself cannot stand, then the Confederacy's failure may have been inevitable, especially under the relentless pressures of war. Most white southerners had opposed secession to begin with, and black southerners could hardly feel much enthusiasm for a government that considered slavery their "natural and normal condition." What early support the Confederacy did have eroded steadily as the passions of 1861 died away.[14]

In the spring of 1862, conscription only accelerated the decline of support for the war. Also devastating to the war effort were the attitudes of planters and the privileges granted them by the government. Not only were they exempt from the draft, but they continued to grow too much cotton and tobacco while their poorer neighbors and Confederate soldiers went hungry. In doing so, planters helped starve the Confederacy out of existence. Hunger in the army and hunger at home contributed to a desertion rate that crippled the war effort early on. Robert E. Lee wrote in the fall of 1862 that desertion and straggling were the main reasons for his army's defeat at Antietam. That loss had far-reaching effects. It spurred Lincoln to announce the Emancipation Proclamation, which made diplomatic recognition and aid for the Confederacy by Britain or France impossible. And it drew over two hundred thousand African Americans, three-fourths of them southerners, into the Union army and navy. Lincoln himself admitted that the Union might not have prevailed without them.[15]

The Union's victory is often attributed to greater northern industry and population. Though it is true that the North had more factories and people than the South, to assume that these were the overriding reasons for Confederate defeat ignores more decisive realities of the battlefield and home front. So successful was the Confederacy's munitions program that never did its forces lose a major battle for lack of war matériel. What they constantly lacked was food. Cotton and tobacco production was largely responsible for that. It was equally responsible for home-front food shortages that contributed to inflation, speculation, food riots, and ultimately desertion. Had it not been for the two-thirds of soldiers who were absent by September 1864, the Confederacy might well have been able to offset the North's population advantage. As it was, Union armies nearly always held the numerical edge—an edge made even greater by the nearly half-million southerners who wore Union blue. Together with hundreds of thousands more who actively and passively resisted the Confederacy, it was southerners themselves as much as anyone else who were responsible for Confederate defeat.

"A deserter" sketched by artist Alfred R. Waud. In October 1863, a Confederate sergeant wrote: "The troops are coming to the conclusion that this is a war for the rich men of the South, and they are determined to get out of it." Added to the two-thirds of soldiers already absent by September 1864, between October 1864 and early February 1865, another 72,000 men deserted from armies east of the Mississippi River. In November, General Robert E. Lee wrote from the Army of Northern Virginia: "Desertion is increasing . . . not withstanding all my efforts to stop it." Ultimately, the decision that soldiers made with their feet sealed the Confederacy's fate. Illustration from the Library of Congress.

Even those who had not grasped the war's base reality in the beginning came increasingly to view the struggle as little more than a rich man's war. Active support for the war among most plain folk inevitably declined once that realization set in. Thousands refused to serve, and thousands more already in the service abandoned their ranks. In October 1863, Confederate Sergeant G.H. Baughn observed: "The troops are coming to the conclusion that this is a war for the rich men of the South, and they are determined to get out of it." Ultimately, as historian Paul Escott put it, "the decision which common soldiers made with their feet sealed the fate of the Confederacy."[16]

For most soldiers, that decision came much earlier and had its impact much sooner than historians have traditionally acknowledged. Some have argued that the fall of Atlanta and Sherman's March to the Sea, along with Lincoln's reelection in late 1864, were the key events leading to southern loss of will and Confederate defeat. Others see July 1863 as the turning point, with Confederate defeats at Gettysburg and Vicksburg. In any case, so the argument goes, it was military defeat that brought a loss of will and doomed the Confederacy. Certainly defeats on the battlefield sapped the Confederacy's will to fight, but those defeats came largely because so many soldiers had already lost their will to fight and deserted the army. Many, perhaps most, had never had any will to fight in the first place. By spring of 1862, with the threat of conscription looming, what volunteering there was reflected more a will to avoid being drafted, losing the $50 enlistment bonus, and being denigrated as a "conscript." While just over half of yeoman farmers who volunteered in the war's first year expressed patriotic sentiments in their letters, only 14 percent of those who enlisted after spring 1862 did so. Small wonder that desertion quickly became such a problem for the Confederacy.[17]

By the time Atlanta was in Union hands, and well before Sherman's March, two-thirds of the Confederate army was absent, "most of them," as Jefferson Davis admitted, "absent without leave." Desertion was at the root of Confederate failures even before the summer 1863 defeats at Gettysburg and Vicksburg, as Robert E. Lee himself wrote just after his September 1862 retreat from Antietam. Soldiers were, in fact, leaving before the war's first year was out, which in large part led to conscription in April 1862.[18] Some left because the army could not feed them. Some left because their families were not being fed. What little food their families had was often hauled away by impressment companies, made up largely of able-bodied men who preferred to stay safely behind the lines. Soldiers left because speculators, too, preyed on their families, often with the backing of corrupt officials. They left because planters grew too much cotton and tobacco—planters who, with government sanction, avoided military service at will. Soldiers left because the Confederacy did little to encourage food production, and its agents lined their pockets with ill-gotten gains. Some left because they had never wanted secession in the first place. Others left because they decided that the cause was not worthy of their families' sacrifice. And, finally, they left because they were tired of fighting a rich man's war.

Even among those who stayed, many did so with little enthusiasm. The rich-man's-war attitude was largely responsible for that. For one young Confederate soldier, his army's short-lived victory in December 1862 at Murfreesboro sparked little enthusiasm. "What is gained anyway?" he asked. "It is a rich man's war and a poor man's fight at best." Thomas Henderson Terry deserted from the Twenty-third Texas Cavalry but grudgingly returned to serve out his enlistment. Family members recalled that for years afterward, Terry "would get very agitated when talking about the war, saying that the slaveholders stayed at home and let the poor whites fight their war for them."[19]

There was little love for the Confederacy even among many of those who never wavered. What loyalty they felt was more for their comrades than for the Richmond regime. Sergeant William Andrews of the First Georgia Volunteers joined the army in February 1861 and remained through the entire war. Few could match his service in the cause of southern independence. Still, only a few weeks after his surrender with Robert E. Lee at Appomattox, he wrote: "While it is a bitter pill to have to come back into the Union, don't think there is much regret for the loss of the Confederacy. The treatment the soldiers have received from the government in various ways put them against it."[20]

"The Results of My Patriotism"

On April 5, 1865, only days before the war's end, Georgia's *Early County News* concluded:

This has been "a rich man's war and a poor man's fight." It is true that there are a few wealthy men in the army, but nine tenths of them hold positions, always get out of the way when they think a fight is coming on, and treat the privates like dogs. . . . there seems to be no chance to get this class to carry muskets.[21]

Though the conflict may have been a rich man's war, it was not as much of a poor man's fight as the rich tried to make it. That was true for North and South. On both sides, the lowest of the lower classes tended to be as adamant as the rich in their refusal to fight—or refusal to fight for their region's dominant regime. In the South, while most Confederate soldiers were nonslaveholders and poorer than their slaveholding neighbors, southerners even poorer still were more likely to dodge the draft, desert, or serve in the Union army. As for the North, James McPherson, in his *Battle Cry of Freedom*, presents evidence suggesting that the poorest northerners were among the least likely to serve. It was in fact their resistance to the draft, and northern dissent generally, that goes a long way toward explaining how a Confederacy at war with itself as well as the North was able to survive for as long as it did.[22]

Lincoln's efforts to maintain popular support for the war were never as successful as most postwar popularizers liked to pretend. Shelby Foote, author of a massive three-volume narrative entitled *The Civil War*, recognized the limits of Lincoln's success when he said, "the North fought that war with one hand behind its back." But Foote was probably mistaken when he added that the North could simply have "brought that other arm out" if it had needed to. Lincoln and Congress tried repeatedly to do just that with such measures as the Militia Act of 1862, which invited blacks to serve, and the Enrollment Act of 1863, which tried to force whites to serve. Lincoln's war policies nearly cost him the presidency in 1864 as it was. He had pushed northerners as far as they were willing to go in support of the war. That "other arm" simply was not coming out.[23]

Despite the North's population advantage of two to one, only about a million native-born northerners served in the Union military—roughly the same as the number of southerners who served the Confederacy. Nearly a fourth of the Union armed forces were made up of immigrants, and almost another fourth were southerners, black and white. It was, in the end, southerners who gave the Union armies their numerical superiority on the battlefield. Given the limits of support Lincoln was able to

muster in the North, the war's resolution largely came down to Southerners themselves. Had all soldiers *from* the South fought *for* the South,
or more precisely for the Richmond regime, the result would have been
at least parity on the battlefield and perhaps Confederate victory.[24]

But that outcome would have required any number of unlikely sce-
narios: planters forgoing cotton and tobacco in favor of food; speculators reining themselves in; southerners volunteering to such an extent
that no draft was necessary; effective government and planter support
for soldiers' families; and the development of a political party system
to keep dissent safely channeled into the electoral process. Finally, and
most unlikely of all, it would have required slaves willing to stay on the
plantations or fight for the Confederacy.

Resistance among slaves, up to and including escape, was on the
rise well before the war. That resistance itself contributed to the slaveholders' push for an independent slavocracy. It is hardly imaginable
that slaves would have become less resistant even had the Confederacy
survived—especially with free nations to the north, west, and south
and no Fugitive Slave Law to force their return. Resistance and escape
would certainly have continued and most likely would have increased.
For the Richmond government to constantly guard every stretch of
the Potomac, Ohio, and Rio Grande rivers, not to mention building a
wall around the rest of its land border, would hardly have been a work-
able response. The Confederacy would eventually have had to end
slavery or lose much of its black labor force. Ultimately, one way or
another, the South's slave-based regime contained the seeds of its own
destruction.

As for nonslaveholding whites, shut out as they were from the ben-
efits of a slave economy, it seems unlikely that they would have supported slavery indefinitely. With limited lands and virtually no
socioeconomic upward mobility, many southern whites, three-fourths
of them nonslaveholders, were already coming to question slavery by
the 1850s. Some, like Hinton Rowan Helper, spoke out forcefully
against it. Such resistance on the part of nonslaveholding whites, like
resistance among slaves, was a strong force driving slaveholder fears
for the future of slavery. And it helped fuel slaveholder demands for
secession and a slaveholders' republic in 1860.

Then there were issues of white disaffection with the Confederacy.
Southern voters had voiced their displeasure at the polls in 1863 and
would surely have done so even more strongly in 1865 had the war not

ended when it did. Frank Lawrence Owsley Sr., the leading authority of his generation on the Old South's plain folk, speculated that "the Confederacy, even had it not suffered military defeat at the hands of the North in 1865, would have been defeated in the next state and congressional elections, which would have disintegrated its armies and brought peace."[25]

But the Confederacy did not last that long. By the winter of 1864–65, social and economic disparities among southerners had taken their toll. Lack of food, speculation, cotton and tobacco overproduction, and government corruption, all in the face of hunger and want, ultimately made the war's outcome a matter of indifference to most southerners. It was a rich man's war in any case. Evidence for that seemed clear enough as the war was winding down. In February 1865, one southerner chastised the rich for their continued hypocrisy and callousness.

> That is right. Pile up wealth—no matter whether bread be drawn from the mouth of the soldier's orphan or the one-armed, one limbed hero who hungry walks your streets—take every dollar you can, pay out as little as possible deprive your noble warriors of every comfort and luxury, increase in every way the necesaries of life, make everybody but yourself and non-producers bear the taxes of the war; but be very careful to parade everything you give before the public—talk boldly on the street corners of your love of country, be a grand home general—and, when the war is over, point to your princely palace and its magnificent surroundings and exclaim with pompous swell, "These are the results of my patriotism."[26]

Patriotism for the Confederacy was a sentiment that most southerners had long since abandoned.

"So Deep That the Hand of Time May Never Resurrect It"

In the spring of 1865, beaten from within and without, the Richmond government was forced to capitulate. But the Confederacy's end hardly brought a close to the South's inner conflicts. Southern blacks and white Unionists found themselves besieged by a resurgent planter power structure, which proceeded to disenfranchise blacks and many poor whites. Largely abandoned by the federal government within a decade of the war's end, blacks and white Republicans were terrorized by the Ku Klux Klan, a guerrilla arm of the Democratic Party. The oppression was economic as well as political. In urban centers, the structure of company towns, company stores, and payment in scrip rather than cash made virtual debt slaves of workers. Rural folk, many of whom had lost their land to larger landholding creditors during the war, found themselves forced into tenancy and sharecropping. Dependent on landholders for lodging and/or credit, poor whites were virtual debt slaves as well. Even those who held a bit of land were kept indebted with liens against their crops and interest rates that averaged 50 percent and more. Opposition parties, such as the Populists, rose to unite oppressed whites and blacks, but racism and lack of financial resources doomed them to failure.

With planters back in control both politically and economically, they moved to shore up the Old Order. Southern state governments, like those of the North before them, passed a series of Jim Crow laws firmly establishing racial segregation. Despite "equal protection of the laws" promised by the Fourteenth Amendment, federal courts, including the Supreme Court, refused to declare Jim Crow unconstitutional in order to appease former slaveholders and ease business relations between northern industrialists and southern landowners.

The Old Order moved to shore up its image as well through a postwar pop-culture movement that came to be known as the Lost Cause. With white supremacy its creed and Robert E. Lee its Christ, the mythological Lost Cause became something of a religion for most white southerners, romanticizing the South's Confederate past and encouraging a racist future. That during the war white southerners had "cursed the Southern Confederacy," that they had fought each other "harder than we ever fought the enemy," all mattered little in the postwar era. What did matter was that the fiction of kind masters, contented farmers, and happy slaves in an idyllic Old South justified the Confederacy, bolstered white supremacy, and fit perfectly with postwar planter politics.

Lost Causers went to great lengths to preserve their rosy image of the past. They erected Confederate monuments all over the South. They named parks, buildings, towns, and counties after Confederate heroes. They enshrined Confederate ideology and icons in novels, in movies, at public events, and on southern state flags. In doing so, they

This unique statue of a Civil War soldier in generic uniform, his left foot placed on the broken blade of his sword as a hopeful sign of peace, is in front of the Winston County courthouse in Double Springs, Alabama. It honors Winston County soldiers on both sides of the conflict and stands as a stark counterpoint to the Lost Cause myth of southern unity. In Winston County, 239 men fought for the Union; 112 fought for the Confederacy. Of them, 21 shared last names. Photo by David Williams.

tried to bury the memory of dissent in a divided Civil War South, as one Mississippi Lost Causer put it, "so deep that the hand of time may never resurrect it."[27]

The Lost Cause and its myth of southern unity were perhaps most firmly cemented in the popular mind with the epic 1939 movie *Gone with the Wind*, based on the novel by Atlanta writer Margaret Mitchell. The film won ten Academy Awards and became the most enduring and widely viewed motion picture in cinema history. Though the film contains no hint of the internal divisions that fatally undermined the Confederate war effort, for many people all over the world *Gone with the Wind* defines the wartime South to this day.

On the whole, Lost Cause myth-makers helped perpetuate a system of class and race oppression that made the New South much like the Old South. In fact, the postwar South was hardly new at all. Though the Civil War is still viewed by many as *the* pivotal event in southern history, little changed in a practical way as a result of the war. Planters remained the South's ruling class both politically and economically. Agriculture, particularly cotton agriculture, remained the region's dominant economic force. And though the Civil War did end chattel slavery, most former slaves were forced into the economic bondage of sharecropping and tenancy, or as some called it, "the new slavery."[28]

Significant change began only in the 1920s after the boll weevil wiped out most of the South's cotton crop. No longer needed to pick cotton, masses of tenant farmers, black and white, were driven off the land and released from the debt slavery so pervasive with tenancy. In a way, the tiny boll weevil freed more slaves in a few seasons of pestilence than Lincoln and the Union army did in four years of war. It would take decades more for federal programs (from the New Deal onward), expanding economic and educational opportunities, farm mechanization, and the Civil Rights Movement to propel the region toward anything like a truly new South.

Most southerners realized well before the Civil War ended that the postwar South would hardly be a new one. Their lives would go on much as they always had, whether ruled from Richmond or Washington. Cornelia McDonald of Winchester, Virginia, wrote that most common people felt "that they would be as well off under one government as another." Most southerners eventually came to feel that they would be better off with the war over and the Union restored. To many, the Confederacy was the real enemy. It conscripted their men, impressed their supplies, and starved them out. It favored the rich and oppressed the poor. It made war on those who dared withhold their support and made life miserable for the rest. One South Carolina farmer, after having his livestock impressed, spoke for many when he insisted that "the sooner this damned Government fell to pieces the better it would be for us."[29]

That feeling led plain folk across the South to work against the Confederacy. Their actions and attitudes, along with those of resistive blacks and dissident Indians, contributed decisively to Confederate defeat, a fact that was well known to southerners of the day. Some had even predicted it. Benjamin Harvey Hill, a soon-to-be Confederate senator from Georgia, warned before the war began that a divided South could not sustain itself. In the fall of 1862, an Atlanta newspaper put it even more bluntly: "If we are defeated, it will be by the people at home." And so the Confederacy was defeated, not only by the Union's military—nearly a quarter of which was comprised of southerners—but also by southerners on the home front.[30]

Notes

Introduction

1. Williams, Williams, and Carlson, *Plain Folk in a Rich Man's War*, 5.
2. Barney, *Secessionist Impulse*, 42, 49.
3. Potter, *Lincoln and His Party in the Secession Crisis*, 208; Escott, *After Secession*, 23–28, 42–44.
4. Escott, "Southern Yeomen and the Confederacy," 157; Kibler, "Unionist Sentiment in South Carolina," 358.
5. Tatum, *Disloyalty in the Confederacy*, 38.
6. Watkins, *Co. Aytch*, 69.
7. Formwalt, "Planters and Cotton Production as a Cause of Confederate Defeat," 272–75.
8. Williams, Williams, and Carlson, *Plain Folk in a Rich Man's War*, 4; Blakey, Lainhart, and Bryant, *Rose Cottage Chronicles*, 307.
9. Williams, *Rich Man's War*, 156; Williams, Williams, and Carlson, *Plain Folk in a Rich Man's War*, 134–35; Meyers, "'The Wretch Vickery' and the Brooks County Civil War Slave Conspiracy," 27–38; Freehling, *South vs. the South*, xiii.
10. Beringer, Hattaway, Jones, and Still, *Why the South Lost the Civil War*, 13.
11. Williams, Williams, and Carlson, *Plain Folk in a Rich Man's War*, 164.

Chapter 1: "Nothing but Divisions Among Our People"

1. Link, *Roots of Secession*, 225; Foner, *History of the Labor Movement*, 299–300.
2. Stutler, *West Virginia in the Civil War*, 6–7.
3. Hannibal Hamlin, U.S. senator from Maine, was Lincoln's vice presidential running mate.
4. Williams, Williams, and Carlson, *Plain Folk in a Rich Man's War*, 13.

5. Reiger, "Secession of Florida," 367; Foner, *History of the Labor Movement*, 299–300.

6. Williams, Williams, and Carlson, *Plain Folk in a Rich Man's War*, 20.

7. Kibler, "Unionist Sentiment in South Carolina," 358.

8. Williams, Williams, and Carlson, *Plain Folk in a Rich Man's War*, 15.

9. Link, *Roots of Secession*, 226; Bolton, *Poor Whites*, 165, 167; Reiger, "Secession of Florida," 360, 363.

10. Phillips, *Wealth and Democracy*, 22; Williams, *Rich Man's War*, 17; Levine, *Half Slave and Half Free*, 37; McKenzie, *One South or Many?* 68.

11. Planters are usually defined by their ownership of twenty or more slaves. The term "yeoman" refers to small farmers and herdsmen ranging from those who owned at least three acres of land and no slaves to those who held up to four slaves. Tenants, sharecroppers, and farm laborers—generally referred to (along with unskilled urban workers) as "poor whites"—worked land owned by someone else. The designation "plain folk" or "common folk," when used in reference to the South, generally means yeomen and poor whites, although most often it includes small merchants and skilled artisans (or "mechanics") as well.

Classification of such groups as yeomen, poor whites, and plain folk varies somewhat from one source to another. Steven Hahn, in *Roots of Southern Populism*, tends to view nonslaveholders as a group, as does Grady McWhiney in *Cracker Culture*. Bill Cecil-Fronsman, in *Common Whites*, treats nonslaveholders and small slaveholders as a group because of their non-elite self-image. In *Masters of Small Worlds*, Stephanie McCurry locates the dividing line between yeomen and planters at ownership of eleven or twelve slaves, the number usually needed to remove a slaveholder from field labor, at least in her South Carolina low-country study region.

Beyond those already mentioned, some of the most insightful works available on the antebellum South's socioeconomic types and their interrelationships are Owsley, *Plain Folk of the Old South*, and Oakes, *Slavery and Freedom*. Two of the very best such studies focusing on particular regions of the South are Harris, *Plain Folk and Gentry in a Slave Society: White Liberty and Black Slavery in Augusta's Hinterlands*, and Bolton, *Poor Whites of the Antebellum South: Tenants and Laborers in Central North Carolina and Northeast Mississippi*.

12. Ware, "Cotton Money," 220; Willoughby, *Fair to Middlin'*, 54, 73.

13. Ford, *Origins of Southern Radicalism*, 87; Bynum, Review, 601–2. In *Poor Whites*, Bolton also points out that although many poor whites migrated west in search of cheap land, few found any real upward mobility. Bynum's comment is from her review of Bolton's work.

14. Aughey, *Iron Furnace*, 226; Oakes, *Slavery and Freedom*, 118; Barney, *Secessionist Impulse*, 4, 39; Foust, *Yeoman Farmer*, 198. The late antebellum years saw a long-term and accelerating decline in the proportion of slaveholders in the South's free population from 36 percent in 1830, to 31 percent in 1850, and finally to 25 percent by 1860. See Wright, *Political Economy of the Cotton South*, 34.

15. Meriwether, *Slavery in Auburn*, 8–9; Rawick, *American Slave*, ser. 2, vol. 13, pt. 3, 1.

16. Stampp, *Peculiar Institution*, 144; Ward, *Civil War*, 9.

17. Clinton, *Harriet Tubman*, 85, 142; Griffler, *Front Line of Freedom*, 95–96; Franklin and Moss, *From Slavery to Freedom*, 188.

18. Williams, *Rich Man's War*, 19; Foner, *History of the Labor Movement*, 252;

Franklin and Moss, *From Slavery to Freedom*, 142. A good general discussion of slave resistance can be found in Genovese, *Roll, Jordan, Roll*, 585–660.

19. Franklin and Moss, *From Slavery to Freedom*, 145.

20. Ibid., 143–45; Aptheker, *American Negro Slave Revolts*, 330; Sellers, *Slavery in Alabama*, 246–47, 248; Douglass, *Narrative*, 81–83.

21. Proctor, "Slavery in Southwest Georgia," 15.

22. Lane, *Rambler in Georgia*, 91; Rawick, *American Slave*, ser. 2, vol. 12, pt. 1, 14–15.

23. Oakes, *Slavery and Freedom*, 69.

24. Stampp, *Peculiar Institution*, 21–22; Morgan, *American Slavery, American Freedom*, 327.

25. Morgan, *American Slavery, American Freedom*, 250–70, 327. See also: Washburn, *Governor and the Rebel*.

26. Morgan, *American Slavery, American Freedom*, 269–70.

27. Ibid., 334–35, 344; Zinn, *People's History of the United States*, 57.

28. Jefferson borrowed this phrase from the English political philosopher John Locke, but because few people in his American target audience had significant landholdings, he replaced Locke's "property" with "pursuit of happiness." See Locke, *Second Treatise of Government*, 70–71.

29. Craven, *Coming of the Civil War*, 119–20, 153–54; Phillips, *Georgia and State Rights*, 158–59; Fleming, *Civil War and Reconstruction in Alabama*, 10. See also: Lamb, "James G. Birney and the Road to Abolitionism."

30. Among the best overviews of Indian removal from the South remains Foreman, *Indian Removal*. For the impact of the southern gold rush on Indian removal, see Williams, *Georgia Gold Rush*.

31. Freehling and Simpson, *Secession Debated*, 93.

32. In the border slave states of Kentucky, Missouri, Maryland, and Delaware, there was the occasional push for slavery's end, to be accompanied by expulsion of all blacks from those states. See Freehling, *South vs. the South*, 24. For good introductions to the role of the yeomen in antebellum southern politics, see Genovese, "Yeomen Farmers in a Slaveholders' Democracy," and Watson, "Conflict and Collaboration: Yeomen, Slaveholders, and Politics in the Antebellum South." See also: Thornton, *Politics and Power in a Slave Society*, and Bolton, *Poor Whites*.

33. Oakes, *Slavery and Freedom*, 80; Bailey, *Class and Tennessee's Confederate Generation*, 76; Standard, *Columbus in the Confederacy*, 20–21.

34. DeBats, *Elites and Masses*, 425; Bolton, *Poor Whites*, 114; Williams, *People's History of the Civil War*, 32.

35. Helper, *Impending Crisis*, 42; Bolton, *Poor Whites*, 115; Oakes, *Slavery and Freedom*, 76.

36. McKenzie, *One South or Many?* 68; Bailey, *Class and Tennessee's Confederate Generation*, 58, 60–61; Bolton, *Poor Whites*, 131.

37. Williams, Williams, and Carlson, *Plain Folk in a Rich Man's War*, 11; Foner, *History of the Labor Movement*, 263–64.

38. Wells, *Origins of the Southern Middle Class*, 183–91; Foner, *History of the Labor Movement*, 260–62; Shugg, *Origins of Class Struggle*, 116.

39. Simons, *Social Forces in American History*, 227.

40. Franklin and Moss, *From Slavery to Freedom*, 146–47; Aptheker, *American Negro Slave Revolts*, 327.

41. Helper, *Impending Crisis*, ix, 22, 32, 43. For the most recent and in-depth biography of Helper, see Brown, *Southern Outcast*.

42. Range, *Century of Georgia Agriculture*, 28; Helper, *Impending Crisis*, 27, 39. For a modern study of the South's antebellum importation of grain, see Lindstrom, "Southern Dependence upon Interregional Grain Supplies."

43. Williams, *Rich Man's War*, 32.

44. McFeely, *Frederick Douglass*, 62.

45. Barney, *Secessionist Impulse*, 42; Harris, *Plain Folk and Gentry*, 40; Walker, *Backtracking in Barbour County*, 177; Potter, *Impending Crisis*, 399; Williams, *Rich Man's War*, 33.

46. Shugg, *Origins of Class Struggle*, 76. Soil depletion and a desire to establish slave-state parity in the Senate were additional factors motivating slaveholders to press for slavery's expansion. And slaveholders were not inclined to limit their expansion demands to territories controlled by the United States. "I want Cuba," insisted Senator Albert Gallatin Brown of Mississippi in 1858. "I want Tamaulipas, Potosí, and one or two other Mexican states. . . . And a footing in Central America will powerfully aid us in acquiring those other States. . . . Yes, I want these Countries for the spread of slavery. I would spread the blessings of slavery, like the religion of our Divine Master, to the uttermost ends of the earth." See Genovese, *Political Economy of Slavery*, 97–98, 247, 257–58, 266–67; Hummel, *Emancipating Slaves, Enslaving Free Men*, 96. See also: May, *Southern Dream of a Caribbean Empire*.

47. Gronowicz, *Race and Politics in New York City*, xvi, 60–61; Levine, *Half Slave and Half Free*, 167; Rawley, *Race and Politics*, 14.

48. For an overview of the Kansas issue and its national implications, see Gates, *Fifty Million Acres*, and Rawley, *Race and Politics*.

49. Williams, *Rich Man's War*, 39–40.

50. Bolton, *Poor Whites*, 162.

51. McPherson, *Struggle for Equality*, 23; Sharkey, *Money, Class, and Party*, 176; Perkins, *Northern Editorials*, 469; Potter, *Impending Crisis*, 443–45.

52. Williams, *Rich Man's War*, 43, 45.

53. DeBats, *Elites and Masses*, 260.

54. Robinson, *Bitter Fruits of Bondage*, 62; DeBats, *Elites and Masses*, 260.

55. Bailey, "Disloyalty in Early Confederate Alabama," 527, Harris, *Plain Folk and Gentry*, 67; Fitzhugh, *Sociology for the South*, 162–63, 225.

56. Williams, Williams, and Carlson, *Plain Folk in a Rich Man's War*, 11; Forret, *Race Relations at the Margins*, 137.

57. Foner, *History of the Labor Movement*, 264; Aptheker, *American Negro Slave Revolts*, 345, 347; Wish, "Slave Insurrection Panic of 1856," 211; McKibben, "Negro Slave Insurrections in Mississippi," 83.

58. Holt, *Political Crisis of the 1850s*, 225; Williams, Williams, and Carlson, *Plain Folk in a Rich Man's War*, 12.

59. Aptheker, *American Negro Slave Revolts*, 345–46; Franklin and Schweninger, *Runaway Slaves*, 15; Harding, *There Is a River*, 198.

60. McKibben, "Negro Slave Insurrections in Mississippi," 83; Aptheker, *American Negro Slave Revolts*, 340.

61. Williams, "The 'Faithful Slave' Is About Played Out," 90; Hadden, *Slave Patrols*, 170. See also: White, "Texas Slave Insurrection."

62. Robinson, *Bitter Fruits of Bondage*, 42, 43.

63. For apprehension over disunion among larger slaveholders, see Alexander and Duckworth, "Alabama Black Belt Whigs during Secession," and Scarborough, *Masters of the Big House*, 289–90.

64. Baum, *Shattering of Texas Unionism*, 81; Horton, "Submitting to the 'Shadow of Slavery,'" 118–19; Phillips, *Correspondence of Toombs, Stephens, and Cobb*, 527; Wakelyn, *Confederates Against the Confederacy*, 20; Freehling and Simpson, *Secession Debated*, 82.

65. Williams, *Rich Man's War*, 49–50.

66. Mallard, "I Had No Comfort to Give the People," 79; Storey, *Loyalty and Loss*, 29.

67. Storey, *Loyalty and Loss*, 29; Aughey, *Iron Furnace*, 50–51.

68. Potter, *Impending Crisis*, 496–97, 507–9; Wynne, *Mississippi's Civil War*, 27; Barney, "Secession," 1379; Davis, *Look Away!* 264–65; Johnson, *Toward a Patriarchal Republic*, 63. Those who ran in opposition to secession labeled themselves "cooperationists" to indicate their feeling that any southern response to Lincoln's election should be made in cooperation with the slave states as a whole. Beyond that, however, their position was uncertain and ill-defined. More likely, their position represented an attempt to thwart secession by garnering the undecided vote. For a discussion of the "confused and ambiguous" nature of the cooperationist message, see Johnson, *Toward a Patriarchal Republic*, 26.

69. Bolton, *Poor Whites*, 143; Shugg, *Origins of Class Struggle*, 165; Degler, *The Other South*, 170; Horton, "Submitting to the 'Shadow of Slavery,'" 118; Baum, *Shattering of Texas Unionism*, 47; Potter, *Impending Crisis*, 503–04.

70. Williams, Williams, and Carlson, *Plain Folk in a Rich Man's War*, 15. For a general treatment of the conventions and their composition, see Wooster, *Secession Conventions of the South*. Later that year, the Confederacy did hold a formal presidential election, though the voters were not given much to decide. Davis's name was the only one on the ballot.

71. Pickering and Falls, *Brush Men and Vigilantes*, 14; Williams, Williams, and Carlson, *Plain Folk in a Rich Man's War*, 18; Storey, *Loyalty and Loss*, 39–40; Bailey, "Disloyalty in Early Confederate Alabama," 526; Thompson, *Free State of Winston*, 19–20.

72. Williams, Williams, and Carlson, *Plain Folk in a Rich Man's War*, 14.

73. Bynum, *Free State of Jones*, 98; Reiger, "Secession of Florida," 363; Storey, *Loyalty and Loss*, 18.

74. Shugg, *Origins of Class Struggle*, 163–64; Williams, Williams, and Carlson, *Plain Folk in a Rich Man's War*, 20; Johnson, *Toward a Patriarchal Republic*, 63; Johnson, "A New Look at the Popular Vote for Delegates to the Georgia Secession Convention," 259–75. Though Johnson laid the issue of Georgia's popular vote to rest in the 1970s, Georgia historians are taking their time catching up to him. The latest edition of Coleman's *History of Georgia* (1991), the leading history of the state, still cites Governor Brown's fraudulent claim that secessionists won the popular vote by a margin of over thirteen thousand. See Coleman, *History of Georgia*, 150.

75. Baum, *Shattering of Texas Unionism*, 42; Shugg, *Origins of Class Struggle*, 169–70; Potter, *Lincoln and His Party in the Secession Crisis*, 210.

76. Potter, *Lincoln and His Party in the Secession Crisis*, 208. Potter's conclusions are supported by Paul Escott's study, *After Secession*, 23–28, 42–44. The most recent examination of the ways in which secessionists maneuvered a reluctant South into secession is Freehling's *Road to Disunion*, vol. 2.

77. Potter, *Impending Crisis*, 473; Poole, *South Carolina's Civil War*, 21; Williams, Williams, and Carlson, *Plain Folk in a Rich Man's War*, 16.

78. Williams, *People's History of the Civil War*, 62, 65.

79. Mitchell, *Civil War Soldiers*, 5; McPherson, *What They Fought For*, 52–53; Kruman, "Dissent in the Confederacy," 296.

80. Groce, *Mountain Rebels*, 33; Ash, *Secessionists and Other Scoundrels*, 61; Fisher, *War at Every Door*, 34, 37; Atkins, *Parties, Politics, and the Sectional Conflict in Tennessee*, 248. The leading biography of Brownlow remains Coulter, *William G. Brownlow*. See also: Kelly, "William Gannaway Brownlow," parts 1 and 2.

81. Bolton, *Poor Whites*, 145, 151–52; Trotter, *Bushwhackers!* 9–11.

82. Wooster, *Secession Conventions of the South*, 199; Trotter, *Bushwhackers!* 35.

83. Dotson, "Grave and Scandalous Evil," 397; Horst, *Mennonites in the Confederacy*, 26–27.

84. Crofts, *Reluctant Confederates*, 321; Perkins, *Northern Editorials*, 907; Stutler, *West Virginia in the Civil War*, 4–5, 13; Curry, *House Divided*, 46, 70–71.

85. Groce, *Mountain Rebels*, 36; Moneyhon, "1861," 6–8; Worley, "Arkansas Peace Society," 445.

86. Shugg, *Origins of Class Struggle*, 172; Williams, *Rich Man's War*, 56–57; Whites, "Civil War as a Crisis in Gender," 14.

87. Bailey, *Class and Tennessee's Confederate Generation*, 77–78, 80; Lufkin, "Divided Loyalties," 174.

88. Bolton, *Poor Whites*, 158; Shugg, *Origins of Class Struggle*, 171–72.

89. Wiley, *Johnny Reb*, 124; Escott, *After Secession*, 115.

90. Edwards, *Scarlett Doesn't Live Here Anymore*, 87–88; Thompson, *Free State of Winston*, 39; Williams, Williams, and Carlson, *Plain Folk in a Rich Man's War*, 23.

91. Williams, Williams, and Carlson, *Plain Folk in a Rich Man's War*, 21; Dotson, "Grave and Scandalous Evil," 402.

92. Williams, *Rich Man's War*, 58.

93. Taylor, *Divided Family*, 45, 46.

94. Ibid., 15, 41.

95. Ibid., 86, 87; Bailey, "Disloyalty in Early Confederate Alabama," 525.

96. Thompson, *Free State of Winston*, 38–39; Bailey, "Disloyalty in Early Confederate Alabama," 524–25.

97. Dodd, "Free State of Winston," 10.

98. Escott, *After Secession*, 97–98; Storey, *Loyalty and Loss*, 39–40; Current, *Lincoln's Loyalists*, 145.

99. Escott, *After Secession*, 94; Baum, *Shattering of Texas Unionism*, 42; Bailey, "Disloyalty in Early Confederate Alabama," 525.

100. Escott, *After Secession*, 115–16.

101. Cecil-Fronsman, *Common Whites*, 205; Tatum, *Disloyalty in the Confederacy*, 144; Williams, Williams, and Carlson, *Plain Folk in a Rich Man's War*, 18, 19–20.

102. Storey, *Loyalty and Loss*, 59–60; Bailey, "Disaffection in the Alabama Hill Country," 189.

103. Thompson, *Free State of Winston*, 3–4; Dodd and Dodd, *Winston*, 76, 87–88.

104. Turner, "Cause of the Union in East Tennessee," 369–70; McKinzie, "Prudent Silence," 83.

105. Bolton, *Poor Whites*, 178; McKibben, "Negro Slave Insurrections in Mississippi," 87.

106. McKibben, "Negro Slave Insurrections in Mississippi," 87; Williams, Williams, and Carlson, *Plain Folk in a Rich Man's War*, 134.

107. Cleveland, *Alexander H. Stephens*, 721; Williams, "The 'Faithful Slave' Is About Played Out," 95–96; Aptheker, *American Negro Slave Revolts*, 94, 360, 363–65.

108. McPherson, *Ordeal By Fire*, 264; Harris, *Making of the American South*, 189.

109. Harding, *There is a River*, 229–30.

110. Williams, Williams, and Carlson, *Plain Folk in a Rich Man's War*, 20; Tatum, *Disloyalty in the Confederacy*, viii.

Chapter 2: "Rich Man's War"

1. Storey, *Loyalty and Loss*, 59–60; Thompson, *Free State of Winston*, 33; Robinson, *Bitter Fruits of Bondage*, 79; Williams, Williams, and Carlson, *Plain Folk in a Rich Man's War*, 18; Baggett, *Scalawags*, 83; Fisher, *War at Every Door*, 42; Ash, *Secessionists and Other Scoundrels*, 115. For a study of divisions in Browlow's Knoxville, see McKenzie, *Lincolnites and Rebels*.

2. Williams, Williams, and Carlson, *Plain Folk in a Rich Man's War*, 23–24.

3. Robinson, *Bitter Fruits of Bondage*, 237; Williams, Williams, and Carlson, *Plain Folk in a Rich Man's War*, 21, 22.

4. Williams, Williams, and Carlson, *Plain Folk in a Rich Man's War*, 21.

5. Ibid., 22; Reiger, "Deprivation, Disaffection, and Desertion in Confederate Florida," 291.

6. Escott, *After Secession*, 63–64; Wiley, *Johnny Reb*, 124–25; Martin, *Rich Man's War*, 75.

7. Williams, Williams, and Carlson, *Plain Folk in a Rich Man's War*, 91–92. Kirkland was fortunate to survive his amputation ordeal. One in four Civil War amputees did not. It is also fortunate for this author that Kirkland survived. He sired six more children after he returned home, one of whom was the author's great-grandfather.

8. Wiley, *Johnny Reb*, 126; Moore, *Conflict and Conscription*, 29–30; Williams, *Rich Man's War*, 130; Robertson, *Soldiers Blue and Gray*, 38; Martin, *Rich Man's War*, 123. For a discussion of wealthy planters who did serve, see Scarborough, *Masters of the Big House*, 317–72. Scarborough notes that, of the Confederacy's 272 largest slaveholders (owning 250 slaves or more), 31 (11.4 percent) saw military service. Four of them (1.5 percent) died on duty. That loss pales in comparison to losses among those not so wealthy. Nearly half the South's military-age white males served at one time or another. A third of those who served did not survive the war.

9. Carlson, "Loanly Runagee," 607–08; Moore, *Conscription and Conflict*, 37, 41, 112.

10. Carlson, "Distemper of the Time," 14–21; Davis, *Look Away!* 237; Escott, *Many Excellent People*, 39; Moore, *Conscription and Conflict*, 56–57; Williams, Williams, and Carlson, *Plain Folk in a Rich Man's War*, 102; Escott, *After Secession*, 116.

11. Watkins, *Co. Aytch*, 69; Escott and Goldfield, *Major Problems in the History of the American South*, 365.

12. Williams, *People's History of the Civil War*, 78.

13. Forret, *Race Relations at the Margins*, 224; Williams, Williams, and Carlson, *Plain Folk in a Rich Man's War*, 100; Poole, *South Carolina's Civil War*, 52; Horton, "Submitting to the 'Shadow of Slavery,'" 133; Moneyhon, *Impact of the Civil War and Reconstruction on Arkansas*, 114.

14. Kruman, "Dissent in the Confederacy," 305; Poole, *South Carolina's Civil War*, 47.

15. Mitchell, *Civil War Soldiers*, 158.

16. Williams, Williams, and Carlson, *Plain Folk in a Rich Man's War*, 94; Rable, *Civil Wars*, 108; Bolton, *Poor Whites*, 156.

17. Rable, *Civil Wars*, 76–77; Williams, Williams, and Carlson, *Plain Folk in a Rich Man's War*, 103.

18. Cumming, *Journal*, 243.

19. Williams, *Rich Man's War*, 131–32; Escott, *After Secession*, 119; Williams, Williams, and Carlson, *Plain Folk in a Rich Man's War*, 100.

20. Williams, *Rich Man's War*, 130.

21. Wallenstein, *From Slave South to New South*, 100; Escott, "The Cry of the Sufferers," 234.

22. Beringer, Hattaway, Jones, and Still, *Why the South Lost the Civil War*, 433; Lebergott, "Why the South Lost," 65–66.

23. Gates, *Agriculture and the Civil War*, 107; Wise, *Lifeline of the Confederacy*, 221; Hill, *State Socialism in the Confederate States*, 4–7; Johnson, *Red River Campaign*, 50.

24. Williams, Williams, and Carlson, *Plain Folk in a Rich Man's War*, 26, 27; Coulter, *Confederate States of America*, 241; Moneyhon, *Impact of the Civil War and Reconstruction on Arkansas*, 107; Reiger, "Deprivation, Disaffection, and Desertion in Confederate Florida," 279–80; Williams, *Rich Man's War*, 99.

25. Robinson, *Bitter Fruits of Bondage*, 202–3.

26. Phillips, *Correspondence of Toombs, Stephens, and Cobb*, 595; Williams, Williams, and Carlson, *Plain Folk in a Rich Man's War*, 28.

27. Williams, *Rich Man's War*, 99–100; Williams, Williams, and Carlson, *Plain Folk in a Rich Man's War*, 34.

28. Gates, *Agriculture and the Civil War*, 30, 33; Williams, *Rich Man's War*, 101; Moneyhon, *Impact of the Civil War and Reconstruction on Arkansas*, 107; Williams, Williams, and Carlson, *Plain Folk in a Rich Man's War*, 31; Coulter, *Confederate States of America*, 241.

29. Moneyhon, *Impact of the Civil War and Reconstruction on Arkansas*, 107; Blair, *Virginia's Private War*, 73; Burton and Kamerling, "Tobacco," 1598.

30. Tyler, "Cotton on the Border," 456, 461, 463, 466.

31. Scarborough, *Masters of the Big House*, 352–54; Gates, *Agriculture and the Civil War*, 105; Coulter, "Commercial Intercourse," 384; Johnson, *Red River Campaign*, 263.

32. Williams, *Rich Man's War*, 102; Williams, Williams, and Carlson, *Plain Folk in a Rich Man's War*, 32.

33. Williams, Williams, and Carlson, *Plain Folk in a Rich Man's War*, 33.

34. Ibid., 32.

35. Ibid., 31–34; Lebergott, "Why the South Lost," 62; Taylor, "Discontent in Confederate Louisiana," 420.

36. Williams, Williams, and Carlson, *Plain Folk in a Rich Man's War*, 31–34; Lebergott, "Why the South Lost," 62, 69; Lebergott, "Through the Blockade," 882–83. Figures rounded to the nearest 100,000 in table 10 of Lebergott's "Through the Blockade" show that of the 6.8 million bales produced in the South during the war, 0.4 were used in the South, 0.5 went to the United Kingdom and Europe, 0.9 went to the North, and 3.8 were destroyed by neglect, the Union army, or southerners themselves. The remaining 1.8 million bales were sold after the war. Cotton production had averaged about 3.5 million bales annually during the late 1850s, reaching just over 3.8 million bales in 1860. See Gray, *History of Agriculture in the Southern United States to 1860*, 2: 1026; Wright, *Political Economy of the Cotton South*, 96.

37. Johnson, "Trading with the Union," 309.

38. Martin, *Rich Man's War*, 133.

39. Robinson, *Bitter Fruits of Bondage*, 149; Williams, *Rich Man's War*, 82–83; Williams, Williams, and Carlson, *Plain Folk in a Rich Man's War*, 34–35.

40. Standard, *Columbus, Georgia, in the Confederacy*, 46; Amos, "All-Absorbing Topics," 19–21; Williams, Williams, and Carlson, *Plain Folk in a Rich Man's War*, 35.

41. Williams, *Rich Man's War*, 84; Williams, Williams, and Carlson, *Plain Folk in a Rich Man's War*, 35.

42. Hill, *State Socialism in the Confederate States*, 8; Gates, *Agriculture and the Civil War*, 34–35; Escott, *After Secession*, 123.

43. DeCredico, *Patriotism for Profit*, 56.

44. Reiger, "Deprivation, Disaffection, and Desertion in Confederate Florida," 281; McKinney, "Women's Role in Civil War Western North Carolina," 49.

45. Tripp, *Yankee Town, Southern City*, 137; Bynum, *Unruly Women*, 120; Marten, *Texas Divided*, 90; Williams, Williams, and Carlson, *Plain Folk in a Rich Man's War*, 43.

46. Bynum, *Unruly Women*, 126; Williams, *Rich Man's War*, 109.

47. Williams, Williams, and Carlson, *Plain Folk in a Rich Man's War*, 69–70.

48. Ibid., 70; Gates, *Agriculture and the Civil War*, 53; Williams, *Rich Man's War*, 109.

49. Gates, *Agriculture and the Civil War*, 54; Moneyhon, *Impact of the Civil War and Reconstruction on Arkansas*, 105. The Confederate Congress did finally pass an act in 1864 forbidding the use of Union currency by anyone but government officials or their agents. The prohibition was largely ignored. See Johnson, "Trading with the Union," 312.

50. Gates, *Agriculture and the Civil War*, 68; Williams, *Johnny Reb's War*, 60–61. See also: Mohr, "Slavery and Class Tensions in Confederate Georgia." For a complete treatment of tax in kind, see Ball, *Financial Failure and Confederate Defeat*.

51. Williams, Williams, and Carlson, *Plain Folk in a Rich Man's War*, 50; McMillan, *Disintegration of a Confederate State*, 88; Morgan, *Planters' Progress*, 61, Taylor, "Discontent in Confederate Louisiana," 417; *War of the Rebellion*, ser. 4, vol. 3, 413.

52. Gates, *Agriculture and the Civil War*, 48; Williams, Williams, and Carlson, *Plain Folk in a Rich Man's War*, 46, 50–51. James Bush, one of Early County's richest planters, contributed to alienation from the government himself by refusing to accept Confederate currency.

53. Williams, Williams, and Carlson, *Plain Folk in a Rich Man's War*, 48–49, 52; Gates, *Agriculture and the Civil War*, 37.

54. Williams, Williams, and Carlson, *Plain Folk in a Rich Man's War*, 49.

55. Williams, *Rich Man's War*, 85.

56. Williams, *People's History of the Civil War*, 92.

57. Faust, "Altars of Sacrifice," 1212; Williams, *Rich Man's War*, 81; Hill, *State Socialism in the Confederate States*, 9–10. For the most complete modern study of blockade running, see Wise, *Lifeline of the Confederacy*.

58. Otto, *Southern Agriculture*, 22.

59. Williams, *Johnny Reb's War*, 17; Williams, *Rich Man's War*, 4; Mitchell, *Civil War Soldiers*, 163.

60. Williams, *Rich Man's War*, 113.

61. Rable, *Civil Wars*, 107; Williams, Williams, and Carlson, *Plain Folk in a Rich Man's War*, 27–28; Haynes, *Thrilling Narrative*, 5–6.

62. Escott, *After Secession*, 122; Bynum, *Unruly Women*, 121; Edwards, *Scarlett Doesn't Live Here Anymore*, 89.

63. Wiley, *Plain People of the Confederacy*, 45.

64. Rable, *Civil Wars*, 83.

65. Faust, "Altars of Sacrifice," 1223; Wiley, *Plain People of the Confederacy*, 66; Rable, *Civil Wars*, 73.

66. Williams, *Rich Man's War*, 113–14.

67. Escott, *After Secession*, 122.

68. Wietz, *More Damning than Slaughter*, 69; Moneyhon, *Impact of the Civil War and Reconstruction on Arkansas*, 116, 119; Tyson, "Texas," 145.

69. Williams, Williams, and Carlson, *Plain Folk in a Rich Man's War*, 54–55.

70. Ibid.

71. Martin, *Rich Man's War*, 129; Ayers, *In the Presence of Mine Enemies*, 334; Williams, *Rich Man's War*, 112–13; Williams, Williams, and Carlson, *Plain Folk in a Rich Man's War*, 65.

72. Cecil-Fronsman, *Common Whites*, 203; Wiley, *Plain People of the Confederacy*, 45–46.

73. Escott, *Many Excellent People*, 40; Williams, *Rich Man's War*, 111–12.

74. Rable, *Civil Wars*, 108; Williams, Williams, and Carlson, *Plain Folk in a Rich Man's War*, 65.

75. Williams, Williams, and Carlson, *Plain Folk in a Rich Man's War*, 58–59.

76. Beringer, Hattaway, Jones, and Still, *Why the South Lost the Civil War*, 13. The Confederate Ordnance Bureau's operation under Josiah Gorgas is most fully explored in Vandiver, *Ploughshares into Swords*. See also: Wilson, *Confederate Industry*.

77. Rogers, *Confederate Home Front*, 81–82.

78. Williams, Williams, and Carlson, *Plain Folk in a Rich Man's War*, 59.

79. Ibid.

80. Massey, *Women in the Civil War*, 148; Faust, *Mothers of Invention*, 90; Williams, *People's History of the Civil War*, 148.

81. Wilson, *Confederate Industry*, 216; Williams, Williams, and Carlson, *Plain Folk in a Rich Man's War*, 59–60.

82. Coulter, *Confederate States of America*, 236–38; Green, *This Business of Relief*, 78; Tripp, *Yankee Town, Southern City*, 138. For a discussion of the writ of habeas corpus and other civil liberties issues in the Confederacy, see Neely, *Southern Rights: Political Prisoners and the Myth of Confederate Constitutionalism*. See also: Williams, "Civil Liberties, C.S.A." and Williams, "Class Conflict, C.S.A."

83. Davis, *Look Away!* 242; Williams, *Rich Man's War*, 143; Williams, Williams, and Carlson, *Plain Folk in a Rich Man's War*, 60, 95.

84. Williams, Williams, and Carlson, *Plain Folk in a Rich Man's War*, 5, 151.

85. Ibid., 94.

86. Baum, *Shattering of Texas Unionism*, 82.

87. Williams, Williams, and Carlson, *Plain Folk in a Rich Man's War*, 152.

88. Harris, *Plain Folk and Gentry*, 151; Faust, *Creation of Confederate Nationalism*, 37; Williams, Williams, and Carlson, *Plain Folk in a Rich Man's War*, 152–53.

89. Inscoe and McKinney, *Heart of Confederate Appalachia*, 153; Williams, Williams, and Carlson, *Plain Folk in a Rich Man's War*, 152; Lonn, *Desertion*, 70; Bynum, *Free State of Jones*, 126; Dotson, "Grave and Scandalous Evil," 420; Mallard, "I Had No Comfort to Give the People," 85.

90. Crawford, *Ashe County's Civil War*, 224; Baum, *Shattering of Texas Unionism*, 42, 113–14; Kruman, "Dissent in the Confederacy," 297; Baggett, *Scalawags*, 91; Tatum, *Disloyalty in the Confederacy*, 125; Williams, *Rich Man's War*, 135; Escott, *After Secession*, 155; Fitzgerald, "Poor Man's Fight," 17; McMillan, *Disintegration of*

a Confederate State, 65; Degler, *The Other South*, 169; Martis, *Historical Atlas*, 82, 83, 84, 87, 118.

91. Williams, *Rich Man's War*, 135–36.

92. Ibid., 136–37. A full-text version of this letter appears in Zinn and Arnove, *Voices of a People's History of the United States*, 202–4.

93. Harris, *Making of the American South*, 208; Massey, *Women in the Civil War*, 171; Williams, Williams, and Carlson, *Plain Folk in a Rich Man's War*, 80; Gates, *Agriculture and the Civil War*, 38–39.

94. Wiley, *Plain People of the Confederacy*, 47–48.

95. Bynum, *Unruly Women*, 133; Gates, *Agriculture and the Civil War*, 39.

96. Cecil-Fronsman, *Common Whites*, 212; Bynum, *Unruly Women*, 134; Thomas, *Confederate Nation*, 204.

97. Friedheim and Jackson, *Freedom's Unfinished Revolution*, 103.

98. Chesson, "Harlots or Heroines?" 131–75; Rable, *Civil Wars*, 108–10; Thomas, *Confederate Nation*, 202–5; Blair, *Virginia's Private War*, 74; Coulter, *Confederate States of America*, 422–23.

99. Amos, "All-Absorbing Topics," 22–23; Gates, *Agriculture and the Civil War*, 39, 40; Coulter, *Confederate States of America*, 241, 243.

100. Williams, Williams, and Carlson, *Plain Folk in a Rich Man's War*, 82–83. For a study of the Georgia riots, see also: Williams and Williams, "Women Rising."

101. *War of the Rebellion*, ser. 4, vol. 2, 468; Green, *This Business of Relief*, 78; Williams, *Rich Man's War*, 84.

102. Williams, Williams, and Carlson, *Plain Folk in a Rich Man's War*, 85.

103. Ibid.

104. Ibid., 85–88.

105. Reiger, "Deprivation, Disaffection, and Desertion in Confederate Florida," 285; Dotson, "Grave and Scandalous Evil," 419; Coulter, *Confederate States of America*, 423; McKinney, "Women's Role in Civil War Western North Carolina," 47; Gates, *Agriculture and the Civil War*, 40; Revels, *Grander in Her Daughters*, 74; Marten, *Texas Divided*, 92.

106. Williams, Williams, and Carlson, *Plain Folk in a Rich Man's War*, 88.

107. Ibid., 83–84.

108. Ibid., 83; Green, *This Business of Relief*, 78.

109. Williams, Williams, and Carlson, *Plain Folk in a Rich Man's War*, 84.

110. Ibid., 88–89.

111. Williams, *Rich Man's War*, 115.

112. Williams, Williams, and Carlson, *Plain Folk in a Rich Man's War*, 89.

113. Mitchell, *Civil War Soldiers*, 165.

114. Thomas, *History of the Doles-Cook Brigade*, 593–95; Faust, "Altars of Sacrifice," 1224.

115. Edwards, *Scarlett Doesn't Live Here Anymore*, 92–93; Williams, Williams, and Carlson, *Plain Folk in a Rich Man's War*, 161.

116. Blakey, Lainhart, and Stephens, *Rose Cottage Chronicles*, 307; Jimerson, *Private Civil War*, 215; Levine, *Confederate Emancipation*, 24; Bynum, *Free State of Jones*, 101, 103.

117. Gates, *Agriculture and the Civil War*, 36.

118. Escott, *Many Excellent People*, 43–44.

119. Robinson, *Bitter Fruits of Bondage*, 244; Martin, *Rich Man's War*, 149.

120. Martin, *Rich Man's War*, 127.

121. Faust, *Mothers of Invention*, 243.

122. Martin, *Rich Man's War*, 148; Chesnut, *Mary Chesnut's Civil War*, 773.

123. Tatum, *Disloyalty in the Confederacy*, 118; Dotson, "Grave and Scandalous Evil," 406–7; Blair, *Virginia's Private War*, 64; Escott, *After Secession*, 127; Radley, *Rebel Watchdog*, 148; Williams, Williams, and Carlson, *Plain Folk in a Rich Man's War*, 162.

124. Mann, "Civil War and Localism," 78–79; Robinson, *Bitter Fruits of Bondage*, 205; Tatum, *Disloyalty in the Confederacy*, 58; Poole, *South Carolina's Civil War*, 61–62; Dotson, "Grave and Scandalous Evil," 409.

125. Blair, *Virginia's Private War*, 65; Casler, *Four Years in the Stonewall Brigade*, 114.

126. Martin, *Rich Man's War*, 17; Radley, *Rebel Watchdog*, 157; Andrews, *Footprints of a Regiment*, 39.

127. Crawford, *Ashe County's Civil War*, 108; *War of the Rebellion*, ser. 1, vol. 53, 380–81; Escott, *After Secession*, 132.

Chapter 3: "Fighting Each Other Harder Than We Ever Fought the Enemy"

1. Edwards, *Scarlett Doesn't Live Here Anymore*, 93; Williams, Williams, and Carlson, *Plain Folk in a Rich Man's War*, 182; Lonn, *Desertion*, 69, 70.

2. Williams, Williams, and Carlson, *Plain Folk in a Rich Man's War*, 152, 160.

3. Tatum, *Disloyalty in the Confederacy*, 158, 43–44.

4. Williams, *People's History of the Civil War*, 284; Aughey, *Iron Furnace*, 266; Williams, Williams, and Carlson, *Plain Folk in a Rich Man's War*, 5.

5. "Dobbin" was a colloquialism referring to a workhorse.

6. Williams, Williams, and Carlson, *Plain Folk in a Rich Man's War*, 179–80.

7. Wood, "Union and Secession in Mississippi," 146–47; Escott, *After Secession*, 131.

8. Moneyhon, "Disloyalty and Class Consciousness in Southwestern Arkansas," 233; Escott, *After Secession*, 120.

9. Escott, *After Secession*, 124–25; Wiley, *Plain People of the Confederacy*, 66.

10. Williams, Williams, and Carlson, *Plain Folk in a Rich Man's War*, 188; Davis, *Look Away!* 271.

11. Bynum, *Unruly Women*, 137; Mallard, "I Had No Comfort to Give the People," 80.

12. Storey, *Loyalty and Loss*, 57–58; Naron, *Chickasaw*, 23.

13. McMillan, *Disintegration of a Confederate State*, 63; Ellis, *Thrilling Adventures*, 337.

14. Aughey, *Iron Furnace*, 267; Dotson, "Grave and Scandalous Evil," 416.

15. Aughey, *Iron Furnace*, 197–98.

16. Williams, *Rich Man's War*, 148.

17. Chesebrough, "Dissenting Clergy in Confederate Mississippi," 119–20; Mallard, "I Had No Comfort to Give the People," 82–83.

18. Mallard, "I Had No Comfort to Give the People," 79–80; Aughey, *Iron Furnace*, 6.

19. Williams, "Civil Liberties, C.S.A.," 441.

20. Chesebrough, "Dissenting Clergy in Confederate Mississippi," 118; Lathrop, "Disaffection in Confederate Louisiana," 309–10.

21. Moore, *Conscription and Conflict*, 53; Williams, *Rich Man's War*, 124.

22. Moore, *Conscription and Conflict*, 54–56; Williams, *Rich Man's War*, 133; Baggett, *Scalawags*, 72; Tatum, *Disloyalty in the Confederacy*, 82–83.

23. Williams, *Rich Man's War*, 134; Storey, *Loyalty and Loss*, 69.

24. Moore, *Conscription and Conflict*, 68; Dotson, "Grave and Scandalous Evil," 400, 415; Ayers, *In the Presence of Mine Enemies*, 252; Schlabach, *Mennonites and Amish*, 190, 191, 192.

25. Horst, *Mennonites in the Confederacy*, 80.

26. Ibid., 30, 32–33; Schlabach, *Mennonites and Amish*, 190. Though Good entered service on July 8, 1861, nine months before the Confederate draft commenced, he and many others were effectively state draftees. Horst explains: "The prewar militia system of Virginia required all males from eighteen to forty-five years of age to drill several times a year unless exempted. There was no exemption for persons who professed conscientious scruples against military activities. Most Mennonites and Dunkers would not attend these drills but would instead pay a nominal fine of fifty or seventy-five cents. When the war broke out in the spring of 1861, the militia was called and Mennonites whose names were on the muster rolls found themselves no longer excused by paying muster fines. . . . Most of the men went into the militia under protest, vowing among themselves, to their families, and to the church that they would not use weapons placed in their hands to kill the enemy." Horst, *Mennonites in the Confederacy*, 28–29.

27. Schlabach, *Mennonites and Amish*, 191.

28. Wright, *Conscientious Objectors*, 115–20.

29. Marten, *Texas Divided*, 93–94, 122; Bailey, "Defiant Unionists," 215–18.

30. Moneyhon, "Disloyalty and Class Consciousness in Southwestern Arkansas," 228–29; Tatum, *Disloyalty in the Confederacy*, 41; Williams, *Rich Man's War*, 132; Williams, *People's History of the Civil War*, 295.

31. Inscoe and McKinney, *Heart of Confederate Appalachia*, 193; Lonn, *Desertion*, 69; Dotson, "Grave and Scandalous Evil," 411.

32. Bynum, *Free State of Jones*, 105; Conversations with Harold O. Williams, the author's father, and other family members.

33. Tatum, *Disloyalty in the Confederacy*, 46, 140, 141; Williams, Williams, and Carlson, *Plain Folk in a Rich Man's War*, 171–72.

34. Williams, Williams, and Carlson, *Plain Folk in a Rich Man's War*, 160; Sarris, *Separate Civil War*, 89; McMillan, *Disintegration of a Confederate State*, 41; Thompson, *Free State of Winston*, 93–97.

35. Williams, Williams, and Carlson, *Plain Folk in a Rich Man's War*, 160; Sarris, *Separate Civil War*, 95–96.

36. Davis, *Look Away!* 233, 448 n. 25; Blair, *Virginia's Private War*, 66; Taylor, "Discontent in Confederate Louisiana," 416.

37. Tatum, *Disloyalty in the Confederacy*, 115; Poole, *South Carolina's Civil War*, 60–61; Williams, Williams, and Carlson, *Plain Folk in a Rich Man's War*, 183; Dotson, "Grave and Scandalous Evil," 416–17.

38. Martin, *Rich Man's War*, 199; Bailey, "Defiant Unionists," 215; Bailey, "Far Corner of the Confederacy," 218.

39. Cecil-Fronsman, *Common Whites*, 207; Inscoe and McKinney, *Heart of Confederate Appalachia*, 127.

40. Storey, *Loyalty and Loss*, 107.

41. Dotson, "Grave and Scandalous Evil," 416–17, 427.

42. Thompson, *Free State of Winston*, 68; Dodd, "Free State of Winston," 16.

43. Fellman, *Inside War*, 28; Schultz, *Quantrill's War*, 4–5.

44. O'Brien, *Mountain Partisans*, 60–62; Mackey, *Uncivil War*, 197.

45. Thompson, *Free State of Winston*, 68–69.

46. Ellis, *Thrilling Adventures*, 105–9.

47. Ibid., 322–26, 344–45.

48. Ibid., 291–93.

49. Williams, Williams, and Carlson, *Plain Folk in a Rich Man's War*, 170–71.

50. Lonn, *Desertion*, 234–35; Williams, Williams, and Carlson, *Plain Folk in a Rich Man's War*, 162.

51. Berlin, Favreau, and Miller, *Remembering Slavery*, 228–29.

52. Trotter, *Bushwhackers!* 47–49.

53. Paludan, *Victims*, 84–85, 96–98.

54. Bynum, *Unruly Women*, 135, 145, 148; McKinney, "Women's Role in Civil War Western North Carolina," 44–45; McCaslin, *Tainted Breeze*, 57; Fisher, *War at Every Door*, 74.

55. Bynum, *Unruly Women*, 143.

56. Ibid., 143–44.

57. Ibid., 142; Fellman, "Women and Guerrilla Warfare," 156–57.

58. Blakey, Lainhart, and Stephens, *Rose Cottage Chronicles*, 311–12.

59. Williams, *Rich Man's War*, 142; Storey, *Loyalty and Loss*, 79.

60. Bynum, *Unruly Women*, 142; Blakey, Lainhart, and Stephens, *Rose Cottage Chronicles*, 311–12.

61. Tatum, *Disloyalty in the Confederacy*, 90.

62. Aughey, *Iron Furnace*, 192–200.

63. Ibid., 7, 64.

64. Taylor, "Discontent in Confederate Louisiana," 411; Rogers, *Confederate Home Front*, 105–6; Dyer, *Secret Yankees*, 163; Berlin et al., *Free at Last*, 161–64.

65. Tatum, *Disloyalty in the Confederacy*, 24–25, 36; Worley, "Arkansas Peace Society," 446; Degler, *The Other South*, 171.

66. Smith, "Limits of Dissent and Loyalty in Texas," 137–38; McCaslin, *Tainted Breeze*, 211–12.

67. McCaslin, *Tainted Breeze*, 87–88. Bourland continued his murderous ways long after the hangings, often executing prisoners without even the pretense of a trial. The murders finally stopped in 1864 only after some of Bourland's own men threatened to call for his court-martial. See Smith, "Limits of Dissent and Loyalty in Texas," 146–47.

68. Marten, *Texas Divided*, 58.

69. Pickering and Falls, *Brushmen and Vigilantes*, 23. Pickering and Falls give the following evidence for their conclusion: "Census records of 1860 for those later indicted in five 1862 hanging deaths show average worth (both real and personal property combined) of $8,605, with the comparable figure for victims being $807. The 1860 census records for those indicted in four 1863 hanging deaths show average worth of $19,100, with a comparable figure for the victims of $1,269. The difference is such that the vigilantes were wealthier and their victims poorer than the average Texan of that time, whose worth was about $6,000."

70. Fleming, *Civil War and Reconstruction in Alabama*, 138; McMillan, *Disintegration of a Confederate State*, 131.

71. Williams, *Rich Man's War*, 139–40.

72. Tatum, *Disloyalty in the Confederacy*, 29.

73. Williams, *Rich Man's War*, 140; Tatum, *Disloyalty in the Confederacy*, 29–30; Dodd and Dodd, *Winston*, 112.

74. Longstreet, *From Manassas to Appomattox*, 651; Williams, Williams, and Carlson, *Plain Folk in a Rich Man's War*, 157; Tatum, *Disloyalty in the Confederacy*, 68.

75. Tatum, *Disloyalty in the Confederacy*, 33–34, 123, 157; Otten, "Disloyalty in the Upper Districts of South Carolina," 108–9; Noe, "Red String Scare," 316. See also: Auman and Scarboro, "Heroes of America," and Nelson, "Red Strings and Half Brothers."

76. Tatum, *Disloyalty in the Confederacy*, 120, 154, 158; Dotson, "Grave and Scandalous Evil," 393.

77. Ellis, *Thrilling Adventures*, 430a; Horst, *Mennonites in the Confederacy*, 41–43; Williams, Williams, and Carlson, *Plain Folk in a Rich Man's War*, 163.

78. Williams, *Rich Man's War*, 142; Storey, *Loyalty and Loss*, 100.

79. Schlabach, *Mennonites and Amish*, 191; Storey, *Loyalty and Loss*, 99; O'Brien, *Mountain Partisans*, 54, 88; McKnight, *Contested Borderland*, 34; Williams, Williams, and Carlson, *Plain Folk in a Rich Man's War*, 183.

80. Otten, "Disloyalty in the Upper Districts of South Carolina," 107–8.

81. Inscoe, "Moving Through Deserter Country," 162.

82. Dyer, *Secret Yankees*, 163; Otten, "Disloyalty in the Upper Districts of South Carolina," 99, 106.

83. Inscoe and McKinney, "Highland Households Divided," 57–58; Inscoe and McKinney, *Heart of Confederate Appalachia*, 191–92.

84. Inscoe, "Moving Through Deserter Country," 165.

85. Ibid., 162.

86. Tatum, *Disloyalty in the Confederacy*, 159; Reiger, "Deprivation, Disaffection, and Desertion in Confederate Florida," 293, 296; Forret, *Race Relations at the Margins*, 224; Baggett, *Scalawags*, 88–89.

87. Massey, *Women in the Civil War*, 89; Leonard, *All the Daring of the Soldier*, 50–56. See also: Ryan, *Yankee Spy in Richmond*; and Varon, *Southern Lady, Yankee Spy*.

88. Williams, Williams, and Carlson, *Plain Folk in a Rich Man's War*, 180; Massey, *Women in the Civil War*, 104; Leonard, *All the Daring of the Soldier*, 69.

89. Leonard, *All the Daring of the Soldier*, 57–60; Massey, *Women in the Civil War*, 102; Sizer, "Acting Her Part," 114, 132. Though born in New Orleans and living there at the war's outbreak, Cushman spent much of her childhood in Michigan.

90. Mallard, "I Had No Comfort to Give the People," 83–84.

91. Williams, Williams, and Carlson, *Plain Folk in a Rich Man's War*, 180.

92. O'Brien, *Mountain Partisans*, 55.

93. McKnight, *Contested Borderland*, 123–24.

94. Williams, Williams, and Carlson, *Plain Folk in a Rich Man's War*, 180–81; Sarris, *Separate Civil War*, 105.

95. Williams, Williams, and Carlson, *Plain Folk in a Rich Man's War*, 157; Freehling, *South vs. the South*, xiii; Crawford, *Ashe County's Civil War*, 125, 132; Dotson, "Grave and Scandalous Evil," 406; Storey, *Loyalty and Loss*, 98; Cimprich, *Fort Pillow*, 53; Baggett, *Scalawags*, 78.

96. Bonner, "David R. Snelling," 275–82.

97. Harris, *Plain Folk and Gentry*, 152; Crawford, *Ashe County's Civil War*, 130; Durrill, *War of Another Kind*, 240; Degler, *The Other South*, 170; Glatthaar, *March to the Sea and Beyond*, 147, 150–51.

98. Harris, *Plain Folk and Gentry*, 151; Marten, *Texas Divided*, 122, 123.

99. Mackey, *Uncivil War*, 62; Sutherland, "1864," 139; Durrill, *War of Another Kind*, 116–17, 133; Mallard, "I Had No Comfort to Give the People," 85.

100. Dodd, "Free State of Winston," 16.

101. Gordon, "In Time of War," 45–46.

102. Thompson, *Free State of Winston*, 78–79; Dodd, "Free State of Winston," 13, 15.

103. Buker, *Blockaders, Refugees, and Contrabands*, 115–16, 150–51; Baggett, *Scalawags*, 67.

104. McGee, "Confederate Who Switched Sides," 20–28; Williams, *Rich Man's War*, 145–46.

105. Worley, "Arkansas Peace Society," 451; Barnes, "Williams Clan's Civil War," 192, 195, 199–200.

106. Bynum, *Free State of Jones*, 98, 105, 112.

107. Davis, *Look Away!* 247.

108. Weitz, *More Damning than Slaughter*, 204, 206, 208.

109. Tatum, *Disloyalty in the Confederacy*, 60; McMillan, *Disintegration of a Confederate State*, 41–42; Hoole, *Alabama Tories*, 6.

110. McMillan, *Disintegration of a Confederate State*, 94.

111. Degler, *The Other South*, 154–55; Baggett, *Scalawags*, 76; Frazier, "Out of Stinking Distance," 163; Weitz, *More Damning than Slaughter*, 223; Taylor, "Discontent in Confederate Louisiana," 425, 426. For more on Wells, who became governor of Louisiana in 1865, the best source remains Lowrey, "Political Career of James Madison Wells."

112. Tatum, *Disloyalty in the Confederacy*, 45, 50, 51; Davis, *Look Away!* 264; Marten, *Texas Divided*, 101.

113. Moneyhon, "Disloyalty and Class Consciousness in Southwestern Arkansas," 230; Neely, *Southern Rights*, 105; Fisher, *War at Every Door*, 68–69.

114. Fisher, *War at Every Door*, 85.

115. Weitz, *More Damning than Slaughter*, 190.

116. Trotter, *Bushwhackers!* 148–150.

117. Tatum, *Disloyalty in the Confederacy*, 137–39; Otten, "Disloyalty in the Upper Districts of South Carolina," 102, 104; Poole, *South Carolina's Civil War*, 61; Weitz, *More Damning than Slaughter*, 195–96.

118. Weitz, *More Damning than Slaughter*, 198–99; Dotson, "Grave and Scandalous Evil," 410, 416, 422.

119. Fisher, *War at Every Door*, 64; Bolton, *Poor Whites*, 160.

120. Current, *Lincoln's Loyalists*, 137.

121. Ibid., 137–38; Durrill, *War of Another Kind*, 108–9; Auman and Scarboro, "Heroes of America," 345. For an excellent study of guerrilla conflict focusing on Pasquotank County and northeastern North Carolina, see Myers, "Executing Daniel Bright" (a master's thesis to be published by Louisiana State University Press). Myers is currently working on a doctoral dissertation examining the hardcore Unionist population in North Carolina and the origins of guerrilla conflict statewide.

122. Carlson, "Loanly Runagee," 600.

123. Williams, Williams, and Carlson, *Plain Folk in a Rich Man's War*, 176–77.

124. Ibid., 164.

125. Ibid., 164–65.

126. Bohannon, "They Had Determined to Root Us Out," 98–106.

127. Williams, Williams, and Carlson, *Plain Folk in a Rich Man's War*, 166–67; Sarris, *Separate Civil War*, 97.

128. Carlson, "Loanly Runagee," 589; Williams, Williams, and Carlson, *Plain Folk in a Rich Man's War*, 174.

129. Turner, *Navy Gray*, 130–31, 325 n. 6; Tatum, *Disloyalty in the Confederacy*, 87.

130. Reiger, "Deprivation, Disaffection, and Desertion in Confederate Florida," 288, 295.

131. Ibid., 293; Weitz, *More Damning than Slaughter*, 218.

132. Buker, *Blockaders, Refugees, and Contrabands*, 98–99, 106–7; Tatum, *Disloyalty in the Confederacy*, 83–84.

133. Reiger, "Deprivation, Disaffection, and Desertion in Confederate Florida," 292.

134. Aptheker, *American Negro Slave Revolts*, 361; Tatum, *Disloyalty in the Confederacy*, 88.

135. Aptheker, *American Negro Slave Revolts*, 360–61; Escott, *Many Excellent People*, 77; Taylor, "Discontent in Confederate Louisiana," 426; Williams, Williams, and Carlson, *Plain Folk in a Rich Man's War*, 140–41.

136. Williams, *Rich Man's War*, 157; Williams, "The 'Faithful Slave' Is About Played Out," 92–93.

Chapter 4: "Yes, We All Shall Be Free"

1. Berlin, Favreau, and Miller, *Remembering Slavery*, 275–76.

2. Williams, *Rich Man's War*, 154.

3. Ibid.

4. Taylor, *Reminiscences*, 8.

5. Berlin, "Slaves Were the Primary Force Behind Their Emancipation," 279; Howard, *Black Liberation*, 17.

6. Schwalm, *Hard Fight for We*, 84; Williams, Williams, and Carlson, *Plain Folk in a Rich Man's War*, 138; Williams, "The 'Faithful Slave' Is About Played Out," 97; Marten, *Texas Divided*, 111.

7. Williams, Williams, and Carlson, *Plain Folk in a Rich Man's War*, 138; Camp, *Closer to Freedom*, 131; Messner, "Black Violence," 21.

8. Schwalm, *Hard Fight for We*, 77; Harris, *Making of the American South*, 203–04; Williams, "The 'Faithful Slave' Is About Played Out," 86.

9. Williams, Williams, and Carlson, *Plain Folk in a Rich Man's War*, 71–72.

10. Faust, *Mothers of Invention*, 57, 59–60.

11. Faust, "Altars of Sacrifice," 1213; Camp, *Closer to Freedom*, 129; Schwalm, *Hard Fight for We*, 105; Williams, Williams, and Carlson, *Plain Folk in a Rich Man's War*, 71–72; Williams, "The 'Faithful Slave' Is About Played Out," 96; Hadden, *Slave Patrols*, 182, 186.

12. Aptheker, *American Negro Slave Revolts*, 363.

13. Williams, "The 'Faithful Slave' Is About Played Out," 99.

14. Bryan, *Confederate Georgia*, 124–25; Marten, *Texas Divided*, 111–12.

15. Williams, *Rich Man's War*, 155.

16. Cimprich, *Slavery's End in Tennessee*, 24; Wish, "Slave Disloyalty," 444; Williams, *Rich Man's War*, 155; Botkin, *Lay My Burden Down*, 175.

17. Williams, *Rich Man's War*, 156; Marten, *Texas Divided*, 111; Faust, *Mothers of Invention*, 58; Newton, "African Americans Resist the Confederacy," 58; Jordan, *Black Confederates and Afro-Yankees*, 177; Robinson, *Bitter Fruits of Bondage*, 180.

18. Cimprich, *Slavery's End in Tennessee*, 26; Wish, "Slave Disloyalty," 449; Crist and Dix, *Papers of Jefferson Davis*, 7: 175; Williams, *Rich Man's War*, 158.

19. Mohr, *On the Threshold of Freedom*, 51, 310 n. 86; Bryan, *Confederate Georgia*, 127; Williams, *Rich Man's War*, 158.

20. Aptheker, *American Negro Slave Revolts*, 95, 367; Wish, "Slave Disloyalty," 443; Jordan, *Tumult and Silence at Second Creek*, 5–6.

21. Williams, Williams, and Carlson, *Plain Folk in a Rich Man's War*, 134.

22. Ibid.

23. Ibid., 134–35.

24. Meyers, "'The Wretch Vickery' and the Brooks County Civil War Slave Conspiracy," 27–38; Williams, Williams, and Carlson, *Plain Folk in a Rich Man's War*, 144–50.

25. Williams, Williams, and Carlson, *Plain Folk in a Rich Man's War*, 140; Mitchell, *Civil War Soldiers*, 4; Aptheker, *American Negro Slave Revolts*, 363–64, 365–66.

26. Durrill, *War of Another Kind*, 132–33; Bynum, *Unruly Women*, 123.

27. Quarles, *Negro in the Civil War*, 62–63.

28. Ibid.; Berlin, Favreau, and Miller, *Remembering Slavery*, 227–28, 264–65; Marten, *Texas Divided*, 110–11.

29. Quarles, *Negro in the Civil War*, 62; Mohr, *On the Threshold of Freedom*, 87–88.

30. Williams, "The 'Faithful Slave' Is About Played Out," 94.

31. Ibid.

32. Jordan, *Black Confederates and Afro-Yankees*, 69; Aptheker, *American Negro Slave Revolts*, 361–62.

33. Bynum, *Free State of Jones*, 109–10.

34. Storey, *Loyalty and Loss*, 80.

35. Williams, Williams, and Carlson, *Plain Folk in a Rich Man's War*, 131; Berlin et al., *Free at Last*, 124.

36. Inscoe and McKinney, *Heart of Confederate Appalachia*, 228.

37. Taylor, *Reminiscences*, 68.

38. Dyer, *Secret Yankees*, 87–89; Berlin et al., *Free at Last*, 124.

39. Otten, "Disloyalty in the Upper Districts of South Carolina," 98–99; Camp, *Closer to Freedom*, 136–37.

40. Inscoe, "Moving Through Deserter Country," 166, 170.

41. Williams, "The 'Faithful Slave' Is About Played Out," 100.

42. Neely, *Southern Rights*, 135; Quarles, *Negro in the Civil War*, 84.

43. Quarles, *Negro in the Civil War*, 84.

44. Poole, *South Carolina's Civil War*, 104; Jordan, *Black Confederates and Afro-Yankees*, 284; Leonard, *All the Daring of the Soldier*, 54–55, 70.

45. Wertheimer, *We Were There*, 137–38; Jordan, *Black Confederates and Afro-Yankees*, 283–84.

46. Wills, *War Hits Home*, 40.

47. McPherson, *Negro's Civil War*, 154–57. After the war, Smalls served several terms as a congressman from South Carolina in the U.S. House of Representatives. In 1899, he was appointed customs collector for Beaufort and held the position until 1913. Two years later, he died of natural causes in the home where he and his mother had once been enslaved. See Uya, *From Slavery to Public Service*.

48. Grant, *The Way It Was in the South*, 83; Quarles, *Negro in the Civil War*, 71; Franklin and Moss, *From Slavery to Freedom*, 209; Williams, *People's History of the Civil War*, 345; Poole, *South Carolina's Civil War*, 104.

49. Messner, "Black Violence," 31.

50. Ripley, *Slaves and Freedmen in Civil War Louisiana*, 17.

51. Wish, "Slave Disloyalty," 442.

52. Chesnut, *Mary Chesnut's Civil War*, 407; Moneyhon, *Impact of the Civil War and Reconstruction on Arkansas*, 137; Escott, "Context of Freedom," 85.

53. Fields, *Slavery and Freedom*, 112; Goodrich, *Black Flag*, 52.

54. Goodrich, *Black Flag*, 54.

55. Balser, *Collected Works of Abraham Lincoln*, 5: 423. The Reverend William Brownlow, a leading Tennessee anti-secessionist, was not so reluctant to see blacks in the military. Brownlow wrote: "If we had the power . . . we would arm and uniform . . . every negro in the Southern Confederacy, and every devil in Hell, and turn them loose upon the Confederacy." Melton, "Disloyal Confederates," 17.

56. Sterling, *We Are Your Sisters*, 237.

57. Freehling, *South vs. the South*, 96; Quarles, *Negro in the Civil War*, 65.

58. Messner, "Black Violence," 21; Fields, *Slavery and Freedom*, 116.

59. Voegeli, "A Rejected Alternative," 775.

60. Ibid., 766–87.

61. Gallman, *North Fights the Civil War*, 126–27, 130; Quarles, *Negro in the Civil War*, 76.

62. Ward, *Civil War*, 150.

63. *War of the Rebellion*, ser. 1, vol. 15, 621–23, 667–69.

64. Blacks in the Union army totaled 178,895. Figures for those in the Union navy, though less exact, were in the neighborhood of 24,000. Burchard, *One Gallant Rush*, xii; Glatthaar, *Forged in Battle*, x; Urwin, "United States Colored Troops," 2002; Ramold, "African-American Sailors,"14; Ward, *Civil War*, 246; Smith, *Trial By Fire*, 309.

65. Goodrich, *Black Flag*, 58; Wilson, *Campfires of Freedom*, 4–5; Poole, *South Carolina's Civil War*, 77–78; Fields, *Slavery and Freedom*, 100.

66. Mohr, "Before Sherman," 339.

67. Wilson, *Campfires of Freedom*, 4; Berlin et al., *Free At Last*, 111–12.

68. Mohr, "Before Sherman," 342–43; Jordan, *Black Confederates and Afro-Yankees*, 163; Glatthaar, *Forged in Battle*, 202.

69. Berlin, Miller, and Favreau, *Remembering Slavery*, 255–56.

70. McPherson, *What They Fought For*, 62.

71. McPherson, *Struggle for Equality*, 92.

72. Ibid., 92–93.

73. Quarles, *Negro in the Civil War*, 180; McPherson, *Negro's Civil War*, 174.

74. Voegeli, *Free but Not Equal*, 101; Ward, *Civil War*, 247; Bailey, "USCT in the Confederate Heartland," 227, 229; Wilson, *Campfires of Freedom*, 39.

75. Berlin et al., *Free at Last*, 440–41; Hollandsworth, *Louisiana Native Guards*, 62.

76. *War of the Rebellion*, ser. 1, vol. 24, pt. 1, 106.

77. Burchard, *One Gallant Rush*, 137–41; Glatthaar, *Forged in Battle*, 140.

78. Berlin et al., *Free At Last*, 444; Blackett, *Thomas Morris Chester*, 115.

79. Lowe, "Battle on the Levee," 125; Speer, *Portals to Hell*, 109.

80. Hollandsworth, *Louisiana Native Guards*, 70–71; Glatthaar, *Forged in Battle*, 156–57; Bailey, "Texas Cavalry Raid," 29; Urwin, "We Cannot Treat Negroes . . . as Prisoners of War," 135–37; Durrill, *War of Another Kind*, 207–8; Suderow, "Battle of the Crater," 203–9; Jordan and Thomas, "Massacre at Plymouth," 190.

81. Cimprich, *Fort Pillow*, 81; Current, *Lincoln's Loyalists*, 141. See also: Castel, "Fort Pillow Massacre," and Frisby, " 'Remember Fort Pillow!' "

82. Coles, " 'Shooting Niggers Sir,' " 74, 75.

83. Glatthaar, *Forged in Battle*, 155–57.

84. Speer, *Portals to Hell*, 108, 113.

85. Levine, *Confederate Emancipation*, 17; Freehling, *South vs. the South*, 191.

86. Williams, Williams, and Carlson, *Plain Folk in a Rich Man's War*, 190.

87. Ibid.

88. Levine, *Confederate Emancipation*, 145; Jordan, *Black Confederates and Afro-Yankees*, 218.

89. Nolan, *Lee Considered*, 175–77.

90. McPherson, *What They Fought For*, 55; Mohr, *On the Threshold of Freedom*, 278.

91. Blomquist and Taylor, *This Cruel War*, 322–23.

92. Mohr, *On the Threshold of Freedom*, 283–84; Williams, *Rich Man's War*, 174.

93. Jordan, *Black Confederates and Afro-Yankees*, 222–25, 246–47; Smith, *Trial By Fire*, 327.

Chapter 5: "Now the Wolf Has Come"

1. Hauptman, *Between Two Fires*, 87, 88, 92.

2. Taylor, "Unforgotten Threat," 300–14.

3. Hauptman, *Between Two Fires*, 66, 69, 73–75; Neely, *Southern Rights*, 134.

4. Finger, *Eastern Band of the Cherokees*, 83; Hauptman, *Between Two Fires*, 76, 87

5. Hauptman, *Between Two Fires*, 87.

6. Finger, *Eastern Band of the Cherokees*, 83, 87, 89; Hauptman, *Between Two Fires*, 103.

7. Finger, *Eastern Band of the Cherokees*, 88, 96–97; Crow, *Storm in the Mountains*, 59; Hauptman, *Between Two Fires*, 109.

8. Gibson, *American Indian*, 366; Debo, *History of the Indians*, 169; Saunt, "Paradox of Freedom," 67; Nichols, *Lincoln and the Indians*, 26–27; Abel, *American Indian as Slaveholder and Secessionist*, 58, 60; Gaines, *Confederate Cherokees*, 8

9. Gibson, *American Indian*, 364, 366–67; Abel, *American Indian as Slaveholder and Secessionist*, 73; Debo, *Choctaw Republic*, 81–82; Debo, *History of the Indians*, 169–70.

10. Josephy, *Civil War in the American West*, 327–28; Debo, *History of the Indians*, 170–71.

11. Gibson, *American Indian*, 366; Debo, *History of the Indians*, 171.

12. Debo, *History of the Indians*, 169; Abel, *American Indian as Slaveholder and Secessionist*, 145, 147, 153–54; Moulton, *John Ross*, 169.

13. Franks, *Stand Watie*, 114–15; Gaines, *Confederate Cherokees*, 8, 21–22; Saunt, "Paradox of Freedom," 64 n. 3; Josephy, *Civil War in the American West*, 326; Hauptman, *Between Two Fires*, 45–46.

14. Gaines, *Confederate Cherokees*, 16–17.

15. Ibid., 11–12; Franks, *Stand Watie*, 118–19.

16. Moulton, *John Ross*, 170; Gaines, *Confederate Cherokees*, 9; Abel, *American Indian as Slaveholder and Secessionist*, 220–224; Franks, *Stand Watie*, 119; Josephy, *Civil War in the American West*, 329.

17. Josephy, *Civil War in the American West*, 228, 330; Gibson, *American Indian*, 367.

18. Gaines, *Confederate Cherokees*, 7; Abel, *American Indian as Slaveholder and Secessionist*, 193–94.

19. Hatch, *The Blue, the Gray, and the Red*, 4; Josephy, *Civil War in the American West*, 327; White and White, *Now the Wolf Has Come*, 16–17.

20. Josephy, *Civil War in the American West*, 328; White and White, *Now the Wolf Has Come*, 23; Hatch, *The Blue, the Gray, and the Red*, 7; Gibson, *American Indian*, 368; Moulton, *John Ross*, 173.

21. Abel, *American Indian as Slaveholder and Secessionist*, 243–44; Gaines, *Confederate Cherokees*, 23.

22. Debo, *Road to Disappearance*, 147–48; Warde, "Now the Wolf Has Come," 68–69.

23. McReynolds, *Seminoles*, 294; Debo, *History of the Indians*, 174–75; White and White, *Now the Wolf Has Come*, 35; Gaines, *Confederate Cherokees*, 38; Banks, "Civil War Refugees from Indian Territory," 286; Hatch, *The Blue, the Gray, and the Red*, 7.

24. White and White, *Now the Wolf Has Come*, 100–107; McReynolds, *Seminoles*, 298–300; Josephy, *Civil War in the American West*, 331–32; Gaines, *Confederate Cherokees*, 46–53.

25. Josephy, *Civil War in the American West*, 332; Gaines, *Confederate Cherokees*, 58–59; Hatch, *The Blue, the Gray, and the Red*, 17–20.

26. McReynolds, *Seminoles*, 302.

27. Ibid., 302–4.

28. Gaines, *Confederate Cherokees*, 55, 57.

29. Ibid., 55–56, 60–61, 94; Franks, *Stand Watie*, 123.

30. Gibson, *American Indian*, 368–69; Hauptman, *Between Two Fires*, 48.

31. Gaines, *Confederate Cherokees*, 97.

32. Ibid., 97, 99.

33. Ibid., 102–4, 106, 112; Franks, *Stand Watie*, 129.

34. Gaines, *Confederate Cherokees*, 108–12.

35. Ibid., 115.

36. Moulton, *John Ross*, 174, 175; Franks, *Stand Watie*, 131, 135; Abel, *Amercian Indian in the Civil War*, 256; Josephy, *Civil War in the American West*, 356–57; Debo, *History of the Indians*, 176–77, 178.

37. Franks, *Stand Watie*, 135–36.

38. Franks, "Confederate States and the Five Civilized Tribes," 440; Franks, *Stand Watie*, 139–40; Gibson, *American Indian*, 370; Gaines, *Confederate Cherokees*, 120.

39. Debo, *History of the Indians*, 178; Warde, "Now the Wolf Has Come," 74; Franks, "Confederate States and the Five Civilized Tribes," 441–42.

40. Warde, "Now the Wolf Has Come," 76.

41. Debo, *Choctaw Republic*, 82; Franks, "Confederate States and the Five Civilized Tribes," 442–46; Franks, *Stand Watie*, 143–45.

42. Hauptman, *Between Two Fires*, 28–29; Franks, *Stand Watie*, 148; Saunt, "Paradox of Freedom," 70; Gaines, *Confederate Cherokees*, 104–5.

43. Gibson, *American Indian*, 370–71.

44. Debo, *History of the Indians*, 179; Hauptman, *Between Two Fires*, 50; Franks, *Stand Watie*, 147, 154.

45. Franks, *Stand Watie*, 141; Franks, "Confederate States and the Five Civilized Tribes," 448; Gibson, *American Indian*, 372.

46. Franks, "Confederate States and the Five Civilized Tribes," 441; Franks, *Stand Watie*, 162–63; Josephy, *Civil War in the American West*, 377; Gibson, *American Indian*, 371–72.

47. McReynolds, *Seminoles*, 302–3.

48. Debo, *History of the Indians*, 176.

49. Banks, "Civil War Refugees from Indian Territory," 291–92.

50. McReynolds, *Seminoles*, 304–5; Banks, "Civil War Refugees from Indian Territory," 292.

51. Banks, "Civil War Refugees from Indian Territory," 293, 295.

52. Nichols, *Lincoln and the Indians*, 22.

53. Ibid., 21–22.

54. Danziger, *Indians and Bureaucrats*, 7; Nichols, *Lincoln and the Indians*, 13, 14, 15, 18.

55. Debo, *History of the Indians*, 176, 179; Moulton, *John Ross*, 176.

56. Gibson, *American Indian*, 382–83; Gibson, *Kickapoos*, 197–98, 202.

57. Gibson, *Kickapoos*, 202–6.

58. Franks, "Confederate States and the Five Civilized Tribes," 452; Franks, *Stand Watie*, 160.

59. Debo, *Choctaw Republic*, 84–85; Franks, *Stand Watie*, 180, 182.

60. Bailey, *Reconstruction in Indian Territory*, 202–3.

Chapter 6: "Defeated . . . by the People at Home"

1. Williams, Williams, and Carlson, *Plain Folk in a Rich Man's War*, 178.

2. Ibid., 185–86.

3. Ibid., 186.

4. Tatum, *Disloyalty in the Confederacy*, xii–xiii; Williams, Williams, and Carlson, *Plain Folk in a Rich Man's War*, 183–84, 186.

5. Williams, Williams, and Carlson, *Plain Folk in a Rich Man's War*, 186; Tatum, *Disloyalty in the Confederacy*, xiii, 106, 163; Lonn, *Desertion*, 70; Sutherland, "1864," 109–110; *War of the Rebellion*, ser. 1, vol. 32, pt. 3, 755; Bynum, *Free State of Jones*, 126; Wood, "Union and Secession in Mississippi," 145; *War of the Rebellion*, ser. 4, vol. 3, 802–4, 812–14; Dotson, "Grave and Scandalous Evil," 424.

6. Berlin et al., *Free at Last*, 151; Wiley, *Plain People of the Confederacy*, 67; Edwards, *Scarlett Doesn't Live Here Anymore*, 85.

7. Davis, *Look Away!* 246; Bynum, *Unruly Women*, 149.

8. Williams, Williams, and Carlson, *Plain Folk in a Rich Man's War*, 182.

9. Ibid., 187.

10. Ibid., 188.

11. Rogers, *Confederate Home Front*, 131; Williams, Williams, and Carlson, *Plain Folk in a Rich Man's War*, 188.

12. Radley, *Rebel Watchdog*, 154.

13. Coulter, *Confederate States of America*, 105, 374.

14. Cleveland, *Alexander H. Stephens*, 721.

15. Johnson, *Abraham Lincoln*, 302–3.

16. *War of the Rebellion*, ser. 1, vol. 30, pt. 4, 180; Escott, *After Secession*, 128.

17. Harris, *Making of the American South*, 201.

18. Escott, *After Secession*, 219; *War of the Rebellion*, ser. 1, vol. 19, pt. 2, 622.

19. Rutledge, "Civil War Journal," 108; Pickering and Falls, *Brushmen and Vigilantes*, 15.

20. Andrews, *Footprints of a Regiment*, 184.

21. Williams, *Rich Man's War*, vii.

22. Harris, *Plain Folk and Gentry*, 152; Crawford, *Ashe County's Civil War*, 130; Durrill, *War of Another Kind*, 240; Degler, *The Other South*, 170; Glatthaar, *March to the Sea and Beyond*, 147, 150–51; McPherson, *Battle Cry of Freedom*, 608.

23. Ward, *Civil War*, 272.

24. Lonn, *Foreigners in the Union Army and Navy*, 582.

25. Owsley, "Defeatism in the Confederacy," 456.

26. Williams, Williams, and Carlson, *Plain Folk in a Rich Man's War*, 193–94.

27. Watkins, *Co. Aytch*, 69; Williams, Williams, and Carlson, *Plain Folk in a Rich Man's War*, 164; Bynum, *Free State of Jones*, 135. Two excellent treatments of the Lost Cause ideology are Foster's *Ghosts of the Confederacy* and Goldfield's *Still Fighting the Civil War*.

28. Grant, *The Way It Was in the South*, 137. Though usually associated with the post–Civil War era, tenant farming and sharecropping were not new at all. In the late 1850s, roughly one in four white farmers in the South worked land owned by someone else. In parts of the antebellum South, landless tenants and sharecroppers made up nearly half the rural white population. But tenancy did see a phenomenal growth after the war. By the early twentieth century, two-thirds of farmers, black and white, in the Deep South were tenants. In Alabama's Barbour County alone, the tenancy rate was over 75 percent. See Williams, *Rich Man's War*, 192; Coleman, *History of Georgia*, 259.

29. Faust, *Mothers of Invention*, 246; *War of the Rebellion*, ser. 4, vol. 3, 413.

30. Williams, Williams, and Carlson, *Plain Folk in a Rich Man's War*, 7.

Bibliography

Abel, Annie Heloise. *The American Indian as Slaveholder and Secessionist.* 1915. Reprinted with new introduction by Theda Purdue and Michael D. Green. Lincoln: University of Nebraska Press, 1992.

———. *The American Indian in the Civil War, 1862–1865.* 1919. Reprinted with new introduction by Theda Purdue and Michael D. Green. Lincoln: University of Nebraska Press, 1992.

Alexander, Thomas B., and Peggy J. Duckworth. "Alabama Black Belt Whigs During Secession: A New Viewpoint." *Alabama Review* 17 (1964): 181–97.

Amos, Harriet E. "'All-Absorbing Topics': Food and Clothing in Confederate Mobile." *Atlanta Historical Society Journal* 22 (1978): 17–28.

Andrews, William H. *Footprints of a Regiment: A Recollection of the First Georgia Regulars, 1861–1865.* Introduction by Richard M. McMurry. Atlanta: Longstreet Press, 1992.

Aptheker, Herbert. *American Negro Slave Revolts.* 1943. Millwood, NY: Kraus Reprint Co., 1977.

Ash, Stephen V., ed. *Secessionists and Other Scoundrels: Selections from Parson Brownlow's Book.* Baton Rouge: Louisiana State University Press, 1999.

Atkins, Jonathan M. *Parties, Politics, and the Sectional Conflict in Tennessee, 1832–1861.* Knoxville: University of Tennessee Press, 1997.

Aughey, John H. *The Iron Furnace: or, Slavery and Secession.* 1865. Reprint. New York: Negro Universities Press, 1969.

———. *Tupelo.* 1888. Reprint. Freeport, NY: Books for Libraries Press, 1971.

Auman, William T., and David D. Scarboro. "The Heroes of America in Civil War North Carolina." *North Carolina Historical Review* 58 (1981): 327–63.

Ayers, Edward L. *In the Presence of Mine Enemies: War in the Heart of America, 1859–1863.* New York: W.W. Norton, 2003.

Baggett, James Alex. *The Scalawags: Southern Dissenters in the Civil War and Reconstruction.* Baton Rouge: Louisiana State University Press, 2003.

Bailey, Anne J. "A Texas Cavalry Raid: Reaction to Black Soldiers and Contrabands." In Urwin, *Black Flag Over Dixie*.

———. "Defiant Unionists: Militant Germans in Confederate Texas." In Inscoe and Kenzer, *Enemies of the Country*.

———. "In the Far Corner of the Confederacy: A Question of Conscience for German-Speaking Texans." In Clinton, *Southern Families at War*.

———. "The USCT in the Confederate Heartland, 1864." In Smith, *Black Soldiers in Blue*.

Bailey, Fred Arthur. *Class and Tennessee's Confederate Generation*. Chapel Hill: University of North Carolina Press, 1987.

Bailey, Hugh C. "Disaffection in the Alabama Hill Country, 1861." *Civil War History* 4 (1958): 183–93.

———. "Disloyalty in Early Confederate Alabama." *Journal of Southern History* 23 (1957): 522–28.

Bailey, M. Thomas. *Reconstruction in Indian Territory: A Story of Avarice, Discrimination, and Opportunism*. Port Washington, NY: National University Publications, 1972.

Ball, Douglas B. *Financial Failure and Confederate Defeat*. Urbana: University of Illinois Press, 1991.

Balser, Roy P., ed. *The Collected Works of Abraham Lincoln*, 9 vols. New Brunswick, NJ: Rutgers University Press, 1953–55.

Banks, Dean. "Civil War Refugees from Indian Territory in the North, 1861–1864." *Chronicles of Oklahoma* 41 (1963): 286–98.

Barnes, Kenneth C. "The Williams Clan's Civil War: How an Arkansas Farm Family Became a Guerrilla Band." In Inscoe and Kenzer, *Enemies of the Country*.

Barney, William L. "Secession." In Current, *Encyclopedia of the Confederacy*.

———. *The Secessionist Impulse: Alabama and Mississippi in 1860*. Princeton, NJ: Princeton University Press, 1974.

Baum, Dale. *The Shattering of Texas Unionism: Politics in the Lone Star State During the Civil War Era*. Baton Rouge: Louisiana State University Press, 1998.

Beringer, Richard E., Herman Hattaway, Archer Jones, and William N. Still. *Why the South Lost the Civil War*. Athens: University of Georgia Press, 1986.

Berlin, Ira. "The Slaves Were the Primary Force Behind Their Emancipation." In *The Civil War: Opposing Viewpoints*, ed. William Dudley. San Diego: Greenhaven Press, 1995.

Berlin, Ira, Barbara J. Fields, Steven F. Miller, Joseph P. Reidy, and Leslie S. Rowland, eds. *Free At Last: A Documentary History of Slavery, Freedom, and the Civil War*. New York: The New Press, 1992.

Berlin, Ira, Marc Favreau, and Steven F. Miller, eds. *Remembering Slavery: African Americans Talk About Their Personal Experiences of Slavery and Freedom*. New York: The New Press, 1998.

Blackett, R.J.M., ed. *Thomas Morris Chester, Black Civil War Correspondent*. Baton Rouge: Louisiana State University Press, 1989.

Blair, William. *Virginia's Private War: Feeding Body and Soul in the Confederacy, 1861–1865*. New York: Oxford University Press, 1998.

Blakey, Arch Fredric, Ann Smith Lainhart, and Winston Bryant Stephens Jr., eds. *Rose Cottage Chronicles: Civil War Letters of the Bryant-Stephens Families of North Florida*. Gainesville: University Press of Florida, 1998.

Blomquist, Ann K., and Robert A. Taylor. *This Cruel War: The Civil War Letters of Grant and Malinda Taylor, 1862–1865*. Macon, GA: Mercer University Press, 2000.

Bohannon, Keith S. "They Had Determined to Root Us Out: Dual Memoirs by a Unionist Couple in Blue Ridge, Georgia." In Inscoe and Kenzer, *Enemies of the Country*.

Bolton, Charles C. *Poor Whites of the Antebellum South: Tenants and Laborers in Central North Carolina and Northeast Mississippi*. Durham, NC: Duke University Press, 1994.

Bonner, James C. "David R. Snelling: A Story of Desertion and Defection in the Civil War." *Georgia Review* 10 (1956): 275–82.

Botkin, B.A., ed. *Lay My Burden Down: A Folk History of Slavery*. Athens: University of Georgia Press, 1989.

Brown, David. *Southern Outcast: Hinton Rowan Helper and* The Impending Crisis of the South. Baton Rouge: Louisiana State University Press, 2006.

Browne, Junium Henri. *Four Years in Secessia: Adventures Within and Beyond the Union Lines*. Hartford, CT: O.D. Case, 1865.

Brownlow, William G. *Sketches of the Rise, Progress, and Decline of Secession; With a Narrative of Personal Adventures among the Rebels*. Philadelphia: G.W. Childs; Cincinnati: Applegate, 1862.

Bryan, T. Conn. *Confederate Georgia*. Athens: University of Georgia Press, 1953.

Buker, George E. *Blockaders, Refugees, and Contrabands: Civil War on Florida's Gulf Coast, 1861–1865*. Tuscaloosa: University of Alabama Press, 1993.

Burchard, Peter. *One Gallant Rush: Robert Gould Shaw and His Brave Black Regiment*. New York: St. Martin's, 1965.

Burton, Orville Vernon, and Henry Kamerling. "Tobacco." In Current, *Encyclopedia of the Confederacy*.

Bynum, Victoria E. *The Free State of Jones: Mississippi's Longest Civil War*. Chapel Hill: University of North Carolina Press, 2001.

———. Review of *Poor Whites of the Antebellum South*, by Charles C. Bolton. *Journal of Southern History* 61 (1995): 601–2.

———. *Unruly Women: The Politics of Social and Sexual Control in the Old South*. Chapel Hill: University of North Carolina Press, 1992.

Camp, Stephanie M.H. *Closer to Freedom: Enslaved Women and Everyday Resistance in the Plantation South*. Chapel Hill: University of North Carolina Press, 2004.

Carlson, David. "'The Distemper of the Time': Conscription, the Courts, and Planter Privilege in Civil War South Georgia." *Journal of Southwest Georgia History* 14 (1999): 1–24.

———. "The 'Loanly Runagee': Draft Evaders in Confederate South Georgia." *Georgia Historical Quarterly* 84 (2000): 589–615.

Casler, John O. *Four Years in the Stonewall Brigade*, 4th ed. Dayton, OH: Morningside Bookshop, 1982.

Castel, Albert. "The Fort Pillow Massacre." In Urwin, *Black Flag Over Dixie*.

Cecil-Fronsman, Bill. *Common Whites: Class and Culture in Antebellum North Carolina*. Lexington: University Press of Kentucky, 1992.

Chesebrough, David B. "Dissenting Clergy in Confederate Mississippi." *Journal of Mississippi History* 55 (1993): 115–31.

Chesnut, Mary. *Mary Chesnut's Civil War*, ed. C. Vann Woodward. New Haven, CT: Yale University Press, 1981.

Chesson, Michael B. "Harlots or Heroines? A New Look at the Richmond Bread Riot." *Virginia Magazine of History and Biography* 92 (1984), 131–75.

Christ, Mark K., ed. *Rugged and Sublime: The Civil War in Arkansas*. Fayetteville: University of Arkansas Press, 1994.

Cimprich, John. *Fort Pillow, a Civil War Massacre, and Public Memory*. Baton Rouge: Louisiana State University Press, 2005.

———. *Slavery's End in Tennessee, 1861–1865*. Tuscaloosa: University of Alabama Press, 1985.

Cleveland, Henry. *Alexander H. Stephens in Public and Private*. Philadelphia: National Publishing, 1866.

Clinton, Catherine. *Harriet Tubman: The Road to Freedom*. New York: Little, Brown, 2004.

Clinton, Catherine, and Nina Silber, eds. *Divided Houses: Gender and the Civil War*. New York: Oxford University Press, 1992.

Coleman, Kenneth, ed. *A History of Georgia*, 2nd ed. Athens: University of Georgia Press, 1991.

Coles, David J. "'Shooting Niggers Sir': Confederate Mistreatment of Union Black Soldiers at the Battle of Olustee." In Urwin, *Black Flag Over Dixie*.

Coulter, E. Merton. "Commercial Intercourse with the Confederacy in the Mississippi Valley, 1861–1865." *Mississippi Valley Historical Review* 5 (1919): 377–95.

———. *The Confederate States of America, 1861–1865*. Baton Rouge: Louisiana State University Press, 1950.

———. *William G. Brownlow: Fighting Parson of the Southern Highlands*. 1937. Reprinted with new introduction by Stephen V. Ash. Knoxville: University of Tennessee Press, 1999.

Craven, Avery O. *The Coming of the Civil War*. Chicago: University of Chicago Press, 1957.

Crawford, Martin. *Ashe County's Civil War: Community and Society in the Appalachian South*. Charlottesville: University Press of Virginia, 2001.

Crist, Lynda Lasswell, and Mary Seaton Dix, eds. *The Papers of Jefferson Davis*, vol. 7. Baton Rouge: Louisiana State University Press, 1992.

Crofts, Daniel W. *Reluctant Confederates: Upper South Unionists in the Secession Crisis*. Chapel Hill: University of North Carolina Press, 1989.

Crow, Vernon H. *Storm in the Mountains: Thomas' Confederate Legion of Cherokee Indians and Moutaineers*. Cherokee, NC: Press of the Museum of the Cherokee Indian, 1982.

Cumming, Kate. *The Journal of Kate Cumming—Confederate Nurse*, ed. Richard Harwell. Savannah, GA: Beehive Press, 1975.

Current, Richard N., ed. *Encyclopedia of the Confederacy*, 4 vols. New York: Simon & Schuster, 1993.

———. *Lincoln's Loyalists: Union Soldiers from the Confederacy*. New York: Oxford University Press, 1994.

Curry, Richard Orr. *A House Divided: A Study of Statehood Politics and the Copperhead Movement in West Virginia*. Pittsburgh: University of Pittsburgh Press, 1964.

Danziger, Edmund Jefferson Jr. *Indians and Bureaucrats: Administering the Reservation Policy during the Civil War*. Urbana: University of Illinois Press, 1974.

Davis, William C. *Look Away!: A History of the Confederate States of America*. New York: Free Press, 2002.

DeBats, Donald A. *Elites and Masses: Political Structure, Communication, and Behavior in Ante-Bellum Georgia*. New York: Garland Publishing, 1990.

Debo, Angie. *A History of the Indians of the United States*. Norman: University of Oklahoma Press, 1986.

———. *The Rise and Fall of the Choctaw Republic*. Norman: University of Oklahoma Press, 1961.

————. *The Road to Disappearance: A History of the Creek Indians*. Norman: University of Oklahoma Press, 1941.

DeCredico, Mary A. *Patriotism for Profit: Georgia's Urban Entrepreneurs and the Confederate War Effort*. Chapel Hill: University of North Carolina Press, 1990.

Degler, Carl N. *The Other South: Southern Dissenters in the Nineteenth Century*. Boston: Northeastern University Press, 1982.

Devens, R.M. *The Pictorial Book of Anecdotes and Incidents of the War of the Rebellion*. Hartford, CT: Hartford Publishing, 1866.

Dodd, Donald B. "The Free State of Winston." *Alabama Heritage* (Spring 1993): 8–19.

Dodd, Donald B., and Wynelle S. Dodd. *Winston: An Antebellum and Civil War History of a Hill County of North Alabama*. Birmingham, AL: Oxmoor Press, 1972.

Dotson, Rand. " 'The Grave and Scandalous Evil Infected to Your People': The Erosion of Confederate Loyalty in Floyd County, Virginia." *Virginia Magazine of History and Biography* 108 (2000): 393–434.

Douglass, Frederick. *Narrative of the Life of Frederick Douglass*. 1845. New York: Signet, 1968.

Durrill, Wayne K. *War of Another Kind: A Southern Community in the Great Rebellion*. New York: Oxford University Press, 1990.

Dyer, Thomas G. *Secret Yankees: The Union Circle in Confederate Atlanta*. Baltimore: Johns Hopkins University Press, 1999.

Edwards, Laura F. *Scarlett Doesn't Live Here Anymore: Southern Women in the Civil War Era*. Urbana: University of Illinois Press, 2000.

Ellis, Daniel. *Thrilling Adventures of Daniel Ellis*. 1867. Reprint. Johnson City, TN: Overmountain Press, 1989.

Escott, Paul D. *After Secession: Jefferson Davis and the Failure of Confederate Nationalism*. Baton Rouge: Louisiana State University Press, 1978.

————. "The Context of Freedom: Georgia's Slaves during the Civil War." *Georgia Historical Quarterly* 58 (1974): 79–104.

————. " 'The Cry of the Sufferers': The Problem of Welfare in the Confederacy." *Civil War History* 23 (1977): 228–40.

————. *Many Excellent People: Power and Privilege in North Carolina, 1850–1900*. Chapel Hill: University of North Carolina Press, 1985.

————. "Southern Yeomen and the Confederacy." *South Atlantic Quarterly* 77 (1978): 146–58.

Escott, Paul D., and David R. Goldfield, eds. *Major Problems in the History of the American South*, vol. 1. Lexington, MA: D.C. Heath, 1990.

Faust, Drew Gilpin. "Altars of Sacrifice: Confederate Women and the Narratives of War." *Journal of American History* 76 (1990): 1200–28.

————. *The Creation of Confederate Nationalism*. Baton Rouge: Louisiana State University Press, 1988.

————. *Mothers of Invention: Women of the Slaveholding South in the American Civil War*. Chapel Hill: University of North Carolina Press, 1996.

Fellman, Michael. *Inside War: The Guerrilla Conflict in Missouri During the Civil War*. New York: Oxford University Press, 1989.

————. "Women and Guerrilla Warfare." In Clinton and Silber, *Divided Houses*.

Fields, Barbara Jeanne. *Slavery and Freedom on the Middle Ground: Maryland during the Nineteenth Century*. New Haven, CT: Yale University Press, 1985.

Finger, John R. *The Eastern Band of the Cherokees, 1819–1900*. Knoxville: University of Tennessee Press, 1984.

Fisher, Noel C. *War at Every Door: Partisan Politics and Guerrilla Violence in East Tennessee, 1860–1869*. Chapel Hill: University of North Carolina Press, 1997.

Fitzgerald, Michael W. "Poor Man's Fight." *Southern Exposure* 18 (Spring 1990): 14–17.

Fitzhugh, George. *Sociology for the South, or The Failure of Free Society*. New York: Burt Franklin, 1854.

Fleming, Walter L. *Civil War and Reconstruction in Alabama*. New York: Columbia University Press, 1905.

Flynn, Charles L., Jr. *White Land, Black Labor: Caste and Class in Late Nineteenth-Century Georgia*. Baton Rouge: Louisiana State University Press, 1983.

Foner, Philip S. *History of the Labor Movement in the United States from Colonial Times to the Founding of the American Federation of Labor*. New York: International Publishers, 1947.

Ford, Lacy K., Jr. *Origins of Southern Radicalism: The South Carolina Upcountry, 1800–1860*. New York: Oxford University Press, 1988.

Foreman, Grant. *Indian Removal*. Norman: University of Oklahoma Press, 1932.

Formwalt, Lee W. "Planters and Cotton Production as a Cause of Confederate Defeat: The Evidence from Southwest Georgia." *Georgia Historical Quarterly* 74 (1990): 269–76.

Forret, Jeff. *Race Relations at the Margins: Slaves and Poor Whites in the Antebellum Southern Countryside*. Baton Rouge: Louisiana State University Press, 2006.

Foster, Gaines M. *Ghosts of the Confederacy: Defeat, the Lost Cause, and the Emergence of the New South, 1865–1913*. New York: Oxford University Press, 1987.

Foust, James Donald. *The Yeoman Farmer and Westward Expansion of U.S. Cotton Production*. Chapel Hill: University of North Carolina Press, 1967.

Frank Leslie's Illustrated Newspaper (New York), 1862–63.

Franklin, John Hope, and Alfred A. Moss Jr. *From Slavery to Freedom: A History of African Americans*, 7th ed. New York: McGraw-Hill, 1994.

Franklin, John Hope, and Loren Schweninger. *Runaway Slaves: Rebels on the Plantation*. New York: Oxford University Press, 1999.

Franks, Kenny A. "The Confederate States and the Five Civilized Tribes: A Breakdown of Relations. *Journal of the West* 12 (1973): 439–54.

———. *Stand Watie and the Agony of the Cherokee Nation*. Memphis, TN: Memphis State University Press, 1979.

Frazier, Donald S. " 'Out of Stinking Distance': The Guerrilla War in Arkansas." In Sutherland, *Guerrillas, Unionists, and Violence on the Confederate Home Front*.

Freehling, William W. *The Road to Disunion, Volume II: Secessionists Triumphant, 1854–1861*. New York: Oxford University Press, 2007.

———. *The South vs. the South: How Anti-Confederate Southerners Shaped the Course of the Civil War*. New York: Oxford University Press, 2001.

Freehling, William W., and Craig M. Simpson, eds. *Secession Debated: Georgia's Showdown in 1860*. New York: Oxford University Press, 1992.

Friedheim, William, with Ronald Jackson. *Freedom's Unfinished Revolution: An Inquiry into the Civil War and Reconstruction*. American Social History Project. New York: The New Press, 1996.

Frisby, Derek W. " 'Remember Fort Pillow.' " In Urwin, *Black Flag Over Dixie*.

Gaines, W. Craig. *The Confederate Cherokees: John Drew's Regiment of Mounted Rifles*. Baton Rouge: Louisiana State University Press, 1989.

Gallman, J. Matthew. *The North Fights the Civil War: The Home Front*. Chicago: Ivan R. Dee, 1994.

Gates, Paul W. *Agriculture and the Civil War*. New York: Alfred A. Knopf, 1965.

———. *Fifty Million Acres: Conflicts Over Kansas Land Policy, 1854–1890*. Ithaca, NY: Cornell University Press, 1954.

Genovese, Eugene D. *The Political Economy of Slavery: Studies in the Economy and Society of the Slave South*. New York: Vintage Books, 1967.

———. *Roll, Jordan, Roll: The World the Slaves Made*. New York: Vintage Books, 1976.

———. "Yeomen Farmers in a Slaveholders' Democracy." *Agricultural History* 49 (1975): 331–42.

Gibson, Arrell Morgan. *The American Indian: Prehistory to the Present*. Lexington, MA: D.C. Heath, 1980.

———. *The Kickapoos: Lords of the Middle Border*. Norman: University of Oklahoma Press, 1963.

Glatthaar, Joseph T. *Forged in Battle: The Civil War Alliance of Black Soldiers and White Officers*. New York: Free Press, 1990.

———. *The March to the Sea and Beyond: Sherman's Troops in the Savannah and Carolinas Campaigns*. New York: New York University Press, 1985.

Goldfield, David. *Still Fighting the Civil War*. Baton Rouge: Louisiana State University Press, 2002.

Goodrich, Thomas. *Black Flag: Guerrilla Warfare on the Western Border, 1861–1865*. Bloomington: Indiana University Press, 1995.

Gordon, Lesley J. " 'In Time of War': Unionists Hanged in Kinston, North Carolina, February 1864." In Sutherland, *Guerrillas, Unionists, and Violence on the Confederate Home Front*.

Grant, Donald L. *The Way It Was in the South: The Black Experience in Georgia*, ed. Jonathan Grant. New York: Birch Lane Press, 1993.

Gray, Lewis Cecil. *History of Agriculture in the Southern United States to 1860*, vol. 2. Gloucester, MA: Peter Smith, 1958.

Green, Elna C. *This Business of Relief: Confronting Poverty in a Southern City, 1740–1940*. Athens: University of Georgia Press, 2003.

Griffler, Keith P. *Front Line of Freedom: African Americans and the Forging of the Underground Railroad in the Ohio Valley*. Lexington: University of Kentucky Press, 2004.

Groce, W. Todd. *Mountain Rebels: East Tennessee and the Civil War, 1860–1870*. Knoxville: University of Tennessee Press, 1999.

Gronowicz, Anthony. *Race and Class Politics in New York City Before the Civil War*. Boston: Northeastern University Press, 1998.

Hadden, Sally E. *Slave Patrols: Law and Violence in Virginia and the Carolinas*. Cambridge: Harvard University Press, 2001.

Hahn, Steven. *The Roots of Southern Populism: Yeoman Farmers and the Transformation of the Georgia Upcountry, 1850–1890*. New York: Oxford University Press, 1983.

Harding, Vincent. *There Is a River: The Black Struggle for Freedom in America*. New York: Harcourt Brace Jovanovich, 1981.

Harper's New Monthly Magazine (New York), 1866.

Harper's Weekly (New York), 1861–65.

Harris, J. William. *The Making of the American South: A Short History, 1500–1877*. Malden, MA: Blackwell Publishing, 2006.

———. *Plain Folk and Gentry in a Slave Society: White Liberty and Black Slavery in Augusta's Hinterlands*. Middletown, CT: Wesleyan University Press, 1985.

Hatch, Thom. *The Blue, the Gray, and the Red: Indian Campaigns of the Civil War*. Mechanicsburg, PA: Stackpole Books, 2003.

Hauptman, Laurence M. *Between Two Fires: American Indians and the Civil War*. New York: Free Press, 1995.

Haynes, Dennis E. *A Thrilling Narrative: The Memoir of a Southern Unionist*, ed. Arthur W. Bergeron Jr. Fayetteville: University of Arkansas Press, 2006.

Heidler, David S., and Jeanne T. Heidler, eds. *Encyclopedia of the American Civil War*, 5 vols. Santa Barbara, CA: ABC-CLIO, 2000.

Helper, Hinton Rowan. *The Impending Crisis of the South*. 1857. Reprint. Cambridge: Harvard University Press, 1968.

Hill, Louise B. *State Socialism in the Confederate States of America*. Charlottesville, VA: Historical Publishing Co., 1936.

Hollandsworth, James G., Jr. *The Louisiana Native Guards: The Black Military Experience During the Civil War*. Baton Rouge: Louisiana State University Press, 1995.

Holt, Michael F. *The Political Crisis of the 1850s*. New York: W.W. Norton, 1978.

Hoole, William Stanley. *Alabama Tories: The First Alabama Cavalry, U.S.A., 1862–1865*. Tuscaloosa, AL: Confederate Publishing, 1960.

Horst, Samuel. *Mennonites in the Confederacy: A Study in Civil War Pacifism*. Scottsdale, PA: Herald Press, 1967.

Horton, Paul. "Submitting to the 'Shadow of Slavery': The Secession Crisis and Civil War in Alabama's Lawrence County." *Civil War History* 44 (1998): 111–36.

Howard, Victor B. *Black Liberation in Kentucky: Emancipation and Freedom, 1862–1884*. Lexington: University Press of Kentucky, 1983.

Hummel, Jeffrey Rogers. *Emancipating Slaves, Enslaving Free Men: A History of the American Civil War*. Chicago: Open Court Publishing, 1996.

Inscoe, John C. "Moving Through Deserter Country: Fugitive Accounts of the Inner Civil War in Southern Appalachia." In Noe and Wilson, *The Civil War in Appalachia*.

Inscoe, John C., and Robert C. Kenzer, eds. *Enemies of the Country: New Perspectives on Unionists in the Civil War South*. Athens: University of Georgia Press, 2001.

Inscoe, John C., and Gordon B. McKinney. *The Heart of Confederate Appalachia: Western North Carolina in the Civil War*. Chapel Hill: University of North Carolina Press, 2000.

Inscoe, John C., and Gordon B. McKinney. "Highland Households Divided: Family Deceptions, Diversions, and Divisions in Southern Appalachia's Inner Civil War." In Inscoe and Kenzer, *Enemies of the Country*.

Jimerson, Randall C. *The Private Civil War: Popular Thought During the Sectional Conflict*. Baton Rouge: Louisiana State University Press, 1988.

Johnson, Ludwell H. *Red River Campaign: Politics and Cotton in the Civil War*. Baltimore: Johns Hopkins University Press, 1958.

———. "Trading with the Union: The Evolution of Confederate Policy." *Virginia Magazine of History and Biography* 78 (1970): 308–25.

Johnson, Michael P., ed. *Abraham Lincoln, Slavery, and the Civil War: Selected Writings and Speeches*. Boston and New York: Bedford/St. Martin's, 2001.

———. "A New Look at the Popular Vote for Delegates to the Georgia Secession Convention." *Georgia Historical Quarterly* 56 (1972): 259–75.

———. *Toward a Patriarchal Republic: The Secession of Georgia*. Baton Rouge: Louisiana State University Press, 1977.

Jordan, Ervin L., Jr. *Black Confederates and Afro-Yankees in Civil War Virginia*. Charlottesville, University of Virginia Press, 1995.

Jordan, Weymouth T., Jr., and Gerald W. Thomas. "Massacre at Plymouth." In Urwin, *Black Flag Over Dixie*.

Jordan, Winthrop D. *Tumult and Silence at Second Creek: An Inquiry into a Civil War Slave Conspiracy*. Baton Rouge: Louisiana State University Press, 1993.

Josephy, Alvin M., Jr. *The Civil War in the American West*. New York: Alfred A. Knopf, 1992.

Kelly, James C. "William Gannaway Brownlow, Part I." *Tennessee Historical Quarterly* 43 (1984): 25–43.

———. "William Gannaway Brownlow, Part II." *Tennessee Historical Quarterly* 43 (1984): 155–172.

Kibler, Lillian A. "Unionist Sentiment in South Carolina." *Journal of Southern History* 4 (1938): 346–66.

Kruman, Marc W. "Dissent in the Confederacy: The North Carolina Experience." *Civil War History* 27 (1981): 294–313.

Lamb, Robert Paul. "James G. Birney and the Road to Abolitionism." *Alabama Review* 47 (1994): 83–134.

Lane, Mills, ed. *The Rambler in Georgia*. Savannah, GA: Beehive Press, 1973.

Lathrop, Barnes F. "Disaffection in Confederate Louisiana: The Case of William Hyman." *Journal of Southern History* 24 (1958): 308–18.

Lebergott, Stanley. "Through the Blockade: The Profitability and Extent of Cotton Smuggling, 1861–1865." *Journal of Economic History* 41 (1981): 867–88.

———. Why the South Lost: Commercial Purpose in the Confederacy." *Journal of American History* 70 (1983): 58–74.

Leonard, Elizabeth D. *All the Daring of the Soldier: Women of the Civil War Armies*. New York: Penguin Books, 1999.

Levine, Bruce. *Confederate Emancipation: Southern Plans to Free and Arm Slaves during the Civil War*. New York: Oxford University Press, 2006.

———. *Half Slave and Half Free: The Roots of Civil War*. New York: Hill and Wang, 1992.

Lindstrom, Diane. "Southern Dependence Upon Interregional Grain Supplies: A Review of the Trade Flows, 1840–1860." *Agricultural History* 44 (1970): 101–13.

Link, William A. *Roots of Secession: Slavery and Politics in Antebellum Virginia*. Chapel Hill: University of North Carolina Press, 2003.

Locke, John. *The Second Treatise of Government*. Indianapolis, IN: Bobbs-Merrill, 1979.

Longstreet, James. *From Manassas to Appomattox: Memoirs of the Civil War in America*. Philadelphia: J.B. Lippincott, 1896.

Lonn, Ella. *Desertion During the Civil War*. 1928. Reprinted with introduction by William Blair. Lincoln: University of Nebraska Press, 1998.

———. *Foreigners in the Union Army and Navy*. New York: Greenwood, 1969.

Lowe, Richard. "Battle on the Levee: The Fight at Milliken's Bend." In Smith, *Black Soldiers in Blue*.

Lowrey, Walter McGehee. "The Political Career of James Madison Wells." *Louisiana Historical Quarterly* 31 (1948): 995–1123.

Lufkin, Charles L. "Divided Loyalties: Sectionalism in Civil War McNairy County, Tennessee." *Tennessee Historical Quarterly* 47 (1988): 169–77.

Mackey, Robert R. *The Uncivil War: Irregular Warfare in the Upper South, 1861–1865*. Norman: University of Oklahoma Press, 2004.

Mallard, M. Shannon. " 'I Had No Comfort to Give the People': Opposition to the Confederacy in Civil War Mississippi." *North & South* 6 (May 2003): 78–86.

Mann, Ralph. "Ezekiel Counts's Sand Lick Company: Civil War and Localism in the Mountain South." In Noe and Wilson, *The Civil War in Appalachia*.

Marten, James. *Texas Divided: Loyalty and Dissent in the Lone Star State, 1856–1874*. Lexington: University Press of Kentucky, 1990.

Martin, Bessie. *A Rich Man's War, A Poor Man's Fight: Desertion of Alabama Troops from the Confederate Army*. 1932. Reprinted with new introduction by Mark A. Weitz. Tuscaloosa: University of Alabama Press, 2003.

Martis, Kenneth C. *The Historical Atlas of the Congresses of the Confederate States of America, 1861–1865*. New York: Simon & Schuster, 1994.

Massey, Mary Elizabeth. *Women in the Civil War*. Lincoln: University of Nebraska Press, 1994.

May, Robert E. *The Southern Dream of a Caribbean Empire, 1854–1861*. Baton Rouge: Louisiana State University Press, 1973.

McCaslin, Richard B. *Tainted Breeze: The Great Hanging at Gainesville, Texas, 1862*. Baton Rouge: Louisiana State University Press, 1994.

McCurry, Stephanie. *Masters of Small Worlds: Yeoman Households, Gender Relations and the Political Culture of the Antebellum South Carolina Low Country*. New York: Oxford University Press, 1995.

McFeely, William S. *Frederick Douglass*. New York: W.W. Norton, 1991.

McGee, Val L. "The Confederate Who Switched Sides: The Saga of Captain Joseph G. Sanders." *Alabama Review* 47 (1994): 20–28.

McKenzie, Robert Tracy. *Lincolnites and Rebels: A Divided Town in the American Civil War*. New York: Oxford University Press, 2006.

———. *One South or Many? Plantation Belt and Upcountry in Civil War–Era Tennessee*. Cambridge, UK: Cambridge University Press, 1994.

———. "Prudent Silence and Strict Neutrality: The Parameters of Unionism in Parson Brownlow's Knoxville, 1860–1863." In Inscoe and Kenzer, *Enemies of the Country*.

McKibben, Davidson Burns. "Negro Slave Insurrections in Mississippi." *Journal of Negro History* 34 (1949): 73–90.

McKinney, Gordon B. "Women's Role in Civil War Western North Carolina." *North Carolina Historical Review* 69 (1992): 37–56.

McKnight, Brian D. *Contested Borderland: The Civil War in Appalachian Kentucky and Virginia*. Lexington: University Press of Kentucky, 2006.

McMillan, Malcolm C. *The Disintegration of a Confederate State: Three Governors and Alabama's Wartime Home Front, 1861–1865*. Macon, GA: Mercer University Press, 1986.

McPherson, James M. *Battle Cry of Freedom*. New York: Oxford University Press, 1988.

———. *The Negro's Civil War*. Urbana: University of Illinois Press, 1982.

———. *Ordeal By Fire: The Civil War and Reconstruction*, 2nd ed. New York: McGraw Hill, 1992.

———. *The Struggle for Equality: Abolitionists and the Negro in the Civil War and Reconstruction*. Princeton, NJ: Princeton University Press, 1964.

———. *What They Fought For, 1861–1865*. Baton Rouge: Louisiana State University Press, 1994.

McReynolds, Edwin C. *The Seminoles*. Norman: University of Oklahoma Press, 1957.

McWhiney, Grady. *Cracker Culture: Celtic Ways in the Old South*. Tuscaloosa: University of Alabama Press, 1988.

Melton, Maurice. "Disloyal Confederates." *Civil War Times Illustrated* 16 (August 1977): 12–19.

Meriwether, Harvey. *Slavery in Auburn, Alabama*. Auburn: Alabama Polytechnic Institute Historical Studies, 1907.

Messner, William F. "Black Violence and White Response: Louisiana, 1862." *Journal of Southern History* 41 (1975): 19–38.

Meyers, Christopher C. "'The Wretch Vickery' and the Brooks County Civil War Slave Conspiracy." *Journal of Southwest Georgia History* 12 (1997): 27–38.

Mitchell, Ried. *Civil War Soldiers*. New York: Viking, 1988.

Mohr, Clarence L. "Before Sherman: Georgia Blacks and the Union War Effort, 1861–1864." *Journal of Southern History* 45 (1979): 331–352.

———. *On the Threshold of Freedom: Masters and Slaves in Civil War Georgia*. Athens: University of Georgia Press, 1986.

———. "Slavery and Class Tensions in Confederate Georgia." *Gulf Coast Historical Review* 4 (1989): 58–72.

Moneyhon, Carl. "1861: 'The Die is Cast.'" In Christ, *Rugged and Sublime*.

———. "Disloyalty and Class Consciousness in Southwestern Arkansas, 1862–1865." *Arkansas Historical Quarterly* 52 (1993): 223–43.

———. *The Impact of the Civil War and Reconstruction on Arkansas: Persistence in the Midst of Ruin*. Baton Rouge: Louisiana State University Press, 1994.

Moore, Albert Burton. *Conscription and Conflict in the Confederacy*. New York: Hillary House, 1963.

Morgan, Chad. *Planters' Progress: Modernizing Confederate Georgia*. Gainesville: University Press of Florida, 2005.

Morgan, Edmund S. *American Slavery, American Freedom: The Ordeal of Colonial Virginia*. New York: W.W. Norton, 1975.

Moulton, Gary E. *John Ross: Cherokee Chief*. Athens: University of Georgia Press, 1978.

Myers, Barton Alan. "Executing Daniel Bright: Power, Political Loyalty, and Guerrilla Violence in a North Carolina Community." Master's thesis, University of Georgia, 2005.

Naron, Levi H. *Chickasaw, A Mississippi Scout for the Union: The Civil War Memoir of Levi H. Naron, as recounted by R. W. Surby*, ed. Thomas D. Cockrell and Michael B. Ballard. Baton Rouge: Louisiana State University Press, 2005.

Neely, Mark E., Jr. *Southern Rights: Political Prisoners and the Myth of Confederate Constitutionalism*. Charlottesville: University Press of Virginia, 1999.

Nelson, Scott Reynolds. "Red Strings and Half Brothers: Civil Wars in Alamance County, North Carolina, 1860–1871." In Inscoe and Kenzer, *Enemies of the Country*.

Newton, Steven H. "African Americans Resist the Confederacy: Two Variations on a Theme." *North and South* 8 (November 2005): 52–60.

Nichols, David A. *Lincoln and the Indians: Civil War Policy and Politics*. Columbia: University of Missouri Press, 1978.

Noe, Kenneth W. "Red String Scare: Civil War Southwest Virginia and the Heroes of America." *North Carolina Historical Review* 69 (1992): 301–22.

Noe, Kenneth W., and Shannon H. Wilson, eds. *The Civil War in Appalachia: Collected Essays*. Knoxville: University of Tennessee Press, 1997.

Nolan, Alan T. *Lee Considered: General Robert E. Lee and Civil War History*. Chapel Hill: University of North Carolina Press, 1991.

Oakes, James. *Slavery and Freedom: An Interpretation of the Old South*. New York: Vintage Books, 1990.

O'Brien, Sean Michael. *Mountain Partisans: Guerrilla Warfare in the Southern Appalachians, 1861–1865*. Westport, CT: Praeger, 1999.

Otten, James T. "Disloyalty in the Upper Districts of South Carolina During the Civil War." *South Carolina Historical Magazine* 75 (1974): 95–110.

Otto, John Solomon. *Southern Agriculture During the Civil War Era, 1860–1880*. Westport, CT: Greenwood Press, 1994.

Owsley, Frank Lawrence. "Defeatism in the Confederacy." *North Carolina Historical Review* 3 (1926): 446–56.

———. *Plain Folk of the Old South*. Baton Rouge: Louisiana State University Press, 1949.

Paludan, Phillip Shaw. *Victims: A True Story of the Civil War*. Knoxville: University of Tennessee Press, 1981.

Perkins, Howard Cecil, ed. *Northern Editorials on Secession*. Gloucester, MA: Peter Smith, 1964.

Pickering, David, and Judy Falls. *Brush Men and Vigilantes: Civil War Dissent in Texas*. College Station: Texas A&M University, 2000.

Phillips, Kevin. *Wealth and Democracy: A Political History of the American Rich*. New York: Broadway Books, 2002.

Phillips, Ulrich B., ed. *The Correspondence of Robert Toombs, Alexander H. Stephens, and Howell Cobb*. Washington, DC: Government Printing Office, 1913.

———. *Georgia and State Rights*. 1902. Reprint, n.p.: Antioch Press, 1968.

Poole, W. Scott. *South Carolina's Civil War*. Macon, GA: Mercer University Press, 2005.

Potter, David M. *The Impending Crisis, 1848–1861*, Completed and edited by Don E. Fehrenbacher. New York: Harper and Row, 1976.

———. *Lincoln and His Party in the Secession Crisis*. Introduction by Daniel Crofts. Baton Rouge: Louisiana State University Press, 1995.

Proctor, William G., Jr. "Slavery in Southwest Georgia." *Georgia Historical Quarterly* 49 (1965): 1–22.

Quarles, Benjamin. *The Negro in the Civil War*. 1953. Reprinted with introduction by William S. McFeely. New York: Da Capo, 1989.

Rable, George C. *Civil Wars: Women and the Crisis of Southern Nationalism*. Urbana: University of Illinois Press, 1989.

Radley, Kenneth. *Rebel Watchdog: The Confederate States Army Provost Guard*. Baton Rouge: Louisiana State University Press, 1989.

Ramold, Steven J. "African-American Sailors." In Heidler and Heidler, *Encyclopedia of the American Civil War*.

Range, Willard. *A Century of Georgia Agriculture: 1850–1950*. Athens: University of Georgia Press, 1954.

Rawick, George P., ed. *The American Slave: A Composite Autobiography*. Series 1 and 2, 19 vols. Supplement, Series 1, 12 vols. Westport, CT: Greenwood Press, 1972 and 1977.

Rawley, James A. *Race and Politics: "Bleeding Kansas" and the Coming of the Civil War*. Philadelphia: J.B. Lippincott, 1969.

Reiger, John F. "Deprivation, Disaffection, and Desertion in Confederate Florida." *Florida Historical Quarterly* 48 (1969–70): 279–98.

———. "Secession of Florida from the Union—A Minority Decision?" *Florida Historical Quarterly* 46 (1968): 358–68.

Revels, Tracy J. *Grander in Her Daughters: Florida's Women During the Civil War.* Columbia: University of South Carolina Press, 2004.

Ripley, C. Peter. *Slaves and Freedmen in Civil War Louisiana.* Baton Rouge: Louisiana State University Press, 1976.

Robinson, Armstead L. *Bitter Fruits of Bondage: The Demise of Slavery and the Collapse of the Confederacy, 1861–1865.* Charlottesville: University of Virginia Press, 2005.

Rogers, William Warren, Jr. *Confederate Home Front: Montgomery During the Civil War.* Tuscaloosa: University of Alabama Press, 1999.

Rutledge, Stephen W. "Stephen W. Rutledge: His Autobiography and Civil War Journal." *East Tennessee Roots* 6 (Fall 1989): 101–12.

Ryan, David D. *A Yankee Spy in Richmond: The Civil War Diary of "Crazy Bet" Van Lew.* Mechanicsburg, PA: Stackpole, 1996.

Sarris, Jonathan Dean. *A Separate Civil War: Communities in Conflict in the Mountain South.* Charlottesville: University of Virginia Press, 2006.

Saunt, Claudio. "The Paradox of Freedom: Tribal Sovereignty and Emancipation during the Reconstruction of Indian Territory." *Journal of Southern History* 70 (2004): 63–94.

Scarborough, William Kauffman. *Masters of the Big House: Elite Slaveholders of the Mid-Nineteenth-Century South.* Baton Rouge: Louisiana State University Press, 2003.

Schlabach, Theron F. *Peace, Faith, Nation: Mennonites and Amish in Nineteenth-Century America.* Scottsdale, PA: Herald Press, 1988.

Schultz, Duane. *Quantrill's War: The Life and Times of William Clarke Quantrill, 1837–1865.* New York: St. Martin's Press, 1996.

Schwalm, Leslie A. *A Hard Fight for We: Women's Transition from Slavery to Freedom in South Carolina.* Urbana: University of Illinois Press, 1997.

Sellers, James Benson. *Slavery in Alabama,* 2nd ed. Tuscaloosa: University of Alabama Press, 1964.

Sharkey, Robert P. *Money, Class, and Party: An Economic Study of Civil War and Reconstruction.* Baltimore: Johns Hopkins University, 1959.

Shugg, Roger W. *Origins of Class Struggle in Louisiana: A Social History of White Farmers and Laborers during Slavery and After, 1840–1875.* Baton Rouge: Louisiana State University Press, 1939.

Simons, A.M. *Social Forces in American History.* New York: International Publishers, 1926.

Sizer, Lyde Cullen. "Acting Her Part: Narratives of Union Women Spies." In Clinton and Silber, *Divided Houses.*

Smith, David P. "The Limits of Dissent and Loyalty in Texas." In Sutherland, *Guerrillas, Unionists, and Violence on the Confederate Home Front.*

Smith, John David, ed. *Black Soldiers in Blue: African American Troops in the Civil War Era.* Chapel Hill: University of North Carolina Press, 2002.

Smith, Page. *Trial by Fire: A People's History of the Civil War and Reconstruction.* New York: McGraw-Hill, 1982.

Speer, Lonnie R. *Portals to Hell: Military Prisons of the Civil War.* Mechanicsburg, PA: Stackpole Books, 1997.

Stampp, Kenneth M. *The Peculiar Institution: Slavery in the Ante-Bellum South.* New York: Vintage Books, 1956.

Standard, Diffie William. *Columbus, Georgia, in the Confederacy: The Social and Industrial Life of the Chattahoochee River Port*. New York: William-Frederick Press, 1954.

Sterling, Dorothy, ed. *We Are Your Sisters: Black Women in the Nineteenth Century*. New York: W.W. Norton, 1984.

Storey, Margaret M. *Loyalty and Loss: Alabama's Unionists in the Civil War and Reconstruction*. Baton Rouge: Louisiana State University Press 2004.

Stutler, Boyd B. *West Virginia in the Civil War*. Charleston, WV: Education Foundation, 1963.

Suderow, Bryce A. "The Battle of the Crater." In Urwin, *Black Flag Over Dixie*.

Sutherland, Daniel E. "1864: 'A Strange, Wild Time.'" In Christ, *Rugged and Sublime*.

———, ed. *Guerrillas, Unionists, and Violence on the Confederate Home Front*. Fayetteville: University of Arkansas Press, 1999.

Tatum, Georgia Lee. *Disloyalty in the Confederacy*. 1934. Reprinted with new introduction by David Williams. Lincoln: University of Nebraska Press, 2000.

Taylor, Amy Murrell. *The Divided Family in Civil War America*. Chapel Hill: University of North Carolina Press, 2005.

Taylor, Ethel. "Discontent in Confederate Louisiana." *Louisiana History* 2 (1961): 410–428.

Taylor, Robert A. "Unforgotten Threat: Florida Seminoles in the Civil War." *Florida Historical Quarterly* 69 (1991): 300–14.

Taylor, Susie King. *Reminiscences of My Life in Camp*. 1902. Reprinted with introduction by Catherine Clinton. Athens: University of Georgia Press, 2006.

Thomas, Emory M. *The Confederate Nation, 1861–1865*. New York: Harper and Row, 1979.

Thomas, Henry W. *History of the Doles-Cook Brigade, Army of Northern Virginia, C.S.A.* Atlanta: Franklin Publishing, 1903.

Thompson, Wesley S. *The Free State of Winston: A History of Winston County, Alabama*. Winfield, AL: Pariel Press, 1968.

Thornton, J. Mills, III. *Politics and Power in a Slave Society: Alabama, 1800–1860*. Baton Rouge: Louisiana State University Press, 1978.

Tripp, Steven Elliott. *Yankee Town, Southern City: Race and Class Relations in Civil War Lynchburg*. New York: New York University Press, 1997.

Trotter, William R. *Bushwackers! The Civil War in North Carolina: The Mountains*. Winston-Salem, NC: John F. Blair, 1988.

Turner, Martha L. "The Cause of the Union in East Tennessee." *Tennessee Historical Quarterly* 40 (1981): 366–80.

Turner, Maxine. *Navy Gray: A Story of the Confederate Navy on the Chattahoochee and Apalachicola Rivers*. Tuscaloosa: The University of Alabama Press, 1988.

Tyler, Ronnie C. "Cotton on the Border, 1861–1865." *Southwestern Historical Quarterly* 73 (1970): 456–77.

Tyson, Carl Newton. "Texas: Men for War; Cotton for Economy." *Journal of the West* 14 (1975): 130–48.

Urwin, Gregory J.W. *Black Flag Over Dixie: Racial Atrocities and Reprisals in the Civil War*. Carbondale: Southern Illinois University Press, 2004.

———. "United States Colored Troops." In Heidler and Heidler, *Encyclopedia of the American Civil War*.

———. "We Cannot Treat Negroes . . . as Prisoners of War." In Urwin, *Black Flag Over Dixie*.

Uya, Okon Edet. *From Slavery to Public Service: Robert Smalls, 1830–1913.* New York: Oxford University Press, 1971.

Vandiver, Frank E. *Ploughshares into Swords: Josiah Gorgas and Confederate Ordnance.* Austin: University of Texas Press, 1952.

Varon, Elizabeth. *Southern Lady, Yankee Spy: The True Story of Elizabeth Van Lew, a Union Agent in the Heart of the Confederacy.* New York: Oxford University Press, 2003.

Voegeli, V. Jacque. *Free But Not Equal: The Midwest and the Negro During the Civil War.* Chicago: University of Chicago Press, 1967.

———. "A Rejected Alternative: Union Policy and the Relocation of Southern 'Contrabands' at the Dawn of Emancipation." *Journal of Southern History* 69 (2003): 765–90.

Wakelyn, Jon L. *Confederates Against the Confederacy.* Westport, CT: Praeger, 2002.

———. *Southern Unionist Pamphlets and the Civil War.* Columbia: University of Missouri Press, 1999.

Walker, Anne Kendrick. *Backtracking in Barbour County: A Narrative of the Last Alabama Frontier.* 1941. Reprint. Eufaula, AL: Eufaula Heritage Association, 1967.

Wallenstein, Peter. *From Slave South to New South: Public Policy in Nineteenth-Century Georgia.* Chapel Hill: University of North Carolina Press, 1987.

War of the Rebellion: A Compilation of the Official Records of the Union and Confederate Armies, 128 parts in 70 vols. and atlas. Washington, DC: Government Printing Office, 1880–1901.

Ward, Geoffrey C. *The Civil War.* New York: Alfred A. Knopf, 1992.

Warde, Mary Jane. "Now the Wolf Has Come: The Civilian Civil War in the Indian Territory." *Chronicles of Oklahoma* 71 (1993): 64–87.

Ware, Lynn Willoughby. "Cotton Money: Antebellum Currency Conditions in the Apalachicola/Chattahoochee River Valley." *Georgia Historical Quarterly* 74 (1990): 215–33.

Washburn, Wilcomb E. *The Governor and the Rebel: A History of Bacon's Rebellion in Virginia.* Chapel Hill: University of North Carolina Press, 1957.

Watkins, Sam R. *Co. Aytch: Maury Grays, First Tennessee Regiment.* 1882. Reprint. Wilmington, NC: Broadfoot Publishing, 1987.

Watson, Harry L. "Conflict and Collaboration: Yeomen, Slaveholders, and Politics in the Antebellum South." *Social History* 10 (1985): 273–98.

Weitz, Mark A. *More Damning than Slaughter: Desertion in the Confederate Army.* Lincoln: University of Nebraska Press, 2005.

Wells, Jonathan Daniel. *The Origins of the Southern Middle Class, 1800–1861.* Chapel Hill: University of North Carolina Press, 2004.

Wertheimer, Barbara Mayer. *We Were There: The Story of Working Women in America.* New York: Pantheon Books, 1977.

White, Christine Schultz, and Benton R. White. *Now the Wolf Has Come: The Creek Nation in the Civil War.* College Station: Texas A&M University Press, 1996.

White, William W. "The Texas Slave Insurrection of 1860." *Southwestern Historical Quarterly* 52 (1949): 259–85.

Whites, LeeAnn. "The Civil War as a Crisis in Gender." In Clinton and Silber, *Divided Houses.*

Wiley, Bell I. *The Life of Johnny Reb: The Common Soldier of the Confederacy.* Baton Rouge: Louisiana State University Press, 1978.

———. *The Plain People of the Confederacy.* 1943. Reprint, with new introduction by Paul D. Escott, Columbia: University of South Carolina Press, 2000.

Williams, David. "Civil Liberties, C.S.A." In Heidler and Heidler, *Encyclopedia of the American Civil War*.

———. "Class Conflict, C.S.A." In Heidler and Heidler, *Encyclopedia of the American Civil War*.

———. " 'The 'Faithful Slave' Is About Played Out': Civil War Slave Resistance in the Lower Chattahoochee Valley." *Alabama Review* 52 (1999): 83–104.

———. *The Georgia Gold Rush: Twenty-Niners, Cherokees, and Gold Fever*. Columbia: University of South Carolina Press, 1993.

———. *Johnny Reb's War: Battlefield and Homefront*. Abilene, TX: McWhiney Foundation Press, 2000.

———. *A People's History of the Civil War: Struggles for the Meaning of Freedom*. New York: The New Press, 2005.

———. *Rich Man's War: Class, Caste, and Confederate Defeat in the Lower Chattahoochee Valley*. Athens: University of Georgia Press, 1998.

Williams, David, Teresa Crisp Williams, and David Carlson. *Plain Folk in a Rich Man's War: Class and Dissent in Confederate Georgia*. Gainesville: University Press of Florida, 2002.

Williams, Teresa Crisp, and David Williams. " 'The Women Rising': Cotton, Class, and Confederate Georgia's Rioting Women." *Georgia Historical Quarterly* 86 (2002): 49–83.

Willoughby, Lynn. *Fair to Middlin': The Antebellum Cotton Trade of the Apalachicola/Chattahoochee River Valley*. Tuscaloosa: University of Alabama Press, 1993.

Wills, Brian Steel. *The War Hits Home: The Civil War in Southeastern Virginia*. Charlottesville: University Press of Virginia, 2001.

Wilson, Harold S. *Confederate Industry: Manufacturers and Quartermasters in the Civil War*. Jackson: University Press of Mississippi, 2002.

Wilson, Joseph T. *The Black Phalanx: A History of the Negro Soldiers of the United States in the Wars of 1775–1812 and 1861–1865*. Hartford, CT: American Publishing Co., 1890.

Wilson, Keith P. *Campfires of Freedom: The Camp Life of Black Soldiers during the Civil War*. Kent, OH: Kent State University Press, 2002.

Wise, Stephen R. *Lifeline of the Confederacy: Blockade Running during the Civil War*. Columbia: University of South Carolina Press, 1988.

Wish, Harvey. "Slave Disloyalty under the Confederacy." *Journal of Negro History* 23 (1938): 435–50.

———. "The Slave Insurrection Panic of 1856." *Journal of Southern History* 5 (1939): 206–22.

Wood, John W. "Union and Secession in Mississippi." In *Southern Unionist Pamphlets and the Civil War*, ed. Jon L. Wakelyn. Columbia: University of Missouri Press, 1999.

Wooster, Ralph. *The Secession Conventions of the South*. Princeton, NJ: Princeton University Press, 1962.

Worley, Ted R. "The Arkansas Peace Society of 1861: A Study in Mountain Unionism." *Journal of Southern History* 24 (1958): 445–56.

Wright, Edward Needles. *Conscientious Objectors in the Civil War*. New York: A.S. Barnes, 1961.

Wright, Gavin. *The Political Economy of the Cotton South: Households, Markets, and Wealth in the Nineteenth Century*. New York: W.W. Norton, 1978.

Wynne, Ben. *Mississippi's Civil War: A Narrative History*. Macon, GA: Mercer University Press, 2006.

Zinn, Howard. *A People's History of the United States*. New York: Harper and Row, 1980.

Zinn, Howard, and Anthony Arnove. *Voices of a People's History of the United States*. New York: Seven Stories Press, 2004.

Zipf, Karin L. *Labor of Innocents: Forced Apprenticeship in North Carolina, 1715–1919*. Baton Rouge: Louisiana State University Press, 2005.

Index

Note: Page numbers in italics indicate images and their captions.